Mi-Lou:
Poetry and the Labyrinth of Desire

Harvard Studies in Comparative Literature
Founded by William Henry Schofield
39

Mi-Lou:
Poetry and the
Labyrinth of Desire

STEPHEN OWEN

Harvard University Press

Cambridge, Massachusetts

London, England · 1989

Copyright © 1989 by the President and Fellows of Harvard College
All rights reserved
Printed in the United States of America
10 9 8 7 6 5 4 3 2 1

This book is printed on acid-free paper, and its binding materials
have been chosen for strength and durability.

Library of Congress Cataloging-in-Publication Data
Owen, Stephen, 1946–
    Mi-Lou: poetry and the labyrinth of desire.
    (Harvard studies in comparative literature; 39)
    Bibliography: p.
    Includes index.
    1. Poetry—History and criticism. 2. Love in literature.
3. Desire in literature. I. Title. II. Series.
PN1076.094   1989   809.1   88–28393
ISBN 0–674–57275–0 (alk. paper)

Page 217 constitutes an extension
of the copyright page.

The author would like to thank the
Guggenheim Foundation and the American
Council of Learned Societies for their
support during the preparation of this book.

Rage and delight, sorrow and joy, anxieties, misgivings, moments of inconstant wavering and moments of rigidity, frivolity, and recklessness, openness and posturing—all are music from the empty spaces, mushrooms forming in ground mist. Day and night each one of these follows upon another, but no one knows from where they sprout. That's all there is! They come upon us from dawn to dusk, but how they came to be—who knows? Without them there is no me, and without me they have nothing to hold on to. That's all there is. But I don't understand how they are set in operation. It may be that there is someone genuinely in control of them, but he leaves no trace for me to find. No doubt that he can act, but I don't see his form; he is there in the circumstance but has no form.

> Master Chuang Chou,
> "Recognizing All Things
> as Equal"

The human affections are, in number, seven: delight, rage, sorrow, fear, love, hate, and desire. They do not come by study.

> *The Book of Rites*

Contents

Mi-Lou, the Palace of Going Astray

In his later years the Emperor Yang of the Sui (569–618) went astray, losing himself in the pleasures of the flesh. One day he addressed his close attendants:

"I, lord of mankind, enjoy the wealth of all the world and now wish to taste the very limits of pleasure in the present, to find fresh satisfactions for my will. Since the world now enjoys peace and wealth, untroubled either within the empire or on the frontiers, such pleasures are mine for the pursuit. Though my palace buildings are magnificent and spacious, it disturbs me that I lack secret chambers and tiny rooms, hidden porches and small doors. If only this sort of thing were to be mine, I could look forward to growing old therein."

Then one of the close attendants, Kao Ch'ang, informed the throne of a friend of his, a native of Che-chiang named Hsiang Sheng, who was said to be a skilled architect. Summoning Hsiang Sheng to an audience the next day, the Emperor questioned him about such an undertaking. Hsiang Sheng begged the Emperor to allow him to draw up plans. Several days later the plans were presented, and His Majesty perused them with great pleasure. On that very day commands were sent out that the appropriate officers should provide the necessary timber. Over twenty thousand laborers were conscripted for the purpose, and within a year the work was completed.

There were towers and mansions high and low, with windows and balconies in gleaming contrast; there were hidden openings, secret chambers, railings of jade and red balustrades, all connecting one with the other, ringing around in all directions. The secret chambers led one into another, with a thousand doors and ten thousand windows all green and gold above and below. Gilt dragons were coiled, lurking beneath the beams, and jade beasts crouched beside the entrances. The walls and the pavements gave off light, while sunbeams shot through the intricately carved window screens. It was the ultimate in craftsmanship, as had never been seen in earlier times. And it came at great expense of jade and gold, so that the royal treasury was left utterly empty. If someone went into it by mistake, he would not be able to find his way out even after a whole day.

When the Emperor first went to tour it, he was greatly pleased, and said to his entourage, "Even an immortal from the other world would go astray wandering through this. In Our eyes it shall be a 'Palace of Going Astray.'" His Majesty then commanded that Hsiang Sheng be awarded an office of the fifth rank, and to show his appreciation he added to this a thousand bolts of silk from the treasury. Next he commanded that several thousand well-born women from the harem be lodged in the palace. Every time he visited the place he would remain inside for an entire month.

Mi-Lou:

Poetry and the Labyrinth of Desire

Introduction

And we may further grant to those of her defenders who are lovers of poetry and yet not poets the permission to speak in prose on her behalf: let them show not only that she is pleasant but also useful to States and to human life, and we will listen in a kindly spirit; for if this can be proved we shall surely be the gainers—I mean, if there is a use in poetry as well as a delight? . . .

If her defense fails, then, my dear friend, like other persons who are enamored of something, but put a restraint upon themselves when they think their desires are opposed to their interests, so too must we after the manner of lovers give her up, though not without a struggle. We too are inspired by that love of poetry which the education of noble States has implanted in us, and therefore we would have her appear at her best and truest; but so long as she is unable to make good her defense, this argument of ours shall be a charm to us, which we will repeat to ourselves while we listen to her strains; that we may not fall away into the childish love of her which captivates the many. At all events we are well aware that poetry being such as we have described is not to be regarded seriously as attaining to the truth; and he who listens to her, fearing for the safety of the city which is within him, should be on his guard against her seductions and make our words his law.

Plato, *Republic*, X (trans. Benjamin Jowett)

It was from the epics of Homer that the children of the city-states received the education and nurture (*trophe*) of which Plato here speaks. But what was the lesson? Despite pious commonplaces about pragmatic knowledge imparted in the epics, despite allegorical ingenuity that discovered serious truths behind the acts of arbitrarily fond and irascible deities, the fact remains that the first epic, the *Iliad*, is a poem of violence and the exultation in violence; it is a poem of destruction brought upon a city, a poem of private honor, of pride, and of desire, all of which work against the community's good and bring it to ruin or near ruin. It is a poem about those forces that cannot be controlled, even by the best nurture and education: it tells splendors of unreasoning impulse and the whims of gods that mock reasonable decisions made by mortals.

> passion was there, and desire,
>   and alluring, intimate words
> that steal away the wits
>   of even the wisest.
>
> *Iliad*, XIV.216–217

The epic antidote to these dangerous impulses of men and gods was the *Odyssey*, a saga about a trickster and man of disguises, who won for himself a fragile measure of control by continuous deception.

Somehow these poems were supposed to prepare a young man to participate in the life of the *polis*, the city-state, and to make, after due consideration, reasonable judgments for the community's general good. The military emblem of such a community was the shield-line, the phalanx, in which a private glory of attack or a private safety of retreat were necessarily subordinated to the collective glory and safety, both of which were assured only by each individual maintaining his place within the line. The individual who acted for himself, who rushed ahead of the line or fled behind it, left a gap, an exposed opening in the hard shield-surface; and through that small space of exposure everyone became soft and vulnerable. Yet Achilles, the *Iliad*'s hero, was somehow always either ahead of the line or behind it.

The peculiar and unreasonable relation between the alluring Homeric world and the values of the *polis* did not escape Plato's reasonable attention, as he gave serious thought to how youths should be best formed to the service of the community. And Plato called poetry to a public trial, as Socrates his teacher had been tried, for corrupting the education of the young. An advocate would be asked to speak for the defense, not eloquently but reasonably.

The publicly wise and all those who make considered judgments for the common good are given the seats of authority in this trial: the judges announce, "It is not we who are on trial here." To come before this tribunal is to tacitly accept its procedures, its standards of proof, its forms of argument. Compelled to conduct the defense according to the rules set by the magistracy, poetry's defenders can make their case only by the most ingenious lies and concealments. If, in this ongoing trial, poetry's defense has never entirely failed and poetry has never been finally thrown out of the Republic, it is perhaps because no community has ever been so rational as to be unwilling to believe attractive and reasonably plausible lies—both the lies poetry itself tells and the lies we advocates tell about it. We have stacks of affidavits and corrupted character witnesses attesting to poetry's respectability. This very willingness of poetry to compromise itself by putting on a mask of scrupulous virtue has enabled poetry to retain its very minor place in the education of the community.

But poetry may indeed lead the citizenry astray. It may speak sweet seductive words, catch us up, work changes upon us. We would legitimately call such an event a straying, dimly recognizing in it the joys of swerving from weary and commonplace values of the community, values to which, when asked, we must always loudly reaffirm our adherence. Do not misunderstand: we affirm those values because they are our own. They seem to appear spontaneously whenever there are two or three of us together. They are precisely the words on which we concur and by which we survive as a community. Yet each of us possesses a liberty of desire that renounces nothing and wants all. We tire of our own virtuous restraints, and we hunger. There may be something in great poetry, even and most perilously in its soothing disguises, that betrays those values we believe we ought to hold; there may be something that subverts the common good and pays honor to the beast.

Though poetry may undermine the community and corrode its worthy values, poetry offers no alternative vision of utopian order: the revolution can never be permitted to succeed—if only because we would then be compelled to renounce our liberty of desire. Poetry envisages no single Republic; it is incapable of choosing one good from many possible and contradictory goods. Furthermore, poetry draws strength from a reflux against the rituals of humiliation and submission daily imposed upon the beast by the world outside of poetry. By words the community binds us, and poetry fights back with words: perfect words, double-edged words, weighted words, words made to rebel against the drudgery to which the community commonly puts them. With these words poetry addresses us and quietly tries to compromise all who are so incautious as to listen. Perilous conditions may be taken for granted, and unreasonable enthusiasms may become, for a moment, our own; words can cast a glow of desire around some shapes and expose others to anger and disgust. Most of all, poetry may seduce us with a freedom of opposition that can hold all contradictory and unrealized possibilities together in one fierce countermotion.

The experiments of spirit that we pass through in poetry pose no immediate or pragmatic danger to the community, but they may work secret changes in the heart; they give sustenance to the beast so that it does not die of our public habits. We live in limitations, imposed by ruthless Nature and by a human society that desperately aspires to equal Nature's inevitability. But there is in each of us a beast that does not love its chains. Poetry would feed the beast with words, calling it back to resistance and desire.

Nature is inexplicably indifferent to the opposition awakened within us; it does not punish us for so deeply resenting its laws and finding them unfair. But the community is uneasy and fears. To such fears poetry will answer at once with hymns to the public gods, praise of princes, maxims in verse, along with other uninteresting truths and prudent lies, soothing the community that sits in judgment.

As Plato saw clearly, the defense of poetry must turn on the question of education, which is our ability to be changed. Poets and poetry's advocates once rested their defense on a claim that poetry made better citizens, that it imparted "culture"; but that initially expedient lie (what else could we do, dragged so unceremoniously before the bench, but deny all the charges?) was far too brazen to last forever. Out of the collapse of that first great untruth arose a new and more hazardous defense: we next claimed that poetry was utterly safe and did not matter, that there is in art a distance from all things of pragmatic consequence and that the beast will not waken to its beguiling words. "Everyone must admit," says Kant in the *Critique of Judgment* (presuming the presence of at least three of us), "that any judgment about beauty in which the least personal interest is mixed will be a very partial and impure judgment of taste"—by which he certified to the community that whatever loveliness we find at the core of art cannot touch our creaturely desires.

Our traditions of public discourse on poetry have repeatedly offered assurances that those who read poetry do indeed have a safe and secure place to stand. The notion that the work of art is a thing, from which we are insulated by aesthetic distance, was both partial truth and expedient deception, set before Plato's jury still in session. Anyone who has experienced art, from the mass ecstasies of popular music to the more laborious and erudite pleasures of older poetry, knows that the studied distances of appreciation and interpretation are not the primary condition of our relation to a poem or song. Such distances, however, are constantly reaffirmed in the reports we make back to the community, assuring the magistracy that we have stood outside art's dangerous embrace. We say that we were not changed, that the virtuous citizen in each of us was not put to shame by the poem, that we did not discover the voice in the song becoming our own.

Privately we may be less certain. Sometimes the lines keep coming back to us, silently mocking the banality of a public duty well performed or evoking desire in a commonplace encounter, desire so palpable that it aches. As we stand in the shield-line, the words whisper in our ears, urging us to dash ahead bravely or throw down our shields and run away. At other times there are no particular words, only the dim awareness that, having been elsewhere in art, we are somehow no longer the same persons that we were. Poetry may call to that part of us that hungers for straying. And as a true straying, it is most forceful when not simply some predictable deviation from the common path or the mere strengthening of some darkness already within us. When we give in to such straying, we encounter the unexpected, the other; and it becomes part of us.

Perhaps the community is right to fear: the citizen's "self" may be found to be soft and plastic and its stability may be precarious; the self may be merely a place secured by habitual and public words. By such words we can live with others; by such words our mutual gestures become predictable; we submit, conceal, hold back, take the customs of the tribe for granted. But those other words, the words of poetry, rearrange relations, disrupt custom, say everything that must not be said.

Countervoice

Don't worry—it is not really true—poems are nothing more than the interpretations we give them, and those interpretations are made by readers who consider the poem from an impregnable distance. I assure you: it all happened long ago and in another country. It is we who look and judge; it is not true that we feel ourselves observed by the poem in return. Don't worry—we "learn" from reading poetry; we "gain" from the experience; it is a mere acquisition, a civilized possession that makes no claim on us. It's safe and fun—only art.

Perhaps this familiar countervoice is now right. Perhaps we have indeed become truly safe from the poems. No contest can remain forever in deadlock; and in this trial of more than two millennia, the defense of poetry may have become an all too successful defense against poetry. Like Odysseus' oarsmen, our ears dulled with wax, we can sail past the Sirens, not only safe from the danger but not even knowing of the windward hazard that made the journey worth the telling. The community approves: all it ever wanted was to have good oarsmen to pull uneventfully through from beginning to end—in this and in all things.

If this is the case, it is for poetry's advocates to consider whether we might not have made some fatal concession. We might detect such a concession in the late eighteenth century, in the dual birth of aesthetics and the modern notion of history. Not only did we ourselves put forward the claim of art's perfect isolation, we also permitted a vision of orderly historical change to be introduced unchallenged; and only now can we see its negative force, its laws of supersession, obsolescence, and forced drafts from the waters of Lethe. In the structure of history the community found the means to extend its most cherished power, the ability to control and define our place. New maps were drawn, new borders outlined, and we were all told where we belonged. We have been informed that we are radically "of" our age, or culture, or gender, or class, and not of another; we can go elsewhere only as tourists, cultural voyeurs. If we believe such a story, we will accept our assigned places, submit to our limitations, and repress the hope that we can go back to where we were, or stay where we choose, or even change and become other, except as we are driven helplessly forward by history's inertial machine.

The community's archaic myth of "us," in its many divisions and subdivisions, has been extended to include an equally mythic "now," protected from all otherness. Words from other times and places and from anyone with unauthorized concerns are safely "understood," contextualized and made charming curiosities or exoticisms to which we can listen without hearing. Those words do not matter, and those others cannot touch us. In the shallow waters of the here and now the subversive forces of art have been reduced to a few genres—film and popular song—where they still struggle nobly, though with limited resources, to lead individuals astray; yet somehow their very subversions have been twisted to the docile service of the community.

This is an unpleasant story. Let's change the ending. Perhaps this recent, most perilous phase of poetry's defense was simply the masterpiece of our dissimulation. The magistracy votes for acquittal. We laugh at them: they were deceived; poetry was guilty of the worst they could imagine. It has always been the subtle enemy. Now we can gloat and pluck the wax from the oarsmen's ears. Poetry meant to lead you astray all along; its intent was to entice you with words, to shame your dullness, to lure you into becoming other, to make you resist each submission, to make you want what you cannot have and suffer not attaining it.

We yawn and renounce that reasonable prose that Plato demanded for the defense. We confess that we never believed in history or in all those finely drawn boundaries between periods, cultures, and languages: we can make our home anywhere. We will no longer obey the laws that tell us we cannot, reasonably and properly, set this poem beside that poem. We are going to empty all the drawers of the museum and scatter the fragments together on the floor, rearranging them in pleasing combinations and creating fanciful stories with them.

No, we won't do any of this. We will start off properly, as we should, with one of the oldest fragments of lyric in the museum, one of the first verses in which the poet speaks for himself.

> Some Thracian tribesman is gloating now
> over that shield of mine which,
> unwilling though I was, I left behind
> by a bush—not a thing
> wrong with it. For my part,
> I was saved, so what do I care
> about the shield—let it go.
> I'll buy another just as good.
>
> Archilochos (ca. 680–640 B.C.)

It can still raise a faint smile of defiance, even in the well-controlled, sophisticated faces of our late age. We want to find the source of this smile, to trace the force of the pulse that pulls the sinew and twists the skin.

The lines were preserved in an anecdote by the Greco-Roman biographer and essayist Plutarch, writing on the institutions of the city-state of Sparta. He tells us that Archilochos, when he came to visit Sparta, was immediately driven out of the city for having been the author of these verses. The Spartans, at least, understood that the poet was truly responsible for the lines, that he could not yet claim the concealing distances of poetry: the lines were a deed of words. Even if there had been some longer poem that framed the lines or mitigated them, it was not heard.

To hold one's place in the line, never to let one's shield fall, was the very essence of citizen honor. There is another famous anecdote, also by Plutarch, about the Spartan mother who told her son as he was going off to war: come home either carrying your shield or dead upon it. If your shield was captured, your enemy had a chance to hoot at you, leap up and down in delight at your humiliation. The shield was the token of personal honor, defined by subordination to the *polis*.

But here at our mythical beginning of the lyric tradition, in one of the earliest poems in which a poet speaks for himself, we find Archilochos proclaiming to one and all that he abandoned his shield on the battlefield. There are no excuses: some half-barbarian Thracian is exulting and boasting and laughing at him, perhaps pointing at him as he runs away, drawing the attention of all his comrades. We have to wonder why anyone would admit such a thing publicly, and wonder even more why he would make the admission in verse, by which it can be remembered verbatim and repeated again and again, passed on to shame him later in Sparta and surviving even today to make a display of his ancient humiliation for our pleasure.

We cannot help noticing that this lyric voice, this voice that says "I" in a way distinct from the professional and divinely authorized voices of Homer and Hesiod, discovers itself by defining itself against the community and its values. The voice declares values for the speaker that are opposed to the values of the community. The community, even one's parents (like the Spartan mother), would rather see him dead in order to preserve the principle of the individual's subordination to the collective good, to the shield-line in which the individual is only a place between others, a place to be filled. Speaking for himself, Archilochos can stand outside the line; staying alive is more important—he can get another shield.

This happened long ago and in another country, even before Plato summoned poets and their advocates to trial (though when he was cast out of Sparta, Archilochos could have guessed that the trial would someday come). Since that age hardly any poet has been able to say "I" with such simplicity and pride, to create a space for himself and honestly speak for values that so openly contravert the community's wisdom. Later voices are driven into hiding and deception; and when they speak for themselves, we feel the pressure of the community's harsh attention: we hear confessional voices haunted by the values of the community rooted within them, or snarling satirical voices, or anxious self-justifying voices, or smooth seductive voices.

This poem repudiates the values of the community and, in doing so, leaves the poet vulnerable to the community's anger. And what is most strange is that such a poem of exposure should concern shields and losing shields, being left uncovered. In these lines Archilochos tells the truth about how he feels; and the Greek word for truth happens to be *aletheia,* "disclosure" or "uncoveredness."

Searching for beginnings, we find a lyric whose values violate social taboo, words that tell how I "really" feel as opposed to the way the community tells me I am supposed to feel, a lyric that declares the value of the single person and individual life over the ideology of the *polis,* a lyric that exposes the poet, tells the kind of truth that means uncovering or disclosure, and tells that truth on the occasion of losing his shield.

What we have discovered so far is only the hard surface of the poem. To "uncover" the poem and tell the truth about it, we must become aware of how Archilochos' truth-telling is a lyric deed. For this lyric tells its truth boldly and in such a way that we all smile, nodding and admitting to ourselves that this is our truth as well as his: hidden from the eyes of comrades, each of us would choose to live; and each of us understands clearly that "death before dishonor" is only what everyone else in the community seems to believe—not me (though I often make the claim as loudly as any, not wanting to be found out). The citizens of Sparta are angered by Archilochos' verses because they recognize a threat that can come only from the truth, something that they must repress, be shielded from. The lines that seem to be a private statement about the self are really a deed, done before the broadest public of all Greece and the future. It was that public declaration of private or alternative values that so disturbed the great community and made the citizens throw Archilochos out of Sparta, and all poets (apart from the the most docile public hymnists) out of Plato's Republic.

If Archilochos had not been bound in some way to the community and its values, he would not have written the poem. Through the poem he constructs new values, a new kind of shield of words to war with and to defend himself against the established values of the community—perhaps even to win them over as they discover those same values in themselves. The brashness of this poem-deed recognizes the anger of the community and braves it. As a public declaration of private values, the lyric fills some gap, answers some need, compensates for the loss of a shield.

No poem is a purely private deed: it is the private speaking back to the public. This poet, who proclaims himself distinct from the community, is at the same time engaging in a most peculiar gesture of rejoining the community. Read the poem carefully: he is not saying that he won't fight alongside them again; he is not refusing to risk his life further; he tells them he will get a new shield and take his place again in the shield-line.

It is this double movement that makes the fragment a great beginning: first proclaiming oneself apart from and opposed to the community, but then in the same moment seeking to rejoin it, either in the shield-line on the battlefield or in a new, subversive community of individuals who unwillingly discover in themselves the values he proclaims. Such individuals may stand in the shield-line and display before all the appearance of "death before dishonor," but they are lying, playing an uncomfortable role, always fearful of being discovered and cast out from the community.

The poems, fragments on the museum floor, are old tokens in some human exchange. Picking them up, we are caught in the exchange. These, like all human exchanges, are double: they are uncoverings, bared truths, shields lost that compel the poet to speak in exposure; at the same time they fill the gap with words, take the place of something missing and desired—lost honor, loss of place in the community in the loss of one's shield. More directly than epic or dramatic poetry, lyric poetry is bound to living circumstance, with its anxieties and pressures of revelation and concealment. When the poet speaks for the self to the community, the act involuntarily engages all those pressures and anxieties. And there is something in us that smiles, caught in such words and answering them.

But I have led you astray. Archilochos was a professional soldier in the seventh century B.C., when the values of the *polis* and the shield-line were in their formative stages. And the story of Archilochos' being driven out of Sparta is probably apocryphal, a fanciful tale generated by the strain between those lines of poetry (if they are indeed by Archilochos) and the values of the age of the shield-line into which those lines had survived. We will never know how those lines first tasted, but the lines kept speaking even as the community changed.

They could not easily be filed away under their historical context, as an example of some primitive lyric license superseded by the more sophisticated ethics of the *polis*.

There is no question that the lines, even when first uttered, in some way defied the community, heroic values, male folkways; but perhaps in the age of Archilochos his companions could more easily join in the uncomfortable laughter. A few centuries later, in the age of the shield-line, this voice of defiance became more disturbing. And it became still different in the age of Plutarch, who looked back wistfully from the Greco-Roman world to a mythic Sparta, a community so firm in its values that it instantly spit out anyone who uttered such dangerous words. This is the final layer and the most troubling irony: our earliest lyric voice, which sets itself so boldly apart, might easily have survived only because of its necessity to the edifying anecdote, publicly virtuous prose that approvingly illustrates the community that disapproves and tries to silence the poem.

The Ballad of Thomas the Rhymer

Of an invitation accepted, the discovery of the third path, an apple eaten, and the poet's uncomfortable reward.

True Thomas lay on Huntlie bank;
  A ferlie he spied wi' his e'e;
And there he saw a ladye bright
  Come riding down by the Eildon Tree.

Her skirt was o' the grass-green silk,
  Her mantle o' the velvet fyne;
At ilka tett o' her horse's mane
  Hung fifty silver bells and nine.

True Thomas he pu'd aff his cap,
  And louted low down on his knee:
"Hail to thee, Mary, Queen of Heaven!
  For thy peer on earth could never be."

"O no, O no, Thomas," she said,
  "That name does not belang to me;
I'm but the queen of fair Elfland
  That am hither come to visit thee.

"Harp and carp, Thomas," she said,
  "Harp and carp along wi' me;
And if ye dare to kiss my lips,
  Sure of your bodie I will be."

"Betide me weal, betide me woe,
  That weird shall never daunten me."
Syne he has kiss'd her rosy lips,
  All underneath the Eildon Tree.

"Noe ye maun go wi' me," she said,
  "True Thomas, ye maun go wi' me;
And ye maun serve me seven years,
  Thro' weal or woe as may chance to be."

She's mounted on her milk-white steed,
  She's ta'en true Thomas up behind;
And aye, whene'er her bridle rang,
  The steed gaed swifter than the wind.

O they rade on, and farther on,
  The steed gaed swifter than the wind;

Until they reach'd a desert wide,
  And living land was left behind.

"Light down, light down now, true Thomas,
  And lean your head upon my knee;
Abide ye there a little space,
  And I will show you ferlies three.

"O see ye not yon narrow road,
  So thick beset wi' thorns and briars?
That is the Path of Righteousness,
  Though after it but few inquires.

"And see ye not yon braid, braid road,
  That lies across the lily leven?
That is the Path of Wickedness,
  Though some call it the Road to Heaven.

"And see ye not yon bonny road
  That winds about the fernie brae?
That is the Road to fair Elfland,
  Where thou and I this night maun gae.

"But, Thomas, ye sall haud your tongue,
  Whatever ye may hear or see;
For speak ye word in Elfyn-land,
  Ye'll ne'er win back to your ain countrie."

O they rade on, and farther on,
  And they waded rivers abune the knee;
And they saw neither sun nor moon,
  But they heard the roaring of the sea.

It was mirk, mirk night, there was nae starlight,
  They waded thro' red blude to the knee;
For a' the blude that's shed on the earth
  Rins through the springs o' that countrie.

Syne they came to a garden green,
  And she pu'd an apple frae a tree:
"Take this for thy wages, true Thomas;
  It will give thee the tongue that can never lee."

"My tongue is my ain," true Thomas he said;
  A gudely gift ye wad gie to me!
I neither dought to buy or sell
  At fair or tryst where I might be.

"I dought neither speak to prince or peer,
  Nor ask of grace from fair ladye!"—
"Now haud thy peace, Thomas," she said,
  "For as I say, so must it be."

He has gotten a coat of the even cloth,
  And a pair o' shoon of the velvet green;
And till seven years were gane and past,
  True Thomas on earth was never seen.

1 Seduction/Invitation

All the bright colors of physical things call out to one another, and how amid all this can a human being find rest?

Liu Hsieh, *The Literary Mind Carves Dragons*
(ca. 500 A.D.)

Invited Out

There are old poems, often the most simple poems, to which we return. Each return in our reading is like repeating the paces of a dance, with a particular pleasure in passing through the same, most simple motions. Whether the dance is simple or difficult, we first began it with a strenuous and awkward mimicry of the dancers, stumbling through the movements, until at last its fine turns and graces became part of us and seemed, in each repetition, to be produced as if by chance from within ourselves. There is service in this, seven years' worth perhaps: in the beginning it was the lure of something remote, being called into the circle of the dancers, then a clumsy excitement in the first motions, followed by growing ease of familiarity, after which came boredom, neglect and forgetting, and the pleasure of return.

We might reflect on how a person becomes bound to the dance and in that binding what happens to both the dance and the person dancing. In some way each dance is changed by our dancing, and the invisible average of all the other dancers bends and reshapes itself to the characteristic motions of the new dancer. We like to say then that we have mastered it, as if we had made it somehow obedient to our will. But we know that it is really we who have let ourselves be slowly changed by the pressure of the dance's strangeness. We wonder why we should do this. There must be some lure here, some invitation that makes us eager to undergo the changes by which the graceful motions become our own.

Ich am of Irlaunde,
and of the holy londe

of Irlande.
Gode sire, pray ich thee
for of sainte charite,
come and daunce wit me
in Irlande.

We guess it was a song; and as songs do, it must have gained much of its force by the repetition. Perhaps it was one of those lyrics that everyone knew, and whenever someone heard it a smile would come, as if hearing the words of an old friend. It became familiar, kin. As kin, there were times we were drawn to it and times we disregarded it, or felt comfortable with it, or were impatiently weary of it; but even when we were weary of it, it was a voice that never entirely lost its claim on us in the repetition.

Yet it is a strange kinship: this familiar voice always begins by introducing itself, declaring that it is a stranger here among us, a voice from somewhere else. In the early fourteenth century, when the song was written down, Ireland was Gaelic-speaking, and to proclaim "ich am of Irlaunde" was already a translation of sorts, an attempt to speak to us that was always arriving from elsewhere. In our time this familiar voice's claim to come from somewhere else is even more strongly confirmed by the archaic pronouns, the spellings, the gracious address. Dancing Ireland far away merges into a remote past where people must have been always dancing.

But let us suppose it was a popular song. The person who stands before us and sings "ich am of Irlaunde" is no stranger but one of our own, a member of the community. Yet to issue her invitation the woman (which is the gender of the voice we most expect to call a "gode sire" to the dance) who begins the song dresses herself in the "I" of someone from far away. If we are not already there, the dance is something to which we must be called, and the call always comes from elsewhere, from another kind of space.

"Ich am of Irelaunde, / and of the holy londe of Irlande." The singer repeats her origins to be certain we have understood that in this present voice she is not a familiar person from here; her home is elsewhere, which is a "holy land." We have never been there, but we know a little of such holy lands, like the shrine of Walsingham in Sir Walter Raleigh's famous song:

"As you came from the holy land
  Of Walsingham,
Met you not my true love

By the way as you came?"
"How should I know your true love,
   That have met many a one
As I came from the holy land,
   That have come, that have gone?"

"How should I know your true love?" The traveler responds to the questioner by requiring some identifying marks. The first question— "Met you not my true love?"—had been innocent, as if the speaker did not understand that by going on a pilgrimage a traveler surrenders his or her place in the familiar community, where everyone is known and knows his true love. On the road all are strangers, requiring close observation and introductions.

In the Elizabethan song mention of the "holy land" identifies the traveler as a pilgrim who, like other pilgrims, has come and gone, and does not really belong to the holy land. But the voice who announces "ich am of Irlaunde" has only come, has left her holy land to enter our common world in order to choose one among us and invite him to return with her.

The familiar person singing a familiar song declares herself to be an outsider, visitor from a holy land. Then she turns to address one of us, establishing a relation and calling the man out of the familiar world and back to her home in the charmed circle of the dance.

Gode sire, pray ich thee,
for of sainte charite,
come and daunce wit me
in Irlande.

The voice is deferential and polite, as befits a stranger in our community who addresses one of us. The stranger wants something of us—strangers often do—and makes her entreaty graciously. "Gode sire, pray ich thee"—spare a penny? take me in among you? But this stranger does not make the common request; she makes one of us the object of her desire.

We have heard the song many times before. We are willing to be surprised, flattered, lured. The stranger will beg what strangers usually do not beg: one of us, our company and partnership, to take us away from this ordinary world of polite social relations and polite language ("gode sire, pray ich thee, for of sainte charitee") back to Ireland and the dance, where the singer claims to be at home. The strangeness of the request is confirmed by this unexpected voice of woman, a woman who places herself outside our community's common roles, not giving herself to be courted by one of us and made to share our dull, too familiar world; instead she chooses, calls one of us back to her magic home. Wherever that place of dancing is, it is not here, nor is it simply another version of here, a place of deferential hierarchy and wariness of strangers. What they do there in Ireland is dance, and even a "gode sire" from here will not be out of place if he goes with her there to the dance.

The song's motions, like the movements of the dance, are circular, repeating: from the opening declaration of her home to the final line which, after a pause, tells him where this dancing will be: "come and daunce wit me / in Irlande." Someone steps out from among the dancers to invite one of the bystanders to return with her into the dance, and the circle closes again. The movement and its song are gestures of great allure, like all promises of magic space elsewhere. It requires no test of fulfillment: in all its repetitions the song remains perpetual approach and invitation. That same movement is again repeated in the act of copying, on an old manuscript where the song is preserved: it is a small, charmed lyric space into which the scribe or monk-copyist longs to flee. The invitation addresses someone with desire, but it may also be displaced into the voice of some merely speculative other, displaced by one who intensely desires to be addressed with such desire and be called away.

Leaving Ireland

Etain, the second wife of the fairy king Midir, was placed under a spell by Midir's first wife and put through various transformations until at last she was born in Ireland as a mortal woman. There she became the wife of the king, Eochaid. To win back Etain, the fairy king Midir challenged Eochaid, king in Ireland, to a game of chess; on winning the match, he demanded a kiss from Etain as his forfeit. The moment they kissed Midir and Etain both changed into swans and flew away to the Great Land. In the saga Midir sings this song to Etain before the chess game:

> Fair lady, will you go with me
> into the land of wonder where there are stars?
> Hair there is like the crown of primroses
> and to its very tip the body is like snow.

Neither mine nor thine exist there;
teeth there are bright; eyebrows black;
the number of our hosts there is a delight to the eye;
each cheek there is the color of the foxglove.

. . . . .

Gentle sweet streams flow across the land,
choice mead and wine;
noble, without flaw are the people;
conception is without sin or guilt.

We see everyone on every side,
and no one sees us;
the darkness of Adam's sin
hides us from being counted.

Woman, if you come to my vigorous people,
a golden crown will be on your head;
fresh pork, ale, milk and drink,
you will have with me there, Fair Lady.[1]

The Great Land that lies still further beyond Ireland seems very much like the dancing Ireland to which we had just been invited. "Neither mine nor thine exist there," where all is pleasure and desires are no sooner proposed than they are fulfilled, without guilt or sin.

We had understood that this space was closed off from the common world, accessible only by magic journeys and invitations that take us by surprise. What we had not realized was that it lay so close by. All around us the dancers watch the children of Adam and Eve, and yet they themselves are not seen. For a moment we feel the discomforting force of those invisible eyes.

Forking Path: Warning

He awaits the invitation that does not come; he grows impatient, sets out on the journey:

> Perhaps you haven't heard of the younger son of a family of Shou-ling who went to the city of Han-tan to learn the famous "Han-tan strut." Not only did he not succeed in learning it, he also forgot how to walk as he had before, and he ended up going back home crawling on all fours.
>
> Master Chuang Chou, "Floods of Autumn"

Invited In

Green, green is the grass by the river,
in garden the willows are all dense and full.
High in the tower a woman so lovely,
she glows in the window, white and so pure.
Rouge on her cheeks, bright in her beauty,
and she puts out a pale and delicate hand.

Once long ago I sang in the barroom,
now I'm the wife of a traveling man.
He travels for pleasure and never comes home now,
A lonely bed can't be kept empty for long.

Chinese, anonymous (ca. second century A.D.)[2]

It is an old poem and a familiar poem, one of those verses that are always fresh but never new; nor can we imagine there was ever a time when it was new. From its first appearance in written history it was already called an "old poem," from a collection called "The Nineteen Old Poems." It all happened long ago and in another country.

It has always been treated with reverence and a due respect for its age; as in an old love letter, a decent haze covers the compulsion of desire and its quiet call to adultery. Of this, "Ich am of Irlaunde" was innocent: it called us away from the polite habits of the community, but took no notice of any ties that might have already been formed, ties that would bind us from departure; we readily suppose the singer free to invite and the "gode sire" free to accept. That song speaks the magic language of dancing Ireland, which has only a present and a future tense. This is as close to Eden's language as we can reach, an invitation with no past: "come and daunce wit me." But it is a language that most poetry cannot speak; our common poetry struggles with the past and hides desire under layers of covering, displacement, and deflection. Even this "old poem" hangs back at the moment just before invitation, and its hesitation is bound up with an acknowledgment of the past, a personal history and the woman's place in the established relations of the community. The poem is "old" and has a past, yet it sets desire against the dead contracts and proprieties of the community. Male desire meets female desire; but desire and the invitation that follows from it are repressed, displaced beneath the poem's surfaces and into the silence that follows the poem.

"Ich am of Irlaunde" called someone out to the dance, to an open space elsewhere; the "old poem" draws someone in, through layers of covering surface. The openness of the former is astonishing; the covering of the "old poem" is more familiar and well understood. Yet poetry lets us see the alluring shape beneath such decent surfaces. It obeys contradictory laws, drawing our attention to what it conceals. We respond to the opposed forces—cloth constraining and flesh straining against it—with our own double motion: we are drawn toward it, and at the same time hold it at a distance—an aesthetic object, only a poem.

It might have once been a tavern song, and could just as easily have been sung by either a man or a woman.[3] Because Chinese version uses no pronouns, we can hear the song in a man's voice, understanding "she" in place of "I" in the last four lines. In such a male voice the poem becomes a report back to the community of what she said or of what she might have said. Even in its first moments, now lost beyond recovery, this may have been the voice of desire deflected into fantasy—like the fantasy of the monk who copies into his manuscript the invitation to the dance.

The poetry of the poem is found in its empty spaces, in what is not said. Each line creates such empty spaces between itself and the preceding line, territories that have been silently traversed. At first such empty spaces are mere physical motions, motions that soon become direction and vectors of attention, until at last the spaces are unspoken motives, anxieties, and anticipations. The poem needs its particular words, but only as clothing, so that they can outline the precise shape of what is hidden, unsaid. Words are the visible points that outline heart's and body's movement, but they are not the movement itself.

The first line, "Green, green is the grass by the river," is a beginning shared by several "old poems" and songs, the signature of some general distance of separation. The later exegetes of this poem have seen in the green expanse of grass stretching along the riverbank the analogy of continuing desire and a scene that draws the attention of someone who feels desire: eyes staring off into hollow distances. Or they tell us that such greenness is the figure of seasonal recurrence, like the longing that returns to the human animal in the warmer seasons. But the scene is also a space across which a body can move, a body invisible in the poem because we move with it, nothing drawing the attention but the line of the river that leads to an undefined somewhere.

Desire is a structure of feeling that is bound to a particular form, either in the eyes or in the heart. To give desire its shape, the scene's initial vacancy must be filled: something blocks our vision and motion, draws attention to what is denied and concealed. When this occurs we have surface and hidden subsurface, covering and the possibility of nakedness.

Summer's willows cover our view. The exegetes remind us that the quality of those willows, *yü-yü,* "dense and full," is a word applied equally to the human heart: cares that seem to swell within and press against the surfaces, longing for expression, trying helplessly to break out. These trees, *liu,* whose very name puns on the invitation to linger, also *liu,* belong to a garden, and the garden must conceal a dwelling; the dwelling must surround a person, and who knows what wonders lie hidden beneath the concealment of the person's clothes or in the heart?

The first four lines of the poem are moments of attention that move us through space and past barriers: passing through the dense willows we see a building, and high in the building another gap opens, the window in which a beautiful woman is framed. Such gaps are the geometry of exposure, openings in the shield line that focus our attention. Let us suppose some other old poem in which this woman is placed before our eyes in the first lines: she would be no less beautiful, but we would be less drawn to her beauty. In this present poem we have discovered her, won through to her, penetrated barriers to what lies hidden. Yet she remains high up, out of reach. We can make no claim on her; we are the stranger, come from afar and from out there where everything is open; here, watching her, we are the voyeur.

It is poetry rather than sharp mortal vision that lets us see her rouged cheeks in the next line. We have the illusion of drawing ever closer, to the thinnest veil of powder covering the skin.

Our seduction depends on not knowing or refusing to notice that it is we ourselves who are seduced: we do not wonder why she stands there at the window or why she has put on that last bright covering of rouge, unless to attract the attention and desire that we give so freely. But she too is playing her role in this dance of distance, concealment, and approach. Now that we have come to her, it is her turn; and her motion is visible to us. Our eyes focus on the bare white flesh, on the hand that comes out through the window. She penetrates a barrier outward, answering our own inward motion: it was all a slow dance. Her moving hand is the focal point of the poem and the only motion that is made visible in the words' surface; it is an ambiguous gesture that we are willing to read as invitation: "tangled in thy beauty's web, / And snared by the ungloving of thy hand."[4]

Having reached bare skin, we are ready to go beneath the sensuous surfaces to the human creature who acts with intent, who possesses desire, history, circumstance. In order to cross this final barrier we require explanations; there is peril in the oncoming sexual encounter. All the implicit shapes of blockage and distance suggest to us that this woman is forbidden, not sexually available—maiden or wife. That was a potent lure, but now that we have won through the barriers and read invitation in her movement, there is another interval of separation, a moment of anxiety that makes us hesitate and want to withdraw. As long as we were merely voyeurs the game was safe and one-sided—we were invisible. But when the hand reaches out, we are seen. The other is no longer merely a desirable surface; when the final layer of covering is passed, we find someone else at home behind those surfaces, someone who make us the reciprocal object of her attention and desire.

> Once long ago I sang in the barroom,
> now I'm the wife of a traveling man.
> He travels for pleasure and never comes home now,
> A lonely bed can't be kept empty for long.

The last four lines answer our hesitation and draw us toward contact, preserving the lure of the forbidden while making it safe and accessible. She is now "covered," housed and hidden away, not displayed before all; but she once "sang in the barroom," and perhaps did more than sing. Male folklore disposes us to suspect that, having been displayed before many men, she will always be willing to encounter one more. And if this information answers an unspoken anxiety in the one who watches, it also exposes her unspoken motive: why she tells him this, knowing how he will understand. Or perhaps it is only his inference as he stares at her, the projection of his desire.

She is married and forbidden now, but her husband, so we are told, is a *tang-tzu,* someone who doesn't give the attention due to the woman at home, who travels far and wide in the open spaces that began the poem and never comes back. Each of these last lines allays an unspoken fear, the clauses of our hesitation. We are given to know that her sexual desire is left unfulfilled by his absence; we know that she has cause (if not, according to traditional morality, justification) for being unfaithful; we know that we are safe from a jealous husband's return.

As it began with empty space, the poem closes with an empty space; but this space, invested with risk and desire, lies concealed within: empty bed.

Counterpoem for Penelope

Here the path forks. We know which branch we will follow. But we glance down the other corridor, which closes the circle and brings us again to the beginning.

> Fair young maid all in the garden,
> Strange young man passes her by,
> Says "Fair maid, will you marry me?"
> This then, sir, was her reply.

> "O no, kind sir, I cannot marry thee,
> For I've a love who sails the sea,
> And he's been gone for seven long years,
> Still no man will marry me."

The young stranger then tries her, suggesting the misfortunes that her beloved, the "traveling man," could have suffered or his possible infidelities in the course of seven years (which is the span true Thomas was bound in the court of the Queen of Elfyn); but she maintains her faith against his invitation.

> Then he picked her up all in his arms,
> And kisses gave her one, two, three,
> Singing, "Weep no more, fair pretty maid,
> I am your lost John Riley."

Hanging Back

When desire is on the point of being fulfilled, there may be a moment of hesitation, of hanging back. The more intense the desire and the longer the path to attainment, the more surely a space will be opened for second thoughts just before the consummation. Desire's trajectory was headlong and commanded our attention: we were our "first thoughts." Desire became the entire form of our life, and beyond its imminent consummation and conclusion we may see an ominous emptiness.

We pause. For a brief or longer time we may be held in a stasis that resists both forward motion and withdrawal. At this moment we hear mocking laughter in the paradox posed by desire: that the end was only a function of the desire itself, and that the value of the end can be sustained only by being continually deferred, missed, kept at a distance. "Come always, come," writes Vicente Aleixandre. At last the beloved approaches; he tells her to stop, to come no nearer:

> Pero tú non te acerques. Tu frente destellante, carbón encendido
>   que me arrebata a la propria conciencia,
> duelo fulgúreo en que de pronto siento la tentación de morir,
> de quemarme los labios con tu roce indeleble,
> de sentir mi carne desharcerse contra tu diamante abrasador.
>
> No te acerques, porque tu beso se prolonga como el choque
>   imposible de las estrellas,
> como el espacio que súbitamente se incendia,
> éter propagador donde la destrucción de los mundos
> es un único corazón que totalmente se abrasa.
>
> But don't come any closer. Your glowing face, live coal that stirs
>   my consciousness,
> the shining pain where all of a sudden I'm tempted to die,
> to burn my lips on your indelible friction,
> to feel my flesh melting, embraced in your burning diamond.
>
> Don't come closer, because your kiss goes on and on like the
>   impossible collision of the stars,
> like space that suddenly catches fire,
> fertile ether where the destruction of worlds
> is a single heart that burns itself out with love.[5]

The moment of contact is desperately postponed. Yet even in the command to halt the approach, the words luridly anticipate fiery dissolution and burning away: fulfillment is extinction. In such close proximity each vector of motion resolves into its opposite, and the oscillation becomes the words of a poem that hold the opposed forces together. In the stanzas that follow Aleixandre breaks through the desperate pause and tells the beloved to resume the approach; but the truth and the solution is hidden in the title: *Ven siempre, ven,* "Come always, come," where in the imperative of the invitation we scarcely hear the qualification that permanently defers arrival: "come always."

Poems often try to hold us on the margin, to perpetuate the contradiction, gratifying and at the same time withholding gratification. In obvious and secret ways they continually make all contrary motions in order to hold great forces in a delicate balance: in their structure, in the art of address, in their topics. Such balancing countermotions often appear in persuasion.

That invitation is best which needs no persuasion: a hand reaches out to draw the bystander into the circle of the dancers or to summon the stranger in the garden into a bed too long empty. It is a permission that acts with confidence in the other's desire. As the voice takes our willing acceptance for granted, so we do as well—no danger, only a poem. But as soon as the voice begins actively to persuade, to define its promises and overwhelm objections, the persuasive voice betrays a lack of faith in its innate allure; we enter into a commerce of desire and the exchange of attractive things.

A person made the object of persuasion is reminded of his or her choices, reminded of doubts and hesitations. The persuasion invokes the distance and resistance that it sets out to overcome. Conjectured wants are answered with lures and promises. The voice is certain that the other will hang back: it ventures and risks disdain, armored with an inventory of imagined attractions. The beloved is effectively silenced. Her part has been written for her: she is supposed to be reluctant, and through reluctance she joins in to defer the conclusion of love and desire. Her role is to sing the songs he has written for her.

> A cask of Alban, nine years old or more,
> Stands full, and in my garden sprays of parsley
> Are prime for weaving crowns; a wealth of ivy
>   Waits, my Phyllis,
>
> For you to wind into your shining hair;
> Burnished silver laughs in the hall, the altar,
> Chastely girt with modest herbs, lacks only
>   The victim's blood;
>
> The house is all alive with tumult, girls
> And boys running in quick confusion, here,
> Everywhere, hearth flames quivering and reeling,
>   Dark soot coiling.
>
> Now hear what merriments I call you to:
> The month of Venus risen from seas, we toast
> The Ides, the day that severs April, twinning
>   Half from half;
>
> For me rightly a day of festival,
> Almost more sacred than my own, marking

The dawn from where Maecenas reckons all
  His gathering years.

But that young man you burn for, Telephus,
His trim transcends your lot; besides, a rich
Swiveling wanton has stormed his towers and keeps him
  In smiling bondage.

The flames that shattered Phaethon hurl terror
On swaggering hopes, and Pegasus dragged down
Under Bellerophon, his earthly rider,
  Sets grim example,

To seek what tallies with yourself, not yearn
For things far and forbidden, but surrender
A paramour so ill matched with you. Come then,
  My last of loves,

For not again hereafter shall a woman
Stir warmth in me; come, learn these songs and sing them
In the voice that summons love; singing can shrivel
  Our black sorrows.

Horace, Odes, IV.11[6]

Poetry is an art of multiple deflections: deflection of passion's trajectory, of address, and here a deflection of her attention away from his aging body into an inventory of lures, things he has that will be shared with the person who comes: the Latin opens with a list, *Est mihi ... est ... est ...,* "There is of mine ... and there is ... and there is ..."[8] Like the songs she will sing to him at the end, the alluring things here promised are common ground on which the lovers can come together, without the terminal union of bodies. Even these deflecting attractions will defer the encounter only temporarily: they are not permanent acquisitions, but wait for the moment when they will be used, fulfilled, consumed, like the cask of Alban wine that has waited nine years.

Diverging Passage: Commodity

Occasions of desire may be bound in a relation to physical form or to the figuring of such form: the object of desire is given as a surface, a surface that is both promise and concealment and which, in its bare spaces or contours, displays what is withheld. This much is well known. However, grasping the function of such form makes it possible to stage

The merriments to which he invites her are the celebrations of the Ides of April, the month of Venus and sexual desire (with a passing acknowledgment of his patron's birthday). This will be a moment of crux, after which everything will be finished, all burning and future love. A person might dance in Ireland forever, but once Phyllis enters the charmed circle of Horace's celebration, everything moves toward one blazing flash. Things will merge and fuse: the wine to be swallowed, the parsley and ivy to be wreathed in her hair that will gleam, reflected in the polished silver that now laughs, and will laugh again in reflecting her laughter. And there is the final unmentioned merging that is the proper end of Venus' festival. As is right for an old poem, here is a vector whose hidden terminus is an empty place in the bed.

Phyllis will be wreathed, and something else is wreathed as well— *casta vincta verbenis*, "chastely girt with modest herbs"—the virginal altar that also awaits its moment, when it will stream with blood from the sacrificial beast. Bloodletting was a proper and customary part of Roman religious rites, a strict formalization of violence that reappears in that strangest of institutions, the games. Horace's poetry often returns to the orderly purity of the sacrifice, just as it subdues all violence, passion, and dangerous forces in controlled form. On

occasions of desire in order to to call forth desire in the other. Within the quotidian world clothing aspires to precisely this event; it is speculatively seeing oneself being seen. All clothing's complicated codes, whether promising ease of attainment or virtuous restraint, seriousness, indifference, or sweet frivolity, are merely variant expediencies to an identical end.

Similar invitations can be made with things, or even with things offered in the words of a poem. Like clothing, such things are intended to be nothing more than surfaces, means to guide the other to the person who claims to have control over the thing. Displayed and offered, the thing becomes the means to focus desire; it glows. The thing becomes like clothing that has retained its alluring shape even though the wearer has stepped out of it: the thing is a surface with nothing inside.

The thing, now an emptied surface, becomes a token, leading to ends displaced or deferred. Once we accept the validity of the token in the currency of desire, the process of token formation is endless—tokens of tokens of tokens of an empty space that was once warm with flesh. By these tokens we hope to barter for affection and make exchanges. If the other takes the token held out, a bargain is made: desire has been elicited.

this altar of woman or stone there will be an end to the beast; and flesh will burn whose smoke is pleasing to the hungry gods.

The aftermath is black soot, black cares, black ash; there is much burning here: hearth flames and warmth for the last time stirred in the heart. Phyllis is already burning for someone else, her flames out of control like those that burned the earth when Phaethon's sun-carriage went out of control and strayed from its course. And the man she loves burns in turn for another; he too is held in bondage, *vinctum,* like the altar bound in herbs and awaiting the victim's blood. In this season destructive and alluring flame is everywhere, immoderate and unequal desire that binds its victims over to slaughter and love's end. Horace too stands on the brink: *Age iam, meorum finis amorum,* "Come then, my last of loves." There is a fierce trajectory in this that needs to be deflected, brought under control, "measured" like the lines of his song and the ripe restraint of his singing voice.

There is no Phyllis of flesh and blood to act upon this invitation or to act outside of the poem's play. Even if there were some Roman girl hiding under the Greek name, it scarcely matters: her part has been written for her. It is this we find most difficult to understand in poetry's strange invitations: the work of art may seek to close itself off

---

The desire to be desired first set in motion this process of token formation, and it can indeed succeed in stimulating responding desire in the other. But in the displacement or deferral of desire, by which the body is able to withdraw from behind the desirable surface, a space is created that can never be crossed. The person who offers the token discovers that if the other does not wisely disdain empty surface, the other may love only surface and can be drawn along further only by proffering yet another, still more alluring surface. And although the beloved can perhaps be drawn on, he or she never comes any closer. Even if, in the bargain made by the token, flesh seems to meet, the thing will always remain a gossamer film between them, preventing perfect union.

Voices that offer things are uninnocent; they fear pain. The wisest of uninnocent voices, Horace's, offers things that will dissolve and disappear on their acceptance, things to be jointly consumed. But we may meet other, more twisted voices that offer tokens to the beloved. There is a honeyed voice that holds out clothing, bargaining away his desire for the beloved's nakedness in exchange for eliciting her own desire, which is to imagine herself seen with desire. And there are dangerous voices that would force the acceptance of the token, either to compromise the beloved or to compensate her.

from those it addresses, both the pretended and the real audiences. It keeps its distance with a melancholy urbanity and fastidious craft, which are countermotions against an intensity, a desire whose consummation will be the end of desire.

> Come then,
>   My last of loves,
> For not again hereafter shall a woman
> Stir warmth in me.

Both her refusal and her acceptance will be equally terminal: sacrificial death and a general conflagration lurk just beneath the surface of all these attractive anticipations. In this trajectory to flame, the only escape is to pause somewhere in the movement, to close off some moment and make it circular. That imperative of eternal delay shifts the sexual invitation to a deflected request: that Phyllis come, learn his songs, and sing them back to him *amanda voce,* "with a voice of loving." He invites her to sing to him songs of invitation—nothing more. The lovers will be left leaning toward one another in perpetual approach.

> Fair youth, beneath the trees, thou canst not leave
>   Thy song, nor ever can those trees be bare;
>   Bold Lover, never, never canst thou kiss,
> Though winning near the goal—yet do not grieve;
>   She cannot fade, though thou hast not thy bliss,
>   For ever wilt thou love, and she be fair!

It is the solution offered in Keats's "Ode on a Grecian Urn," but that particular urn-surface of controlled art may, in another urn-sense, contain only black ashes, with none of the crackling flames that make the solution so imperative here. Horace's songs, which might diminish black sorrow and resist the black ash of burning, are *carmina,* the category of this poem and all the Odes. They are, in their archaic sense, *carmina* that are magic "charms."

In place of the empty bed and the consummation of desire, this poem hangs back before the flames, circling upon itself, singing songs about songs about songs. The Phyllis of Horace's poem is a lyrical cousin to Scheherazade, whose life hangs on an unending thread of story. If the song ends, the frozen momentum will be released, the lovers will go up in flames, and this final love will be finished forever.

Observing with the melancholy of dispassion, we may scorn such deflection, which neither turns back nor rushes ahead but instead bends away on the third path into a charmed circularity of inviting song. This song-space hangs close around the world of the children of Adam and Eve, but there is a barrier of form that holds the song-space apart from the world. Although it seems that at any moment the circle will break and the dancers will be hurled out from their orbits back into the common world, a strict law holds them in repetition. Form's resilience is in direct proportion to desire's force and the fear of losing control. Horace is form's master, but the work's hard surface is only a measure of the strain it must bear. The song is both music and rites: a relation between ecstatic union and holding strictly apart.

Digression: Music and Rites

Music unifies; rites set things apart. In unifying there is a mutual drawing close; in setting things apart there is mutual respect. If music overwhelms, dissolution occurs; if rites overwhelm, there is division. To bring the affections into accord and to adorn their outward appearance is the function of music and rites. When rites and ceremonies are established, then noble and commoner find their own levels; when music unifies them, then those above and those below are joined in harmony.

Book of Rites, "Record of Music"

In earliest antiquity the Sage Kings established music and rites to hold the forces of the ceremony in a precarious balance. In every ceremony each participant, including the audience, is set apart from others, fulfilling a role that is a function of its distinctions from other roles. Just as in our relations in the world, the encounter with others is an estrangement: we recognize difference in desires, motives, intentions. We threaten and are threatened, try to compel and are compelled. Everywhere is division.

But ceremony realizes an alternative possibility that is submerged in the common world. I am not the role I play, this determinate relation to others. In ceremony I know that others have played this role before me and will play it again after me. Moreover, I understand that for all who play against me now the ceremony is a joint venture, a serious game. And even as I play the role seriously, I feel its boundaries dissolve: I know all the words of all the other participants and repeat them silently to myself as the others say them. In the play each actor plays every part as well as playing against all other parts. As at Horace's celebration, the songs are already written.

There is a doubleness here and there are dangers, for which the Sage Kings gave us music and rites. On one side is the danger of difference melting, a loss of self and place in terrifying union in which all the words become entirely my own, an ecstasy (*ekstasis:* to stand outside the self). On the other side is the danger of absolute estrangement, the complete absorption of the participant into the role. Here the other players in the ceremony become truly other, and we find ourselves back in ordinary life rather than in the shared, repeatable venture of ceremony. Music and rites hold these dangers in balance. Music unifies: it is shared by all participants, the common ground of the ceremony, and it constantly reminds us that we are together in the enterprise. The formal gestures and the stylized words of rites reinforce difference, between the roles of the participants and between the participant and his or her role.

The Sage Kings of antiquity knew that poetry was both music and rites. We share the music and stand with those others, speaking or being addressed (even undressed), seeing and being seen. At the same time in poetry there are stylized rites that give us a place apart: we are only reading words, we see nothing; we hear no voices, only a poem.

Music and rites are the tools of compensation. Each age and each poet either puts weight on the stylization of rites or plays the music more loudly, depending on which threat seems greatest. Where the lure of the music is overpowering, the poet hardens the text against it. When the artifice of rites seems too strong, we yearn for music and rashly believe we would rush willingly ahead, answering the invitation to come dance in Ireland.

Rushing Ahead to Eden

Those unnamed old singers included us in their invitations, and they left their songs of invitation so that we could sing them for ourselves or so that we could receive them sung by others. Such songs remain easy for us; they are the joy of the creature playing, and we do not misunderstand their temptations and promised delights. It is otherwise with the later poets. They seem to call to some particular other and allow us only to overhear; but we know that their call is issued only so that we can listen. If there is pleasure in this, it is a strange and concealed pleasure, a pleasure gone somehow astray. The play becomes a dark game: the speaker pretends not to notice our presence, while the person addressed is transformed into a mere landscape, a alluring surface toward which the poet speaks and we listen. This is poetry from a fallen world, a poetry of clothing; and knowing that it is fallen, it longs to strip away the covering of words and bodies and to find its way back to Eden.

Come, Madam, come, all rest my powers defie,
Until I labour, I in labour lie.
The foe oft-times having the foe in sight,
Is tir'd with standing though he never fight.
Off with that girdle, like heavens Zone glittering,
But a far fairer world incompassing.
Unpin that spangled breastplate which you wear,
That th'eyes of busie fooles may be stopt there.
Unlace your self, for that harmonious chyme
Tells me from you, that now it is bed time.
Off with that happy busk, which I envie,
That still can be, and still can stand so nigh.
Your gown going off, such beautious state reveals,
As when from flowry meads th'hills shadow steales.
Off with that wyerie Coronet and shew
The haiery Diademe which on you doth grow:
Now off with those shooes, and then safely tread
In this loves hallow'd temple, this soft bed.
In such white robes, heaven's Angels us'd to be
Receav'd by men; Thou Angel bringst with thee
A heaven like Mahomets Paradise; and though
Ili spirits walk in white, we easly know,
By this these Angels from an evil sprite,
Those set our hairs, but these our flesh upright.
   License my roaving hands, and let them go,
Before, behind, between, above, below.
O my America! my new-found-land,
My kingdome, safeliest when with one man man'd,
My Myne of precious stones, My Emperie,
How blest am I in this discovering thee!
To enter in these bonds, is to be free;
Then where my hand is set, my seal shall be.
   Full nakedness! All joyes are due to thee,

As souls unbodied, bodies uncloth'd must be,
To taste whole joyes. Gems which you women use
Are like Atlanta's balls, cast in mens views,
That when a fools eye lighteth on a Gem,
His earthly soul may covet theirs, not them.
Like pictures, or like books gay coverings made
For lay-men, are all women thus array'd;
Themselves are mystick books, which only wee
(Whom their imputed grace will dignifie)
Must see reveal'd. Then since that I may know;
As liberally, as to a Midwife, shew
Thy self: cast all, yea, this white lynnen hence,
There is no pennance due to innocence.
   To teach thee, I am naked first; why than
What needst thou have more covering then a man.

John Donne, Elegie 19, "Going to Bed"

John Donne undresses his wife for us, never turning his eyes to acknowledge that he knows we are present. We are set up to be voyeurs, or more precisely, set up by this gifted master of oxymoron to be blind voyeurs, who are loudly invited to gather outside the bedroom door and listen. We are never given nakedness itself—a direct and comprehensible creaturely pleasure—rather we are given words in an urgent trajectory toward nakedness, self-dramatizing words in which the poet stands noisily between us and the promised view. We are both included and excluded: he publishes (in several senses) the gradual disrobing of his wife, while at the same time withholding her from our gaze, commenting to his wife within our hearing that we have no right to look. Ours are precisely "th'eyes of busie fooles" that all these falling veils were meant to block.

Although he makes vigorous pretense to address the woman, his words transform her into opaque surface; she is territory, "mine" and

---

Diverging Passage: Suspicions

In the fallen world all poetic address is deflected: words take on an obliquity, and the poet can call to the other only through mediating things, which are instruments of motives concealed and fulfillments deferred. However, when one of those mediating things happens to be another person, the person he only pretends to address, then the corrupting force of concealment becomes apparent. His words to the beloved are shaped by the anticipation of *our* attention, we who listen outside the door. To "a mine" to be quarried for those very jewels that cover her surface, catching our foolish gaze and preventing a thorough reading of her body. But we soon realize that he is not addressing her at all; at every moment he is hearing himself being heard by us, his words and the tone of voice shaped by the pressure of our attention. For his lady these words are less invitation than command, imperative, a sexual haste that promises her but little pleasure. But the voice of command seems almost unaware that she might hear; its interest is to dramatize for us his power, his right over her. There is indeed an erotic event in this, an invitation and a seduction; but it is the poem's audience standing just outside the bedroom door, who are to be seduced.

This is an erotics of possession, produced by a slight twisting of the structure of desire after the Fall. Instead of the simple hope for reciprocal desire, wanting the other to want me and to call to me because of his or her wanting, now the desire is that the other wants to be me, to stand in my place. It is still an erotics: it dreams uncomfortable dreams of being desired and of a kind of union, but it is an erotics of envy and the desire to be envied. However, the possibility of replacement (if the other were actually to take my place) complicates the passion: he must both instigate desire in others and at the same time forcefully resist the threat their desire poses. Such a mutilation of human desire is not at all rare in this world after the Fall.

To sustain such a relation there must be a third thing, invested with desirability and generally desired, something reserved for his enjoyment alone: a *tertium aliquid,* the third actor whose introduction produces mature tragedy. This third term must be displayed to others and withheld from them. The very structure of the relation precludes all possibility of satisfaction: the value of the third term can be sustained only by the continuing desire of others, and it must be constantly displayed before them in order to call forth their desire; at the same time the desire evoked in others is a constant threat that allows the

---

use someone else merely in order to write to all, to an audience, can be an abuse, of which Robert Lowell's *The Dolphin* is the most famous and self-reflective example. Such abuse is often bound together with a secret shame at the abuse, creating a hunger for simple intimacies and a vector back toward Eden and its direct, naked relations.

Suspicions surround the act of address within the poem. Such suspicions can produce a much simpler countermove, and this move also

possessor no peace. The erotic pleasure is twisted: it occurs in successful resistance to the desires of others, ostentatiously covering the third term and hiding it away, then with equal ostentation discovering it while keeping it from the grasp of the others. (Dr. Donne would surely not object to our play on the word "discovery," and might even remind us of the legal "right of discovery" that gives possession.)

Questions of power lie at the heart of an erotics of possession. Such power is theater, seeing oneself being seen, requiring continual display and confirmation. But the performance of power is never simple, and the claim of power can never be disentangled from the revelation that the claimant is himself acting under compulsion. He is in bondage to his props and his audience. He must constantly watch and guard the "thing": his ownership must be active. At the same time he must always gauge the responses of the others, luring them and warding them off. The drama of veiling and display, the act of power in possession, is compulsory and compulsive. And in it the owner becomes the helpless victim of ownership's strenuous demands.

Recognizing at last that the thrill of ownership is flawed, wearying, and unhappy, the wise possessor may hope to turn back to some Eden where there is neither ownership nor the threat of loss. He had not known there was an audience when the fruit was eaten; it was the discovery of that omnipresent attention from the outside that caused him and the beloved to cover themselves, and the commanding force

---

claims compulsion. In this case the poet strenuously denies the power of our attention, of those of us who listen at the door. Here, in a more desperately direct way, the poet tries to reassert the edenic pair. But the very energy with which our attention is denied perversely draws attention to our presence in the shadows, watching and listening all around the lovers. Sir Philip Sidney's "Astrophel and Stella," 90:

> Stella, think not that I by verse seek fame,
> Who seek, who hope, who love, who live but thee;
> Thine eyes my pride, thy lips my history;
> If thou praise not, all other praise is shame.
> Nor so ambitious am I as to frame
> A nest for my young praise in laurel tree;
> In truth, I swear I wish not there should be
> Graved in mine epitaph a poet's name.
> Ne, if I would, could I just title make,

of that attention gradually turned the beloved into a thing, a prop.

To return to Eden he must turn away from such attention, whether from outside the door or from above the Garden; instead of stripping her, he must strip himself, and in doing so strip away all the powers that disempower him and place him under compulsion. At last he awaits her naked. The curtain falls; we who were listening at the door are excluded in the silence that follows the poem.

To make his way back to Eden, however, he must begin from this world. He opens by clamoring for our attention; he is ruthless in his use of this woman. "Come, Madam, come": let's get on with it. "All rest my powers defie": I can't get to sleep until I relieve myself of this nagging burden of sexual desire. He is "in labour," under duress to perform this laborious task, to eject a bodily burden that his wife may at some future date re-eject, also in labor. He passes on these compulsions of his body, compelling her. And we know that all this is said to turn the attention of his readers instantly to such a performance of male dominion and power.

But it is strange how his aggressive voice of power keeps repeating that its actions are carried out under compulsion. He is all too aware of the beast that powers his beastliness. Without such stylized performance of sexual compulsion and without the appeal to the same force in his audience, the poem would lose much of its direct force (imagine for a moment he was commanding his wife to clean the room rather than to undress). "Until I labour I in labour lie": his compulsion cannot be disengaged from sexual aggression, and this

---

That any laud to me thereof should grow,
Without my plumes from others' wings I take;
For nothing from my wit or will doth flow,
Since all my words thy beauty doth endite,
And Love doth hold my hand and makes me write.

He cannot, finally, write us out of the poem; fame comes to this poet who pretends not to see us and not to seek the fame that we so gladly confer. He knows that because he might hunger for our admiration and approval he is untrustworthy. He can remove us only by erasing himself. This he claims to achieve by emptying himself, making himself mirror and medium (like the archaic figure of the poet in *Ion*) through which Stella's beauty is reflected back to her and to the world. There is still a "showing forth" of the person in the poem, but the person shown is Stella. It does not succeed; Stella is invisible in the poem. We read only Sidney's loud assertion that he and we are nothing.

domineering voice seems to try to transfer to his lady the very oppressive forces that are acting on him.

Poets have always been disposed to inventories, and the love poet tends to inventory promised gifts to his lady or, in the *blason,* the parts of her body displayed in celebration. There is a hint of the *blason* in Donne's poem, but his inventory is the wardrobe of the striptease, the loving removal of blocking layer upon layer; its fragmented items disappear in being named, moving toward some wholeness beneath. She is an anticipated landscape that is at once Eden and the discovered New World, the "far fairer world." We recognize easily the terms of colonial conquest, possession, and exploitation; but contending with those terms is a more interesting impulse to emigration.[7] Only now, before the crossing is made, can he take his uneasy joys in the display of possession; once an immigrant in Eden, it is not clear whether he will have the land or the land will have him. As we approach nakedness, authority becomes increasingly uncertain. Acknowledging and dramatizing his compulsion along with his power, the poet can no longer decide questions of freedom and unfreedom. "To enter in these bonds is to be free" (the theological arguments of the day are here given a sexual twist). And if he will treat her as territory to be explored, the explorer must have "license" from her.

He falls into a veritable ecstasy of ownership, bubbling with possessive pronouns, always wanting to close off this territory he has opened up, to ensure that it is "with one man man'd." She is to be "mined," her jewel or jewels extracted, repeatedly stamped with the first person possessive pronoun and touched everywhere with a "seal" that proclaims the territory "mine." These seals also mark covering and closure, as he claims the right to cover her and to keep her hidden from other men. He flaunts before us that approaching "full nakedness." Of course, all this occurs before he reaches those far shores; her nakedness is never attained.

Gems may be mined beneath the surfaces of these newfound lands, but they are also left littered on the surface, hiding without covering, concealing by distracting the attention.

> Gems which you women use
> Are like Atlanta's balls, cast in mens views,
> That when a fools eye lighteth on a Gem,
> His earthly soul may covet theirs, not them.
> Like pictures, or like books gay coverings made

For lay-men, are all women thus array'd;
Themselves are mystick books, which only wee
(Whom their imputed grace will dignifie)
Must see reveal'd.

There is a peculiar sexual inversion of the myth of Atlanta here, and Dr. Donne has forgotten who was in possession of the balls, as it were. Atlanta, renowned equally for her beauty and fleetness of foot, was warned by Apollo never to marry. When suitors came to seek her hand, she set the following conditions:

> I'll be in no man's power unless
> first vanquished in the race: by your feet test it
> with me; for the swifter, wife and bed
> are the rewards; to the slow the prize
> is death.
>
> *Metamorphoses*, X.569–573

Many suitors raced with her, losing both the race and their heads in the process. A certain Hippomenes at first considered the risk too great—until he caught sight of her face and her naked body (her clothing put aside for the race), *ut faciem et posito corpus velamine vidit*. Determined to win her, Hippomenes tried the device of golden apples, casting them down one by one in the race; Atlanta, who had already developed a fatal affection for this young man, allowed herself to be distracted by these baubles, and Hippomenes won the race (as indeed Donne wins the race to nakedness and the condition of Eden at the end of the poem).

Donne transforms edenic apples into "balls"; he switches sexes in the story; and he inverts a conventionally moralized parable of female delight in baubles into an instance of male delight in the same. This suggests strange forces at work. Those forces become somewhat more comprehensible when we recall the secret vector of address in the poem: "th'eyes of busie fooles," outside the bedroom door or blocked from sight of her body by clothes, and now distracted by gems, surface glitter, mere pictures and covering. As he races his Atlanta to nakedness, he also competes with his secret auditors, "outstrips" them; and while we poor busy fools are slowed by the contemplation of Atlanta's balls, he, desire's true priest, reads the hieroglyphs of woman's body as a mystic book. (Recall that the pages of Donne's books are made of white "lynnen," like this last gown).

Donne is a reader, but it is not the secret soul that he wants to read: his attention is drawn to another jewel, a more physical depth, and the edenic site of man's origins: "As liberally, as to a Midwife, shew / Thy self." Before the final veil is thrown down, the poem breaks off. Here is an eagerness that does not offer any hint of hesitation or holding back. And yet there was one dangerous moment when he paused, recognizing how close a neighbor Eden is to a more sinful garden of earthly delights. For a moment he is uncertain of where she is leading him. "Ill spirits walk in white," like this woman in her shift, recalling how in Eden woman's body was made the instrument of demonic powers. At once he overcomes this faltering; still playing to the audience outside the door, he accepts the most physical evidence of nature's compulsion as proof that this woman in white is an angelic apparition. Nature may be God's earthly form, but it is an unorthodox theology that reads conscience's fine ethical decisions in an erect penis. Like wit, nature here is neither neutral nor neutered.

The poet is making his way back to a true Eden, the reunion of the earthly and the divine. But Donne's Eden (slightly tinged with the heresy of Moslem paradise) will also impossibly reunify the world before the Fall with the world after the Fall. It will involve a knowing that is both immediately sexual and reflective, the palpable body read as a book: as Sidney put it, "Stella, in whose body is / Writ each character of bliss." In this second Eden reading and action, looking and touching, are fused. The pleasures of a fallen world—deferring, hesitating, contemplating nakedness—are joined with the pleasure of sexual union.

Donne walks backward into Eden to rewrite the myth and unify the contradictory alternatives produced through the Fall: the pleasurable knowledge that attends the Fall and the innocence that is prior to it. He would both enjoy and know he is enjoying. To undo a charm you say it backward; to undo an act you invert its phases. In the Fall the woman preceded the man in tasting the apple and taught him to put on clothes and deception layer by layer; now he speaks her clothes off, layer by layer, and leads the way, preceding her into full nakedness.

Hearing the last line and the ensuing silence, we chuckle outside the door and go our ways. It was only a game of words, play meant to amuse us. Mrs. Donne wasn't even in the room when John gave his little performance. We knew she was downstairs all the time, doing embroidery. It was a strange game too, so different from what usually is said, and even from what properly should be said in poetic games. Something was working there that was more than simple play—though play it was. We have heard enough truly empty play from poets to understand that this poet dares to evoke the very powers of compulsion that the poem toys with, watching them even as they touch him.

Jewels

La très-chère était nue, et, connaissant mon coeur,
Elle n'avait gardé que ses bijoux sonores,
Dont le riche attirail lui donnait l'air vainqueur
Qu'ont dans leurs jours heureux les esclaves des Mores.

Quand il jette en dansant son bruit vif et moqueur,
Ce monde rayonnant de métal et de pierre
Me ravit en extase, et j'aime à la fureur
Les choses où le son se mêle à la lumière.

Elle était donc couchée et se laissait aimer,
Et du haut du divan elle souriait d'aise
A mon amour profond et doux comme la mer,
Qui vers elle montait comme vers sa falaise.

Les yeux fixés sur moi, comme un tigre dompté,
D'un air vague et rêveur elle essayait des poses,
Et la candeur unie à la lubricité
Donnait un charme neuf à ses métamorphoses;

Et son bras et sa jambe, et sa cuisse et ses reins,
Polis comme de l'huile, onduleux comme un cynge,
Passait devant mes yeux clairvoyants et sereins;
Et son ventre et ses seins, ces grappes de ma vigne,

S'avançaient, plus câlins que les Anges du mal,
Pour troubler le repos où mon âme était mise,
Et pour la déranger du rocher de cristal
Où, calme et solitaire, elle s'était assise.

Je croyais voir unis par un nouveau dessin
Les hanches de l'Antiope au buste d'un imberbe,
Tant sa taille faisait ressortir son bassin.
Sur ce teint fauve et brun, le fard était superbe!

—Et la lampe s'étant résignée à mourir,
Comme le foyer seul illuminait la chambre,
Chaque fois qu'il poussait un flamboyant soupir,
Il inondait de sang cette peau couleur d'ambre!

She was naked, my dearest, and knowing my heart,
wore nothing more than melodious jewels
whose rich allure gave the mastering air
of slaves of Moors in their finest days.

Casting in dance its mocking, sharp sound,
this world that glows of metal and stone

sweeps me away in ecstasy, and frenzied I love
things in which sound is fused with the light.

so she lay down, gave herself to be loved,
from high on the couch she smiled with content
on my loving, as deep and as soft as the sea,
that rose up upon her as though to a cliff.

Her eyes fixed on me, like tiger tamed,
her manner dreamlike, she tried all her poses,
and candour conjoined with wantonness
gave fresh charm to her metamorphoses;

and her arms and her leg and her thigh and her groin,
gleamed as with oil, rippled like swan,
passed by my eyes, clear-seeing, serene;
and her belly, her breasts, the grapes from my vine,

came forward, more seductive than angels of ill,
to trouble the sleep where my soul had been set,
and in order to shake it from crystal cliff
where it was seated, peaceful and very alone.

I thought I saw joined, by some new design,
Antiope's haunches with beardless youth's chest,
so strongly her waist set off her hips.
Stunning, the blush on her dark, tawny flesh.

And the lamp was giving in to die,
with the hearth alone casting light in the chamber,
each time it emitted a flaming sigh,
it engulfed with blood this amber-colored skin.

Charles Baudelaire

Enclosed Expanses

   . . . without the hope of the condition to which I aspire, because I
feel it is my right, I would no longer exist except in memories.

Rousseau, Reveries of a Solitary Walker

La chair est triste, hélas, et j'ai lu tous les livres.
Fuir! là-bas fuir! Je sens que des oiseaux sont ivres
D'être parmi l'écume inconnue et les cieux!
Rien, ni les vieux jardins reflétés par les yeux
Ne retiendra ce coeur qui dans la mer se trempe
O nuits! ni la clarté déserte de ma lampe

Sur le vide papier que la blancheur défend,
Et ni la jeune femme allaitant son enfant.
Je partirai! Steamer balançant ta mâture,
Lève l'ancre pour une exotique nature!

Un Ennui, désolé par les cruels espoirs,
Croit encore à l'adieu suprême des mouchoirs!
Et, peut-être, les mâts, invitant les orages
Sont-ils de ceux qu'un vent penche sur les naufrages
Perdus, sans mâts, sans mâts, ni fertiles îlots . . .
Mais, ô mon coeur, entends le chant des matelots!

Unfortunately the flesh is sad and I
have read all the books. To get away!
To get away out there! I sense birds drunk to be
between unknown sea-spray and the skies!
Nothing, not old gardens reflected in eyes
will hold back this heart, drenched in sea,
o nights!, nor the empty clearness of my light
on the blank paper, guarded by its white, nor
even the young wife nursing her child.
I'm going away! Steamer, masts swaying,
raises anchor for some exotic Nature.

A weariness, by cruel hopes disappointed,
still believes in handkerchiefs and the ultimate
farewell. And are, perhaps, the masts,
which call in the storm, the sort that winds bend
over lost shipwrecks, now without masts or fertile isles . . .
But heart, listen to the sailors' song.

Stéphane Mallarmé, "Ocean Breeze"

He opens with a commonplace, the flesh's melancholy, and comments on the fact, *hélas,* "alas," a rhetorical irony that the translation has transposed into a drier English irony: "Unfortunately the flesh is sad." Beneath that compromise lurks a more rollicking possibility: "The flesh is sad—too bad!" It is indeed too bad, but to say so— *hélas,* "too bad"—is something more. This is a voice filled with conflicting impulses, impulses that Mallarmé learned to hide in the oracular purity of his mature years. It inhabits the space between desire (that the flesh prove not to be sad) and acknowledged fact (that the flesh is, unfortunately, sad). The voice's peculiar irony comes from being at home neither in the desire nor in the acknowledged fact: the former is impossible; the latter, uninteresting.

The sadness of the flesh, though necessarily proven on an unbookish field, is a Latinate and bookish observation: *post coitum omnia animalia* ... The poet's comment on books betrays an irresolution similar to that of his conclusions regarding the flesh. Announcing that he has read "all the books" has a certain finality, as if to confide wearily to us that, after all is said and done, they give no more satisfaction than the flesh. He has been taken in by seductions carnal and poetic and has been disappointed; however much he might wish, he will listen to their blandishments no more. Yet his fantasies are distinctly bookish (and secretly fleshy on fertile isles) in their yearning to get beyond books; and he closes with a rhetorical flourish enjoining his heart, *ô mon coeur*, to listen to the enticing song of the sailors, the bookish image of some transbookish liberty: for "what good is a book that does not carry us beyond all books?"[8] As in Horace's poem, yet more repressed, the desire for the flesh, admittedly melancholy by experience, ends up with songs that hold us permanently on the threshold of possibility.

As Horace's songs defer the encounter with flesh, here song takes the place of an encounter with familiar flesh—which, we note, is presently occupied, being offered to a younger member of the species. There is no one now to invite him into the circle of the dance; he accepted the invitation and now discovers himself back in the habitual world, replaced. There are no more perpetual beginnings. All that remains is to issue an invitation to himself, a bookish invitation, poised between desire and a formal distancing of desire, consequent to disappointment and reluctant disbelief.

The promise of words to provide sensuous pleasures that the senses never provide proved fraudulent; the words become sheer promise. The disjunction between the words and whatever might be promised through words assumes an ever larger role in these invitations; the words are ribbons and wrapping paper around empty spaces. But the proper comment on this fact remains *hélas*, "too bad," never quite yielding up the desire. To redeem these still alluring but ineffectual words, we rename their emptiness "purity." Raw human longing is never absent in these poems; it is always present to be denied: "La chair est triste, hélas," or Rilke:

Dies *ists* nicht, Jüngling, dass du liebst, wenn auch
die Stimme dann den Mund dir aufstösst,—lerne

vergessen dass du aufsangst. Dass verrinnt.
In Wahrheit singen, ist ein andrer Hauch.
Ein Hauch um nichts. Ein Wehn im Gott. Ein Wind.

Being in love is, young man, not it, even if
voice pries your mouth open—study to forget

that you ever sang out. That passes.
To sing in truth is breath of another kind:
breath about nothing, a puff in the god, a wind.

Sonnets to Orpheus, I.3

Irlaunde disappears over the horizon and becomes an abstract *là-bas*, "out there"; even the goal is displaced into attention to the medium of transit, the words of the invitation and the sea, a space of pure transition and perpetual approach.

Encrustations of the past hold us back: the woman in the "old poem" has a husband and a history; Horace and Phyllis come together in a terminal encounter, shadowed by past loves; Mrs. Donne is swathed in the clothing of a fallen world. And Mallarmé names all the things that bind him here by denying their hold on him: the garden reflected in eyes that continue their gazing; the white paper of the unwritten poem, filled now with the present poem that he writes instead of departing; the nursing wife. Action becomes all song, now the sole course for desire, which is at last recognized as pure impotence and is included in the poem as blank paper to be left blank and renounced; but to do so, he finds himself writing a vow of renunciation on the blank paper; the moment never comes of rushing from the house and leaving the blank paper behind.

The *ennui*, the disappointed weariness, claims to still believe in "handkerchiefs and the ultimate farewell"; but by this point we understand that it believes in the scene and not in the event. No empirical flight to the ocean can ever fulfill that scene. Never on shipboard can one experience such a storm, and the masts bent low, carried over submerged shipwrecks, vessels always lost before reaching Ireland and the other fertile isles. The dots of ellipsis break off before reaching any landfall, even in song. We have already come too close to desire: turn back to the purely poetic move, the rhetorical address to the heart and the sailor's song, the faraway instigation of desire.

The rusted and green hull
of the old felucca
rests in the sand . . .
The sail seems, in its shreds,
still to dream in sun and sea.

Antonio Machado, *Canciones*

Human generations continue; there are always young people to take the bait of flesh and book yet one more time. But art is less fortunate. It grows old in the memory of its failures to reach outside itself. Midir and Etain dance naked before the children of Adam and Eve: at first they are delighted that no one from that world could see them; then they discover that no matter how hard they try, still no one can see them. Yet art's vitality remains, twisted but undiminished in the controlled force of its disappointment: *hélas,* "too bad." As if under some curse or compulsion, it continues to make the old moves one more time.

We are still included, but just barely, in Mallarmé's address. Poets have grown accustomed to placing us over to the side or outside the door, pretending that our attention doesn't matter; they want little from us but general approval and admiration for their genius. Many of the modern poets that came after him—by no means all—have demonstrated conclusively that art can be great without mattering very much.

This poem does not catch us in the same way as "Ich am of Irlaunde" or any of those earlier invitations; it does not try. Still the poem bears the one print of his desire, the *hélas,* which invites a wink of complicity and appeals to shared understanding (the smile of shared doubleness that survives perhaps best in the comic translation: "the flesh is sad—too bad!"). The desire may have become purely literary, but that aging art has also become second nature—a distinct faculty within us. What the ears can never hear, the literary heart, *ô mon coeur,* can hear clearly. "There is no Word without a reply, even if it meets no more than silence . . ."[9]

Forking Path: An Alternative to Entering Mallarmé's Chamber

> We know how to say many false things that are very much like the truth; but if we want, we also know how to speak things that are true.
>
> Hesiod, *Theogony,* 27–28

> Syne they came to a garden green,
>   And she pu'd an apple frae a tree:
> 'Take this for thy wages, true Thomas;
>   It will give thee the tongue that can never lee.'
>
> "Thomas the Rhymer"

We must consider the possibility that when she told Thomas that he could never again lie, the Queen of Elfyn was herself lying; she often does. But Thomas the Rhymer believes that he is now under compulsion always to reveal the truth (which is not to say that he will always want to tell the truth). He cannot look forward to a comfortably aging art, a closed chamber with no one listening at the door, a chamber in which again and again he can make for himself songs of flight and the open door. The gift of Elfyn's queen has made art's closure impossible. Thomas's words will take on a life of their own, subject to a force that subjugates his will. The words are no longer his in the sense that he has control over them; but they remain painfully his in the sense that they will represent him to the other; he will be held responsible for them: "I dought neither speak to prince or peer / Nor ask of grace from fair ladye." The words get loose, fly away. He had wanted them to go on missions for him, to "ask of grace from fair ladye," but he can no longer foresee their behavior once they arrive at their destination. He suspects they will go astray and the other will hear things unintended, true things. His words take flight—sent on this mission, they leave only disappearing tracks. Neruda addresses the beloved:

> So that you can hear me
> these words of mine
> at times attenuate
> like gull-prints on the beaches.

Under the curse of truth-telling, he confesses his anxiety and his desire that his words obey his will:

> I want them to say now what I want to say to you,
> so that you can hear me as I want you to hear me.

He tries to speak simply; he dreams of a lovely transparency of words, molded to the exact shape of his intent, apprehended by the other exactly as he wishes. He dreams of words that will be pure rhetoric in a sense other than Mallarmé's; he dreams of words that will be the mind's sheer means.

But they always do go astray. Their straying is not in calling forth some utterly disparate interpretation in the other. These words stray by telling the truth, which is doubled, compelled, and far darker than any clear surface of controlled intent. The would-be seducer is seduced; the words are driven by an engine of desire which glows behind the frail structure of manipulation that is the seduction. What he tried to offer lightly and graciously as invitation becomes entreaty, exposing the truth of all the pain and vulnerability of desire. "Ich am of Irlaunde" was written before Thomas was put under truth's curse: its invitation is successful because there are no gaps in its covering. It is our firm illusion that if the "gode sire" were to refuse the invitation (and how could he?), the dancer would return lightly and unconcerned into the circle of the dancers. Now, under the gift-curse to reveal the truth, he acknowledges the pleading voice behind the gracious invitation:

> Cries of old mouths, blood of old entreaties.
> Companion, love me. Don't leave me. Come with me.
> Come with me, companion . . .

The weight of old words and the voices that survive in poetry do not bring Mallarmé's bemused disenchantment; instead, memories of ancient and inevitable failure ride along with the venture, which will always be made one more time.

Donne wrestled the archaic compulsion into strenuous play; Mallarmé artfully turned the invitation in upon itself and sang seductive songs to himself. In both poems the contours of desire show beneath the clothes. But this voice, Pablo Neruda's, finds the strength not merely to reveal the truth but also to say it.

The truth of the voice is more ominous than the mere fact of compulsion: speaking to the beloved, he looks within and finds there nothing unshaped by the force of the other and his desire: there is no self, no place from which to control the words. He has become pure relation. Worse still, that relation is unstable, composed of contraries: a desire to join and a desire to keep apart, friendship and anger, and a resistance to being no more than this relation. Anger and a charge of guilt are directed to the other, the woman, who places him under compulsion and forces him to confess his powerlessness: "It is you, woman, guilty," *Eres tú la culpable.* He admits that he has lost control of the words: "I see them far away," he says, "those words of mine. / Yours they are more than mine." And: "they grow more darkly dyed with your love, these words of mine. / You occupy everything, everything."

It is one of the oldest motions of the Western love poem, to attribute all power to the woman (or in the case of a woman poet such as Vittoria Colonna, to the man), and with that power the credit for successful art and the blame for suffering. If it is truth, it is monumentally ineffectual. We may justly suspect that no lover's invitation has ever been accepted on these terms, that no human being of either gender has ever been seduced by them. We will always follow the woman or the man who tells neither truth nor lies, who asks one of us to go off and dance forever in Ireland. But this declaration of compulsion, however old it is, is seduction and invitation gone astray, an uncomfortable truth that ensures the other will never "hear me as I want you to hear me."

Yet at last something is won in this poem, the fifth of Neruda's "Twenty Poems of Love":

> Para que tú me oigas
> mis palabras
> se adelgazan a veces
> como las huellas de las gaviotas en las playas.
>
> Collar, cascabel ebrio
> para tus manos suaves como las uvas.
>
> Y las miro lejanas mis palabras.
>
> Más que mías son tuyas.
> Van trepando en mi viejo dolor como las yedras.
>
> Ellas trepan así por las paredes húmedas.
> Eres tú la culpable de este juego sangriento.
> Ellas están huyendo de mi guarida oscura.
> Todo lo llenas tú, todo lo llenas.
>
> Antes que tú poblaron la soledad que ocupas,
> y están acostumbradas más que tú a mi tristeza.
>
> Ahora quiero que digan lo que quiero decirte
> para que tú me oigas como quiero que me oigas.
>
> El viento de la angustia aún las suele arrastrar.
> Huracanes de sueños aún a veces las tumban.
> Escuchas otras voces en mi voz dolorida.
>
> Llanto de viejas bocas, sangre de viejas súplicas.
> Amame, compañera. No me abandones. Sígueme.
> Sígueme, compañera, en esa ola de angustia.
>
> Pero se van tiñendo con tu amor mis palabras.
> Todo lo ocupas tú, todo lo ocupas.

Voy haciendo de todas un collar infinito
para tus blancas manos, suaves como las uvas.

So that you can hear me,
these words of mine
at times attenuate
like gull-prints on the beaches.

Bracelet, drunken bell
for those hands of yours as smooth as grapes.

And I see them far away, those words of mine.
Yours they are more than my own.
Like ivy they climb up old pain.

Up they climb as over damp walls.
It is you, woman, guilty of this blood-sport.
They are fleeing my dark lair.
Everything is filled by you, everything.

Before you, they peopled the loneliness you occupy,
and more than you they were used to my sorrow.

I want them now to say what I want to say to you,
so that you can hear me as I want you to hear me.

The wind of agony still keeps on
    exerting its pull on them.
Dream tempests still overwhelm them from time to time.
You are listening to other voices in my voice of pain.

Cries of old mouths, blood of old entreaties.
Companion, love me. Don't leave me. Come with me.
Come with me, companion, upon this wave of agony.

But they grow more darkly dyed with your love,
    these words of mine.
You occupy everything, everything.

Of them all I am making an infinite bracelet
for those white hands of yours, smooth as grapes.

The ancient compulsion tries to reach the beloved in an invitation or entreaty. But the truth is told, and the poem goes astray, fails, falls back into art. "Unfortunately the flesh is sad." There is then a moment of decision as to what this thing, this poem, may now be: the pure alternative and closed dream, or the remembrance of its genesis, inseparable from the beloved. Neruda accepts remembrance and more: he returns the artwork to the beloved as gift; it is the *collar*, the infinite bracelet of words, the circular work of craft and sole adornment for the naked hand. Because the words are hers as well as his, they return to her now as possession in a new sense; the token is neither mere means nor mediation. And within the gift he still manages to inscribe the first moment of desire that began the failed voyage: a focus of attention on the smooth hand that is encircled but not bound. The hand is Eden's fruit, apple or grape, wreathed in jewels that call attention to the bare skin, the apparel that shows without covering.

Coda: Words of Seduction That Wandered Astray

On the day Yüan Chen reached T'ung-chou and had not yet settled in his office, he saw some lines written on the wall. When he read them, he realized they were an old poem of mine. The last lines went:

> In green waters a red lotus,
>   its single blossom opening,
> at which every other flower and plant
>   lose all loveliness.

But he didn't know who had inscribed it there. Yüan Chen recited the lines with pleasure, then composed a piece of his own, and sent it to me along with a copy of the original poem. When I looked the poem over closely, I recalled that I myself had written it some fifteen years ago, when I first passed the examination, as a quatrain for the singing girl A-juan. When I think of those things that happened so long ago, they seem faint to me, as if in a dream. Reflecting on how things were then and how they are now, I answered Yüan Chen with the following poem:

> Fifteen years ago
>   seems like a journey in dream,
> when with these lines of poetry
>   understanding was reached between lovers.
> My offhand addition to laughter and song,
>   my play with A-juan
> unforeseen have passed from mouth to mouth
>   all the way down to T'ung-chou.
> Back then they compelled the lovely
>   red-sleeved woman to sing;
> now they produce mere melancholy
>   in a blue-gowned magistrate.

Depressing as well to hear
    the place they've been written down:
where rain streams over a river lodge
    on the broken wall.

Like the little books that sometimes transmit them, poems have their own strange destinies: they may be passed on from mouth to mouth, recited and sung until the poet and the poet's original intentions are lost from the singer's memory. Once long ago the circumstances were clear: A-juan, the singing girl at a party with young men, was the lotus, before whose beauty the beauty of all the other girls paled. The lines were part of a passing courtship, a minor gesture of poetic graciousness at a party. He calls it "play with A-juan," that cautious playfulness that hides a sexual invitation.

But once he gave these lines to A-juan for her to sing, they escaped him. Who knows how they came to be used afterward: perhaps they became a common poem of sexual invitation at such parties, and later, when the parties were only memories, perhaps they summoned memory of those sexual encounters long ago; on the lips of any singing girl these lines might have been the proud declaration of her own beauty, and perhaps A-juan sang them to remind all how the famous poet Po Chü-yi had praised her loveliness above all others; a man in exile and disgrace might have recited these words defiantly, asserting his own worth. Perhaps someone even used the lines to describe real lotuses. But most mysterious is how the verses came to be written on the wall there, in the dreary and remote southern town of T'ung-chou. To write them on the wall was to grant them particular importance, a gesture of strong feeling for some unknown circumstance, an ambiguous message left for the next literate traveler. It was written on the wall as a statement of something that no doubt mattered greatly to the person who wrote it—but what?

Then Yüan Chen came, Po's closest friend sent to T'ung-chou in exile; he read the poem, admired it, and wrote his own poem on finding the quatrain there. He sent this new poem to Po Chü-yi along with a copy of the original quatrain, and Po recognized the discovered lines as his own. The poem returns to its author, but like a child who has grown up and had experiences that the parents can never know, it is changed now, with a darkness and a reserve. And the poet-parent, his long-lost lines returning to him once again, is surprised to find how much they have changed. The poem's new complexity is a relation between situations of many moments, some of which must remain in shadow: the original occasion, now long past; its meaning to Yüan Chen; and the mystery of what it has meant passing from mouth to mouth, as a singing girl is passed from man to man. The author cannot escape the claim of care the poem makes on him, but at the same time he realizes that he no longer has authority over the poem. It has become promiscuous, and his long-ago intentions at the composition are not quite irrelevant, but now only a part of what the poem has become.

His first thought on rereading the poem is of the original occasion, fifteen years ago, which now seems as insubstantial as a dream, a dream that the poem brings back. The limitation of the original occasion fascinates him: the poem was a motivated act, a simple message from one person to another, a public declaration of his desire for intimacy with A-juan, but public only within the limited circle of the party, answering the needs of the moment. This was not the sort of thing a poet often saved: it truly was for the moment, something to evaporate with the voice as the singing ended, as the laughter died down and the desire was sated. These lines in praise of A-juan are commonplace; his modest puzzlement at the poem's mysterious life is justified. He stresses how minor it was, an "offhand addition" to the party, part of the social whole. Such a poem was never meant to wander over China all alone. When a poet writes seriously and hopes to retain some authority over his poem, he may frame it with information that compels a reader to take it the way he intended; for example, he may write a long title that explains in great detail the circumstances of the poem's composition. But this first poem lost its occasion and frame; it was *ch'uan-sung,* passed on by recitation, like one of those parlor games in which a sentence is sent around a room in whispers until it returns to its originator, altered beyond recognition. In this case the words, set in the strictness of verse, remain the same; only their significance changes. They must have had some special significance for someone, that he or she wrote them on that wall in T'ung-chou, so far in every way from where the verses began.

For the moment Po passes over this mystery, which is most difficult for the poet to accept and understand. Instead in the third couplet he notes only those moments he can easily grasp. There was the first moment, the initial transmission, when he composed the poem and recited it out loud so that the lovely woman could sing it—but didn't it already begin to change when she first sang those words? At that moment they ceased to be Po's admiration for her beauty, and became in her voice shy pride and recognition of Po's admiration. The private significance of the poem had already left him. Against this is the second, parallel circumstance, Po imagining his friend Yüan Chen finding the poem, imagining what Yüan must have felt. And here too doesn't the poem change between Yüan's reading and Po's feeling for how Yüan Chen must have felt in the reading? Only the text is shared and its power of seduction, but the terms of the invitation change in every reading and recitation.

That separation between human beings, which is deeper than the space between here and T'ung-chou, or the interval between now and a party fifteen years in the past, finds its embodiment in the final couplet of Po Chü-yi's answering poem: the bare, exposed characters, the track of some lost significance that cannot be reached. The poem is no longer the infinitely repeatable text, copied out neatly by Yüan Chen and sent to Po Chü-yi; the poem has become its particular inscription on that broken wall in T'ung-chou. The image of its presence there, crumbling and wearing away in the weather, is not the promiscuous repeatability of the text but a mark of the unguessable circumstance and state of mind of the unknown person who wrote the lines there, the dreary isolation that must have had something to do with the significance of its inscription. And the fact that the wall will crumble or the inscription weather away will not simply be the loss of one copy of a poem that can be written down again and again; it will be the loss of the last trace of one intense and mysterious moment, a moment we can never know except that it must have somehow expressed itself through these words.

2 Interlude: Pastourelle

Every man speculates upon creating a *new* need in another in order to force him to a new sacrifice, to place him in a new dependence, and to entice him into a new kind of pleasure and thereby into economic ruin.

Karl Marx, third "Economic and Philosophical Manuscript"

Come live with me, and be my love,
And we will all the pleasures prove
That valleys, groves, hills and fields,
Woods, or steepy mountain yields.

And we will sit upon the rocks,
Seeing the shepherds feed their flocks
By shallow rivers, to whose falls
Melodious birds sing madrigals.

And I will make thee beds of roses
And a thousand fragrant posies,
A cap of flowers, and a kirtle,
Embroidered all with leaves of myrtle.

A gown made of the finest wool
Which from our pretty lambs we pull,
Fair lined slippers for the cold,
With buckles of the purest gold.

A belt of straw and ivy-buds,
With coral clasps and amber studs,
And if these pleasures may thee move,
Come live with me, and be my love.

The shepherds swains shall dance and sing
For thy delight each May morning.
If these delights thy mind may move,
Then live with me, and be my love.

Christopher Marlowe
"The Passionate Shepherd to His Love"

There is a disarming sweetness in this invitation, perhaps the most famous in English poetry. It barters for the nymph's consent with promises of pastoral goods (though in the end, like Horace, offers her only song). Yet the proposal has an ease, assurance, and forthrightness—a lucid vision of how it will be there, *là-bas*—that makes Marlowe's honeyed bait sound like the invitations of the old unnamed singers. He makes no attempt to conceal that this pastoral Eden is only poetry, the fabric of speculative desire. He proposes a world in which straw belt and golden buckles contribute to a perfectly matched wardrobe; nor are we certain that the madrigals anticipated from the birds are merely metaphorical. And although this poetic world is classless, we observe that emigration there bears some resemblance to passing a class boundary, not simply because of the sumptuous additions to the nymph's wardrobe, but because it promises leisure to sit and watch "the shepherds feed their flocks" and to receive pastoral dance and song as a performance "for thy delight" rather than as a participatory celebration of the community ("come and daunce wit me, in Irlaunde").

Its sweetness disarms, and we cannot help feeling uneasy in our disarmament. The poem has power, and we (perhaps even its singer) are at risk from its illusion. For its invitation is all too fluent, inspiring a corrective distrust by the very force of its allure. Other jewelled pastorals may be easily disregarded, instinctively relegated to the status of mere words; but this poem calls so perfectly to the children of Adam and Eve that it begs a counterspell, protective words of disenchantment. This we find in the equally famous "Nymph's Reply," attributed to Sir Walter Raleigh. The poetic disenchantment is framed by reminders of the suspicions we should have, living in the old age of the world.

> If all the world and love were young,
> And truth in every shepherd's tongue,
> These pretty pleasures might me move
> To live with thee and be thy love.
>
> But Time drives flocks from field to fold,
> When rivers rage and rocks grow cold,
> And Philomel becometh dumb;
> The rest complains of cares to come.
>
> The flowers do fade, and wanton fields
> To wayward Winter reckoning yields;
> A honey tongue, a heart of gall,
> Is fancy's spring, but sorrow's fall.

Thy gowns, thy shoes, thy beds of roses,
Thy cap, thy kirtle, and thy posies,
Soon break, soon wither, soon forgotten,
In folly ripe, in reason rotten.

Thy belt of straw and ivy buds,
Thy coral clasps and amber studs,
All those in me no means can move
To come to thee and be thy love.

But could youth last and love still breed,
Had joys no date, nor age no need,
Then these delights my mind might move
To live with thee and be thy love.

"The Nymph's Reply" answers from another province of poetry's domain, where people tell the truth by exposing lies and illusion; it speaks for the winter of the world, the flesh's sadness, and takes a "hard" look at poetic promises. But even Raleigh's voice of the world's age, in its wise resistance to illusory promises, leaves a small opening, as Plato had, for the possibility of a defense. It cannot finally resist the bait. We note that the last stanza is conditional, an escape clause that might allow poetry to prove its case. If the conditions are met, the nymph will assent. Like the fantastic tasks required for heroes to win their brides in old folktales, the poetic shepherd is set a task of proof that seems all but impossible, but which, in the very proposal of conditions, leaves hope as desire's support.

The nymph's reply resists the invitation, but it is not a definitive turn of the back and a silent walking away. It is another poetic construct of words, given as the woman's answer, a gendered voice of the other that uses a disillusionment of words to parry the barb of illusion that the first words create. She tells the truth to embarrass and expose the powerful art-shapes produced by desire, to show the emptiness beneath their surfaces. She is firm, even hard—hard-headed but not necessarily hard-hearted.

In this double motion of provoking and resisting desire, of illusion and disillusion, Marlowe's shepherd and Raleigh's nymph perform a very old dance. These Elizabethan performances are true pastoral, reinvented from the model of classical antiquity, in which the class and power of nymph and shepherd are roughly matched. But the roots of the dialogue go back to the medieval pastourelle, in which a powerful, highborn male rides out one morning and with fine words tries to seduce a young woman of the people. The first stage of pastourelle corresponds roughly to Marlowe's poem; but there are many versions of the woman's response and the consequences. Sometimes his desire is met with desire, a hunger for the very illusions he uses as currency. Sometimes, when she resists his illusions, the sweet mask falls away, revealing the raw force beneath the surface and she is raped. But in some cases, as in Raleigh's answer, the woman successfully resists his illusions of what she might desire by a counterforce of words that disenchant.

In the first stage the man's words are always rooted in the pretense that she is in some way his equal, with the power of choice; and we always see through the lie. His use of fine and courtly words are part of his apparel, the sumptuary mark of class power: male force and the force of the nobility are masked in deference to the woman, conditional submission to the rules of courtship's game, gentleness.

She answers with plain words that expose the realities of class and power to which she would be submitting were she to accept his illusions of equality in the courtly love game. The twelfth-century Provençal troubadour Marcabru, who as a child "was left at the door of a rich man," takes particular pleasure in the battle of these two languages.

> I met a shepherdess the other day,
> beside a hedge, a common girl,
> but full of verve and wit;
> and as peasant girl does,
> cloak and coat and furs she wore,
> and thick linen shift,
> shoes and woolen stockings.

The young man, highborn, is always in transit, chancing to pass by, a sexual prowler and "traveling man." He meets a young woman. They have no relation outside the words they exchange. But the invitation is corrupted: power is in play. She is always young and desirable, promising the easy availability of the lowborn and powerless: a medieval *vilana*. In the European versions of this poem she is often roughly dressed, as a peasant should be, and the young man, like Marlowe's shepherd, may offer to dress her in finery. Marcabru tells us that she is "full of verve and wit," as we shall hear for ourselves; but first he inventories the surface, the container of such plenitude, and every item of her clothing confirms *filla de vilana,* "peasant girl."

This is not the Renaissance pastoral, where straw belt and golden buckles combine for a fashionably rustic charm; this is a real nose-holding pastoral, whose heroine wears thick protective layers to keep off the assaults of the cold, a rough surface to match the fresh roughness of nature within. Yet these clothes are certainly warm enough to give an edge of irony to his concern in the following stanza.

> I came to her across the meadow,
> "Maid," said I, "exquisite creature,
> it pains me how the cold doth sting you.
> And the peasant said to me "Good sire,
> thank God and the woman who gave me suck,
> wind in my hair doesn't bother me,
> being quite cheerful and in good health.

When he began this poem saying "I," we had believed the poet was speaking for himself, but now we see that he has no allegiance to his own deceptive words. He exposes to us the game: he plays it only to elicit truth from the other, to test her. She is "cheerful and in good health," and her words show the pretense of his own. He plays the knight only to draw her out, to let her display her strength. She meets his words politely and ignores the motives that are so apparent behind his concern for her comfort. She shows no reticence, nor will she give the predator the whiff of the kill by taking flight. Neither does she reveal a secret desire for the "gentleness" he offers, a desire that would deliver her up to the beast. She stands her ground, deflects his words. He tries again.

> "Maid," said I, "sweet thing,
> here I've gone out of my way
> just to keep you company;
> for pretty peasant maids like you
> should not, without companion by,
> graze so many animals
> in such a place, and all alone."

This is the serpent's language in pastoral Eden: sweet surfaces and malice within, dangerous intent dressed in fine clothing. His offer of protection is a barely veiled threat, reminding her of the vulnerability of her situation, her sex, and her class. In this erotic feudalism the roles of protector and despoiler are separated by only the thinnest line of her forced consent; both roles are the same in the power they would work upon her. Her consent would only give the illusion of equal power. Still she stands her ground, striking back with words: she neither submits to the threat nor lets herself be drawn into belief in appearances. Rather, she exposes the hollowness of the promise.

> "Lord," said she, "whoever I be,
> I know what's wise, I know what's folly;
> so let your lordly company
> stay where it ought,"
> so said the peasant girl to me,
> "whoever believes to command such company
> has nothing more than appearance."

We try to grasp what is happening here, the mysterious relation between the threat of force and play. There is no pragmatic danger: the poem is only a game of words, the fabrication of a conventional literary encounter that never has and never could occur quite like this. Within the larger poetic game a man and woman game with words, and these words hold the contest of power in play and undecided. Yet beneath the light banter it is a tense, desperate game; so long as words can be be kept in play, force can be held at bay.

She understands the reality of "whoever I be," *qui que'm sia*. This classless truth can declare the facts of class and power: let the nobleman companion the nobly born. He only pretends to empower her, and any woman who accepts that gift of words has accepted only words, illusion, appearance. Checked, he hears the hint of an opening in "whoever I be" and tries a new attack with a fresh, enticing illusion that, if she accepts it, will undermine her class objections and make their anticipated mating one of like with like. He rewrites her geneology to make her his equal. But still she stands firm, proudly proclaiming the truth of her birth and turning the hierarchy of class against him.

> "Maid, by condition well-born,
> your father was a knight,
> who got you in your mother,
> for she was peasant of courtly grace,
> You seem more lovely the more I look,
> I brighten through your good cheer—
> if only you'd be a bit more kind."
>
> "Lord, I observe all my lineage
> and origins traced back

to the sickle and the plow,
good sire," said the girl to me;
"and he who acts at being knight
would do better to act as we,
six working days of the week."

She plays on *faire,* to act. He plays the role of knight, *se fai caval-
gaire,* a disjunction between the person and the social role well suited
to someone who dresses himself in fine words. Better she and her
peasant kin, who work, *faire,* act without "acting as" anything. Hers
is a voice whose surface and depth are the same, where there are no
illusions, and because there is no surface of illusion, she is impenetrable, hard as stone. Yet her voice, the voice of truth, cannot stand
alone; it requires his voice of illusion in order to appear. It needs his
commonplace deceptions to call forth its powers of unmasking. Poetic
truth is an act, the dissolution of untruth and the return to truth in a
fallen world. His remains a double world and a language of double
entendre:

"Maid," said I, "some noble sprite,
endowed you when you were born
with a beauty that dazzles
beyond all other peasant girls,
and a loveliness well doubled
if just once I saw myself
on top and you below."

Her challenge induces him, in his own poetic and doubled way, to
tell the truth about the doubling of bodies: "myself on top and you
below," a lecherous wink that brings social hierarchy, gender hierarchy, and sexual position together.

"Good sire, you've praised me so
that I'll be the envy of all;
and since you've upped my value, you,
good sire," this peasant said to me,
"will get this reward for our parting:
'Stand and gawk, you ass!'
and wait for nothing all afternoon."

Now she shows that, if pressed, she also can speak the language of
doubleness, but her dialect is different. There is nothing sly here, only

a sarcasm in which figural language instantly exposes its own lies, shows its emptiness. He bargains with her, but his currency is only appearances, an illusion of words. She enters the game, giving value for value, nothing for nothing. She displays herself to him and pays him with a taunt: gape and gawk in desire at what you can't have; I offer you the appearance, the view, the impenetrable surface. The harder he presses, the harder she becomes. She is unbreachable. He reads her as nature, waiting only to be tamed by his human social power. Now he barters, still with words, but with promises of a substantial exchange beyond words. She refuses the trade, refuses to be purchased, and the grounds of her refusal are almost mocking: it would damage appearances.

> "Maid, a wild heart that holds apart
> a man domesticates by use.
> Well I know in passing here
> a man may make 'rich' companionship
> for such a peasant girl as you,
> from affection in the spirit,
> if one doesn't betray the other."

> "Lord, it's a man hard-pressed by madness
> that swears, pleads, gives guarantees:
> such is the 'homage' you offer me,
> Lord," said the peasant girl to me;
> "but I have no desire at all to barter
> maidenhead for whore's name
> at such small admission price."

> "Maid, each creature
> turns back to its nature: and we
> should be mated and mating,
> you and I, peasant girl,
> in the copse down by the pasture
> for there you'll be safer
> to do something very sweet."

The last of these stanzas is the strangest: an appeal to nature and the classless relation of the creatures beneath the clothes. Social power may mediate and corrupt the proposal, but the motive behind the seduction is a desire that knows no class. He claims shared animal nature unclothed: fellow creature matched and mating with fellow creature. But still she stands firm. The realities of class and power are

also part of the truth, and although she agrees with value of being
mated each to its own kind, to her it is a class statement. Those who
have power can all too easily renounce power, especially to suit the
conditions of the moment; but those who fall into the power of others
cannot so easily forget.

> "You're right, good sire, but as is just,
> a fool chases his foolishness,
> a man of court, courtly adventure,
> a peasant boy his peasant girl;
> Good sense is lacking where
> men don't keep the proper measure—
> so said the ancients."

She turns his argument against him, pointing out the finer distinctions that mate like with like, distinctions that will keep their mating
apart. In frustration he comes to his final misuse of language, an anger that calls her honesty deception and her faith falseness:

> "Maid, I never saw another girl
> more deceiving in appearance,
> or more false in her heart."
> "Lord, the owl augurs for you:
> one stands gawking at the painting,
> the other hopes for manna."

It is a cryptic conclusion that understandably puzzles commentators. Called "deceptive," she offers him a unique mode of figural language—the oracular language that reveals truth behind veils, nature's
language. She offers neither the smooth lie nor the winking double
entendre, but a figure for reflection: a man gawking at a mere appearance, a painted surface, and the hope for sustenance falling free from
heaven, so that a human being need not work six days of the week.

In the Chinese versions of pastourelle it is never the seducer who
speaks fine words of seduction.[1] Instead the singer entraps us with the
image of the woman's beauty and seduces the listeners to share the
desire that the highborn passer-by will feel. Thus we begin in "Officer
of the Guard":

> A bondsman of the house of Huo,
> Feng by name, Feng Tzu-tu,
> hid behind the Lord General's power,

> trifling with the Turkish tavern girl.
> Fifteen was the Turkish maid
> alone at the bar one day in spring,
> a long-hung skirt, sash of twisted ribbons,
> billowing sleeves, vest with love-twined patterns.
> On her head she wore Lan-t'ien jade,
> in her ears she wore pearls from Rome,
> her hair in two knots, so lovely
> there was nothing like them in the world:
> one knot was worth five million in gold,
> and the two together, more than ten.

Feng Tzu-tu works with borrowed power, power on loan; everyone knows him in terms of his subordination ("Look, there goes Feng Tzu-tu, the Lord General's bondsman"). But power is a contagious disease. Someone made the object of power will seek relief by passing his or her submission on to another. In the transmission small hierarchies appear, and each new would-be master borrows from his own immediate master the authority to enforce submission. This craving for mastery is compulsion, and it must deny the forces at work through illusions of unconcern and "freedom" (which is the same name that we give to the final, negative moment in the experience of compulsion). So Feng Tzu-tu trifles with the tavern girl; as with Marcabru's knight, the appearance of play is the essential demonstration that the would-be master is not himself mastered by need.

The Turkish tavern girl is placed on poetic display, as the singer draws our attention to her surfaces, the clothing and adornment that elicit desire for all that is wrapped within. In the seductive game of the song, she plays along by returning the appraising look.

> I never expected this dashing guard
> to stop by our tavern so gallantly,
> his silver saddle sparkling,
> his blue-covered coach waiting empty.
> And he comes to me wanting clear wine:
> I brought him a rope-handled jugful.
> And he comes to me wanting fine things to eat;
> a golden plate with fillet of carp.
> And he gives me a mirror of green bronze
> That he ties to my skirts of red gauze.

We have been shown her loveliness through the eyes of Fen Tzu-tu; and now she speaks back to the officer of the guard with a tone that suggests womanly desire meeting man's desire, an assessment of his bearing and equipment that encourages us. We are ready to go ahead, to "make advances," crossing this perilous space toward the other. The transactions of tavern business anticipate desires made known and desires gladly fulfilled. Then the seduction gift enters the system of exchange. It is a commodity unequal to the price and a most peculiar token: the mirror in which she can see herself as she is seen, in which she can recognize her own worth outside the flirtatious exchange of words and gifts.

> I would gladly have murdered
> the man who first made the mirror.
> When I think about it,
> I don't have a worse enemy.
> The second she looks at herself
> and realizes how much she's worth,
> it won't be me who enjoys
> her or her love.
>
> Bernart de Ventadorn[2]

The mirror opens a distance that cannot be crossed: stand and gawk. That same distance is simultaneously produced in the physical gesture of touching, which violates the game of mutual admiration and pretends to cross the space to the other. He gives way to compulsion, reaches out to lay hold of the person, and the other suddenly recedes beyond his grasp. Appearances become mere appearances.

> I don't care if my red gauze gets torn,
> nor even this poor body:
> a man always wants a new woman,
> but a woman values the man she has;
> in human life there are new things and old,
> one highborn does not mix with one born base.
> No thank you, officer of the guard,
> private love is passion wasted.

Advance is blocked, cast back, humiliated: speculative fantasy meets hard-headed sense, sticking to what one has, holding to class boundaries. There is someone at home inside this surface who cannot be touched, cannot be grasped with the hand of power.

The strangest thing is our delight in this resistance, in the officer's discomfort, even though we ourselves have been drawn in. Where can we stand, especially the poem's male readers, in this game of desire and desire thwarted? There is an answer in the rarest and most lovely of pastourelles, "Mulberries on the Path."

Sunrise in southeast
shines on the halls of our house of Ch'in,
and the house of Ch'in has a lovely girl
whose name, we shall say, is Lo-fu.
Lo-fu is skilled with the silkworms
and picks mulberry leaves south of the wall.
The straps of her basket are made of blue silk,
its handle, a branch of cinnamon;
Her hair has a trailing pony-tail,
in her ears are bright moon pearls.
Her skirt below is saffron damask,
of purple damask her vest above.
When passers-by see Lo-fu, they
set down their loads, they stroke their beards;
and when young men see Lo-fu,
their hats fall off and their headbands show.
Men at the plow forget the share;
men with the hoe forget the hoe,
and when they go home there's always a fight,
and all because of seeing Lo-fu.

From the south the lord governor came,
and he halted his five-horse team;
and the lord governor's sent a runner
to ask who that maiden is:
"The house of Ch'in has a lovely girl
whose name, we shall say, is Lo-fu."
"And just how old is this Lo-fu?"
"Not yet up to twenty,
but well beyond fifteen."
The governor invites Lo-fu:
"Now will you ride along with me?"
Lo-fu came forward and said these words:
"The lord governor is a fool:
the lord governor has his own wife;
I, Lo-fu, have my own man.
In the east are a thousand riders and more,
and my husband is head of them all.
How can you tell which my husband is?—
he rides a white horse, a black colt behind,
and the horse's tail is wound in blue silk,
and gold is the halter upon its head,

at his waist is a wound-pommel sword,
worth perhaps a million or more.
At fifteen he was a county runner,
by twenty, an officer of the court,
by thirty, in the emperor's entourage,
by forty, the master of a city.
His skin is smooth, his skin is white,
his beard is wispy and fine,
he walks with slow pace through the courts,
with stately steps he goes through the halls.
There are thousands that dine at his table,
and all of them say how splendid he is!"

This poem opens new territories beyond the simple play of advances made and repulsed. The first addition is a gallery for the audience, the initial displacement of desire that points toward art's cultivated distances: we, the listeners, are situated within a general populace that can gaze on this woman with desire and at the same time laugh at the reflections of that desire all around us. We have learned, perhaps painfully, to be content to stand and gawk. This is no simple dispassion: Lo-fu's beauty disrupts the social order; work stops as she passes by; domestic squabbles arise because she reminds the men that the women at home are not so lovely as Lo-fu, and every woman resents the man's desire. This epidemic of desire and disruption is both real and comic; a chuckle is born in the tense space between the inclination and its impossibility. We are proprietary about that space; it may not be crossed. Everyone may gawk, but no one makes advances. The woman is magically protected within a frame created by the distance of collective admiration.

Then comes the lord governor, a stranger and passing traveler, the man with power. He oversteps the boundary. As always his advances are repulsed, and we delight in the repulse. Yet in this case the voice that comes from behind the impenetrable and alluring surface of woman is not that of the conservatrix of good sense and class standards. Lo-fu overwhelms the lord governor with her own counter-illusion, words that evoke a lover whose greater power and desirability humble the governor. It does not matter whether there is such a husband or not: he exists in her words. She contests the poetry of desire with the poetry of desire.

3 Woman/Stone, Man/Stone

Of this worlds Theater in which we stay,
My love, lyke the Spectator, ydly sits:
Beholding me, that all the pageants play,
Disguysing diversly my troubled wits.
Sometimes I joy when glad occasion fits,
And mask in myrth lyke to a Comedy:
Soone after, when my joy to sorrow flits,
I waile, and make my woes a Tragedy.
Yet she, beholding me with constant eye,
Delights not in my merth, nor rues my smart:
But, when I laugh, she mocks; and, when I cry,
She laughs, and hardens evermore her hart.
    What then can move her? If nor merth nor mone,
    She is no woman, but a senceless stone.

Spenser, *Amoretti,* 54

. . . we imagined a statue organized internally like ourselves, and animated by a spirit deprived of any kind of idea whatsoever. We further supposed that the surface, all of marble, did not allow it the usage of any of its senses; and we reserved for ourselves the liberty to open those senses as we chose to the various impressions to which they are susceptible.

Abbé de Condillac, *Treatise on the Sensations* (1754)

Woman/Stone

This is the first story of stone. Touched, the flesh of woman yields; she is penetrated. This touch is a test of difference, for of all the senses touch alone is said to permit no deception. If it were so simple, we could pass it by. But genital flesh, which meets on brief and anxious occasions, becomes figured in the hardness and softness of entire bodies; it becomes an ideology of hardness, affirmed at difficult moments and multiplied in the metaphors of our world.[1] The ideology of hardness most concerns that gender whose hardness or softness is in question, and the male fears the possibility of any physical or spiritual flaccidity.

Softness, feared and repressed, takes on gender and is given over to woman. On this tender field male hardness is to be tested and proven. Womanly softness is to be taken, and the taking must be an active penetration, the ostentatious exercise of male will. Folkways require that this softness be a quality of more than body: all things that surround woman must be soft, as hardness is reserved as the signature of the male.

The restaging of the distinction in each contested encounter is a rite to ward off the threatened inversion: woman/stone, an impenetrable hardness of body and heart. The woman who refuses her lover is hard-hearted, as hard as stone, as cold and hard as ice. At the other extreme is the woman who takes rather than allowing herself to be taken, a woman promiscuous in her desires or unwilling to be passive in her passion: such a woman has become "hardened," or even metallically "brazen."

The hardness of woman has its complementary inversion: the man melts, softens, weakens, is made impotent and is "unmanned." He may become a shape-changer beneath her hard and unmoved gaze:

> My love, lyke the Spectator, ydly sits:
> Beholding me, that all the pageants play,
> Disguysing diversly my troubled wits.

The intense desire, which should produce the requisite hardness in the man, is blocked and brings instead softness and plasticity. Spenser saw clearly the theater here, a desperate art of changing appearances, thrown against the shell of the beloved in the vain hope of softening stone. She is the statue; he, the metamorph, who tries in his various shapes to touch her, to open some aperture to contact.

Reciprocal myths of metamorphosis are also told over the skin of the beloved: one story is of tender flesh turning to stone, the other is of a hard surface softening, yielding. The two myths are found paired in the tenth book of Ovid's *Metamorphoses*. Ovid first tells how certain women, the Propoetides, defied the power of Venus. The goddess, slighted, worked a change upon them: the Propoetides were taught the force of lust, and became the first women to take men promiscuously. By doing this they lost the ability to blush, or, as Ovid says, "the blood in their faces hardened," *sanguisque induruit oris*. Venus then completed her curse by a small supplementary metamorphosis, hardening them still more until they passed utterly into stone.[2]

The adjacent myth tells of the artist Pygmalion, who was disgusted with the randiness of the Propoetides (which also inspires the other artist, Ovid, to gratuitous misogyny):

> Pygmalion saw them, whose lives were passed in wickedness,
> and repelled by their vice (which to female mind
> nature gave full share), he thus lived a single life,
> wifeless, and long lacked companion for his bed.
>
> Meanwhile with great success in wondrous art, he
> carved the snowy ivory to beauty that no woman born
> might have, and fell in love with his own work.
> A real maiden's face—you might believe it lived and
> longed to be moved, held back by decent modesty alone,
> so well did art conceal his art.
>   Pygmalion marveled,
> and fire for body's simulacrum seized his chest.
> Often testing hands were placed upon the work to see
> if it be body, or of ivory, nor could he call it ivory;
> gave kisses, thought himself kissed back, spoke, held,
> convinced his touching finger sank into those limbs,
> and fearful lest on fondled joints a bruise appear.

There is much touching of the submissive ivory in this story, much kissing and love banter (she is such a good listener!); and when his fingers press the hard surface, he is worried lest he leave a bruise: there are subtle acts of force, the touch that penetrates and wounds. He tries to soften that ivory and searches for marks of yielding. She might "long to be moved" (the sensual and emotional qualities of being moved are in the Latin as well as the English) but she is decently passive, her desire withheld even under the stimulation of his caress. This woman is pure surface, and Pygmalion's passion, however intense, is sheltered from any but imagined response: he is granted a reflective education in the flesh.[3]

The conclusion of the story is well known. On the festal day of Venus, the artist, suffering the torments of desire for this beloved all too literally hardened against him, prays to the goddess—not for the statue itself, but for a bride just like the ivory woman he has created. He would have preferred to ask for the statue, but he shows *reverentia*, a "decent modesty" like the statue's own—he is not yet hardened—and in his prayer he deflects his true desire into a counterfeit image of that desire. But Venus knows the artist's intent, and just as she hardened women into stone, she can also soften stone into woman: at last the impenetrable bride-to-be yields.

> tested now, ivory softened, its hardness set aside,
> yielded to his fingers, gave in, as Hymettian wax
> resoftens in the sun and to many shapes is bent
> with thumb-work, made useful by the use.

As Ovid tells it, the couple lived happily ever after.

This too raw relation between desire and art is a disturbing myth: a statue crosses the boundary between art and our ordinary world, and Pygmalion's touching of the statue touches perhaps too closely on our own acts of fantasy that are rooted in both worlds:

> It is most true, what we call Cupid's dart
> An image is, which for ourselves we carve,
> And, fools, adore in temple of our heart.
>
> Sir Philip Sidney, "Astrophel and Stella"

In both the myth of Pygmalion and Sidney's lines the moment of unease comes when fantasy's artifact ceases to be only a surface, when another human being is discovered at home beneath the shell. Who that person in the statue might have been when she came to life is beyond our imagining and beyond Ovid's.[4]

It should make us uneasy. The myth of Pygmalion giving life to stone raises a possibility that haunts art: the work of art might be nothing more than the bare image of the artist's craving and the cravings of the audience. In an increasingly repressive world any suggestion of such shocking gratifications must be ever more vigorously denied. Kant offered the classic codification of the modern defense: the apparition of true beauty can occur only in the absence of all interest, appetite, and desire. And yet we hunger.

The denial of our hunger requires ingenious indoctrination. We view nude paintings and sculptures, as alluring to the touch as Pygmalion's, and are instructed to see only form. The eyes are drawn to breast, nape, buttocks, groin. The hand longs to caress the cold chest or to reach under the fig leaf, to see if anything lies on the other side of the hard and icy surface, something that can be caressed, squeezed, touched, perhaps softened or made to stir. Desire runs to the marble's erogenous zones; the indoctrination of art compels us to a reflective distance that grasps the whole (rather than its particular "parts").

And if the statue were to look back at our looking, it would surely see an impenetrable surface of cool appreciation.[5]

These are reciprocal motions of a dance: the dream of touching and being touched (touching being the only purely reciprocal sense, in which the one who touches is at the same time touched); or an approach checked, followed by recoil and contemplative reserve or frustrated yearning. Such phases outline the mythology of the affections; their motions are focused on an uncertain surface of skin—a barrier, a wall, a garment—where hardness or softness will be tested and proven.

Woman/stone enters the mythology of the affections: the object that resists possession and being made object, a hardness that defies penetration and in doing so gives life to desire.

> e'l mio disio però non cangia il verde,
> si è barbato ne la dura petra
> che parla e sente come fosse donna.
>
> yet my desire does not loose its green,
> so rooted it is in that hard stone
> which speaks and feels as if it were woman.

The lines are from Dante's "stone rhymes," *rime petrose,* a complaint against the woman/stone whose refusal sustains his desire and art, woman/stone in which he is rooted against his will, as a soft green vegetation that somehow stubbornly thrives. Out of her hardness and his blocked desire comes a second hardness in the act of art, the poem. Throughout the Western tradition the poem's technical mastery was described with the metaphor of sculpture, Horace's *limae labor,* "the toilsome work of the file." The Chinese tradition used the figure of woodcarving.

Forking Passage

It might be that the figure of the beloved who appears in the hard statue is not entirely other, but also a mirror image of the self. Moreover, the self that would appear in such a mirror would be no neutral matrix of identity, but rather the self as a longing gaze fixed upon the image of the other. There is no little confusion and indecision here regarding the boundary between self and other. One forking of the way will lead to the metamorphosis of the artist Pygmalion into Narcissus, of whom the late Latin poet Pentadius wrote: *quodque amat ipse facit,* "what he loves, he himself makes" (compare Ovid on Pygmalion: "fell in love with his own work"). The other fork is Neruda's, in which nothing that the artist produces is truly his own:

> But they grow more darkly dyed with your love,
>   these words of mine.
> You occupy everything, everything.

At this forking of the ways, we will allow Michelangelo, the sculptor, to speak:

> S'egli è che 'n dura pietra alcun somigli
> Talor l'immagin d'ogni altri a se stesso,
> Squallido e smorto spesso
> Il fo, com'i' son fatto da costei.
> E par ch'esempio pigli
> Ogni or da me, ch'i' penso di far lei.
> Ben la pietra potrei
> Per l'aspra sua durezza,
> In ch'io l'esempio, dir ch'a lei s'assembra;
> Del resto non saprei,
> Mentre mi strugge e sprezza,
> Altro scolpir che le mie afflitte membra.
> Ma se l'arte rimembra
> Agli anni la beltà, per durare ella,
> Farà me lieto, ond'io le' farò bella.

> If it is so, that in hard stone
> one likens every other's image to oneself,
> ashen and often pale I make it,
> just as I am made by her.
> And thus I ever take model from me,
> intending it be she.
> Well one might say that stone
> resembles her, model for me
> through her sharp hardness;
> as for the rest, I,
> consumed and mocked, only know
> to carve my own tormented limbs.
> But if art recalls
> beauty to the years, I will be glad
> to make her lasting, whereby I'll make her lovely.

Rime, 109.53

The statue is no longer Pygmalion's simple image of desire: it has become something else altogether, something which is both fusion and confusion of self and other. Indeed this may be the only place, here on the artwork's hard surface without depth, that the broken halves of the androgyne can meet and become one again. Yet the distinguishing trait of the other that is preserved in the statue is the very quality of the medium: the hardness of stone, which represents the beloved only in her relation to the sculptor-lover. Likewise, the primary trait of the self that meets and fuses with the beloved is the pale skin reappearing in the pale marble, his own surface as it has been transformed by relation to her. Each survives entirely in the quality of their mutual relation; and the visible cause and consequence of blocked desire are bound together in perpetual unfulfillment: writhing limbs that do not stir.

The statue is a strange thing in which contraries meet. It is both consummation and consummation perpetually deferred. She is hard, *dura,* and in the hard surface of the stone the artist chooses to make her hardness last, *durare.* The loveliness that he imparts to this statue is only the expedient means to perpetuate this fusion of the two lovers in one body, or in a surface that figures desire's permanence in its permanent impenetrability.

The myth of Pygmalion is often retold in later ages; in its variations it is always deflected before its conclusion, the softening into life and the "happily ever after." The stone sculpture produced from blocked desire is finely polished, the very image of woman/stone. But the age of magic has passed; no kindly goddess looks down to see the artist's secret desires and answer his prayers by softening the impenetrable surface of the stone. The artwork is left perpetually incomplete, a dark hope unfulfilled—*ars interrupta:* we are kept at a distance; we may not touch. (There are complex balances here. We are forbidden by custom to touch the tactile artform, the naked sculpture, but the taboo can be overcome by abstracting the form. Thus modern sculpture that we are invited to touch has succeeded in hiding the body.)

Pygmalion differed from all later artists in the need to exercise his art only once; his art was fulfilled, by which he could "have" the object of his desire a thousand times. Sculptors of later times produced statues by the hundreds and poets, poems by the thousands, always trying to get it right, yet never achieving what they wanted even once. As Petrarch says in *Rime 78:*

Pygmaliòn, quanto lodar ti dei
de l'imagine tua, se mille volte
n'avesti quel ch'i' sol una vorrei.

Pygmalion, you are due much praise
for the image you made: a thousand times
you had what I would have just once.

Such later artists inevitably produced surfaces without depth, planes, the "shadow" that is the mere image or representation:

Compare me to Pygmalion with his image sotted,
For, as was he, even so I am deceived.
The shadow only is to me allotted,
The substance hath of substance me bereaved.

Bartholomew Griffin,
"Fidessa, More Chaste Than Kind," 25

It is a strange event, the missing substance swallowing the artist's substance in the repeated production of the "shadow." The art, constantly ventured again despite all its former failures, gradually destroys the artist:

For hapless lo, even with my own desires
  I figured on the tablet of my heart
  And so did perish by my proper art.

Samuel Daniel, "Delia," 13

Glimpse into a Parallel Chamber

Of how the god might bring the soul from the caverns of the stone
and how an almost successful act of art is ruined just before completion because the artist softened and looked back with desire. Or perhaps the event is only figured in the stone of a bas-relief, an event that
the poet seeks to animate.

That was the deep uncanny mine of souls.
Like veins of silver ore, they silently
moved through its massive darkness. Blood welled up
among the roots, on its way to the world of men,
and in the dark it looked as hard as stone.
Nothing else was red.

There were cliffs there,
and forests made of mist. There were bridges
spanning the void, and that great gray blind lake
which hung above its distant bottom
like the sky on a rainy day above a landscape.
And through the gentle, unresisting meadows
one pale path unrolled like a strip of cotton.
Down this path they were coming.

In front, the slender man in the blue cloak—
mute, impatient, looking straight ahead.
In large, greedy, unchewed bites his walk
devoured the path; his hands hung at his sides,
tight and heavy, out of the falling folds,
no longer conscious of the delicate lyre
which had grown into his left arm, like a slip
of roses grafted onto an olive tree.
His senses felt as though they were split in two:
his sight would race ahead of him like a dog,
stop, come back, then rushing off again
would stand, impatient, at the path's next turn,—
but his hearing, like an odor, stayed behind.
Sometimes it seemed to him as though it reached
back to the footsteps of those other two
who were to follow him, up the long path home.
But then, once more, it was just his own steps' echo,
or the wind inside his cloak, that made the sound.

He said to himself, they had to be behind him;
said it aloud and heard it fade away.

They had to be behind him, but their steps
were ominously soft. If only he could
turn around, just once (but looking back
would ruin this entire work, so near
completion), then he could not fail to see them,
those other two, who followed him so softly:

The god of speed and distant messages,
a traveler's hood above his shining eyes,
his slender staff held out in front of him,
and little wings fluttering at his ankles;
and on his left arm, barely touching it: *she*.

A woman so loved that from one lyre there came
more lament than from all lamenting women;
that a whole world of lament arose, in which
all nature reappeared; forest and valley,
road and village, field and stream and animal;
and that around this lament-world, even as
around the other earth, a sun revolved
and a silent star-filled heaven, a lament-
heaven, with its own, disfigured stars—:
So greatly was she loved.

But now she walked beside the graceful god,
her steps constricted by the trailing graveclothes,
uncertain, gentle, and without impatience.
She was deep within herself, like a woman heavy
with child, and did not see the man in front
or the path ascending steeply into life.
Deep within herself. Being dead
filled her beyond fulfillment. Like a fruit
suffused with its own mystery and sweetness,
she was filled with her vast death, which was so new,
she could not understand that it had happened.
She had come into a new virginity
and was untouchable; her sex had closed
like a young flower at nightfall, and her hands
had grown so unused to marriage that the god's
infinitely gentle touch of guidance
hurt her, like an undesired kiss.

She was no longer that woman with blue eyes
who once had echoed through the poet's songs,
no longer the wide couch's scent and island,
and that man's property no longer.

She was already loosened like long hair,
poured out like fallen rain,
shared like a limitless supply.

She was already root.

And when, abruptly,
the god put out his hand to stop her, saying,
with sorrow in his voice: He has turned around—,
she could not understand, and softly answered
Who?

                                        Far away,
dark before the shining exit-gates,
someone or other stood, whose features were
unrecognizable. He stood and saw
how, on the strip of road among the meadows,
with a mournful look, the god of messages
silently turned to follow the small figure
already walking back along the path,
her steps constricted by the trailing graveclothes,
uncertain, gentle, and without impatience.

Rainer Maria Rilke, "Orpheus, Eurydice, Hermes"[6]

Going Astray

Non ha l'ottimo artista alcun concetto,
Ch'un marmo solo in sé non circoscriva
Col suo soverchio, e solo a quello arriva
La man che ubbidisce all'intelletto.

Il mal ch'io fuggo e'l ben ch'io mi prometto,
In te, Donna leggiadra, altera e diva,
Tal si nasconde; e perch'io più non viva,
Contraria ho l'arte al disiato effetto.

Amor dunque non ha, né tua beltate,
O durezza, o fortuna, o gran disdegno,
Del mio mal colpa, o mio destino o sorte,

Se dentro del tuo cuor morte e pietate
Porti in un tempo, e ch'el mio basso ingegno
Non sappia, ardendo, trarne altro che morte.

The finest artist has no intent
    that marble block does not contain
    abundantly within itself: to this attains
    alone the hand obedient to mind.

The ill I flee, the good that I propose
  hide this very way in you, capricious lady,
  proud lady, goddess; and since I live no more,
  contrary runs my art to the desired effect.

Then this my ill's no fault of Love,
  nor of your beauty, hardness, or disdain,
  or fortune, or my destiny or luck:

You bear both death and grace together
  in your heart, whence my low talent, set ablaze,
  no better knew than from it to snatch death.

Michelangelo, *Rime,* 83

"The finest artist has no intent that marble block does not contain." Pride in mastery speaks here. The skilled and obedient hand perfectly transmits the clear reflection of the artist's intention and peels it from the three-dimensional stone, which contains all that the artist can conceive. But, as in Pygmalion's story, acts of art can be only imperfectly distinguished from human desire. In the performance of the intention something goes awry. "Contraria ho l'arte al disiato effetto:" contrary runs my art to the desired effect. The lover is sculptor, the woman is stone, with a heart of stone; love's possibility resides in that stony heart, but must be shaped to love and gracious consent by the conjunction of artistic intent and talent that guides the sculpting hand. Yet somehow the sculptor's mastery fails.

Sculpture in stone is an art of risk: each blow of the chisel decides conditional success or complete ruin, grace or death. He speaks now from failure and death, having miscarried where Pygmalion succeeded, in his attempt to shape woman/stone to life and responding desire. The failure recoils upon him: not the "finest artist," but a flawed talent, "set ablaze," his master craftsman's dispassionate control led astray by passion's force. He lacked aesthetic distance; he was ablaze. The chisel slipped, and the block of marble cracked.

Or the artist holds a mirror up to nature, a mirror which is also his protective shield, and the mirroring shield's polished surface shows the Medusa her own gaze, which turns her to stone. The myth has many variations.

Common poets will blame the lady for her hardness; the poet suffers death by fire in her stony glance. But stone is Michelangelo's medium, and he has faith in the power of his art to produce the perfect images of his will. In Vittoria Colonna he encounters the intractable and impenetrable other; artistic control falters, and he can only blame himself: *basso ingegno,* a "low talent" that has revealed itself inadequate.

Theorists of art in his age spoke often of the artist's work as carried through on the model of creative divinity: the artist is a minor deity, producing poetic heterocosms or physical forms from formlessness. Like the divinity, the artist exercises absolute control, a diminutive Aristotelian First Mover that remains itself unmoved.

Not merely artist and work are in play here, however: there is someone else. Let us imagine her reading this finely crafted sonnet that reaffirms the artist's absolute control in a strange way: as an intent to work a second creation upon an independent being of the first creation. He denies her even the power that the common sonneteer grants his beloved. It is an unkind absolution of her guilt to say that there is no deciding power in her beauty, or in her hardness, or in her ability to command his obedience through the force of love; to the sculptor her stoniness is inert stuff. We watch her face as she reads, and we see that somehow the art of this sonnet has strayed from its intent as a love poem: "contrary runs my art to the desired effect." The art of the poet-lover misses its mark even as it tells her how the art of the sculptor-lover has missed its mark.

A love sonnet was a stylized token within a ceremony of courtship, real or pretended. In its strict language, shared by women and men, difficult desires might be declared, understood, and negotiated. The commonplace moves of such a sonnet could be so arranged that the lover's intent was exposed, but he neither created nor fully controlled the poem; rather, he learned to speak through its stringent rules. By doing so the lover submitted to the shared language of poetic ceremony, and acknowledged to the beloved that he accepted its restraints (the rules of courtly "service" and disempowerment pretending to compensate for the male's social power). Each phrase of such a sonnet was shaped by anticipations of her reading eyes, her listening ears.

But for this poet the words are not merely stylized tokens in the courtship ceremony; they are blank material, like a block of marble, to be cut to shape by will alone. For him the words are not address; he cannot hear how the other must hear them. He is the divine artist of mere stuff, gauging the properties of words, insensible to the operation of the artwork in the human world. In her fury she rips the sonnet into pieces. But he has kept a copy. He plans to continue working on the phrasing.

The art of this sonnet fails as an act of address to another person even as it speaks of the failure of another, metaphorical act of art. It is precisely at this moment of a double failure to execute intentions that the sonnet becomes art in a different sense. We understand easily that it reaches something finer by withdrawing from the transparent game of persuasion that is the courtship sonnet; but that can only occur by a simultaneous withdrawal from the perfect execution of artistic intentions in the mind of this mock divinity. In asserting the possibility of unqualified control, it loses control and becomes more than he could ever have hoped it be. It is cursed always to reveal more than it intends. "I dought neither speak to prince or peer, / Nor ask of grace from fair ladye"—.

Such sonnets were often identified by their first line: "Non ha l'ottimo artista alcun concetto," the finest artist has no intent. The unwitting truth is discovered in the most radical claim for the power of artistic intention. The double negative that finally empowers all artistic intent is deferred too long. Complete power and complete loss of power are given together.

The intent that should govern the act of art is *concetto,* what Sir Philip Sidney called the poet's "foreconceit," the work of art as a fully realized idea in the mind. All external products of art are supposed mere execution. This radical view of art suits sculpture, Michelangelo's art of choice, in which the external material is a block of stone that somehow contains the artwork as a latent possibility to be discovered. Woman/stone, Vittoria Colonna, is for him figured as such material, and the expression in her face and feelings in her heart will be the desired shape he discovers within her.

The artist in this version is one who works changes on outer material without himself being changed; if he is touched by another and set aflame, his control is compromised, and he may become an incompetent deity who botches his metamorphoses. It was desire's unsteadiness that caused Orpheus to lose control and look back. But there is another story told about the collapse of the artist's control: in the dialogue *Ion,* Socrates concludes that the poet's art is perfect only when he is as much out of control as Michelangelo's artist believes he should be in control. In Socrates' potentially ironic version, greatness comes only when the poet's flawed and mortal intentions are bypassed and the god speaks through him. "The finest artist has no intent."

Such is also the conventional claim of the common sonneteer, though made with the secret and manipulative intent of bringing his lady to bed. The god that is supposed to shape the words of the common lover is Eros, or the powerful beloved through whom Eros works:

> For anything I can speak or do
> the thanks is hers, who's given me
> the knowledge and judgment by which I
> am poet of grace; and
> so much as I fashion fittingly
> I derive from her body, fair and sweet—
> as many concerns as from fine heart come.
>
> Peire Vidal, Canso

The poet may claim that his art is determined by the beloved and not under his control. In making such a claim, he submits to the rules of a courtship exchange; however, in doing so he may also realize his prior intent and desire, and win his lady. Perhaps it is Love the god or the goddess speaking through Michelangelo in this sonnet as well, in which he tells of artistic intention going awry, compelling him to say the wrong thing in the most beautiful way. We may not be able to decide whether the artist is utterly in control or utterly out of control, but we realize that here in love and art the question of complete power is the stake for which we roll the dice.

Once rolled, the dice will come up one way or another. A decision will emerge that will suppress one of the contrary terms: an interpretation. But each interpretation, if pressed only gently, will resolve into its opposite.

We become easily tangled in the question of power, where behind every claim of being mastered by passion we can see the shadows of manipulative control, behind which stands a force of desire that manipulates the manipulations; a claim of mastery, by its insensibility to the beloved, becomes failure of mastery. Opposites continually change places, and our only certainty is that control, both mastery and being mastered, matters very much. This question of control is the consequence of the encounter with woman/stone (or in the case of Vittoria Colonna's sonnets, of the encounter with man/stone). The hard, concealing surface, the barrier to contact, is not only the physical shape of desire, it is also the shape of uncertainty and threat; as the lover is forcefully drawn to and repelled from that impassible surface he learns lessons in the question of power.

The work of art is a ground on which the question may be posed. But among the many forms of art in which the deflected forces of desire and artistic mastery contend, the literary art of the love poem occupies a strange double position: it is both a thing of art and an address to the beloved; it removes the dance of desire to its own world and then returns to our common world to dance here.

Pause: *The Fantasy of Ends Attained and Gone Wrong*

Pygmalion presses on the hard surface; Michelangelo chisels out the disposition of the beloved's heart. But the darkest hope of art's power is to get beneath the skin. Thus Ronsard dreams of working Venus' vitalizing magic to journey into the ice-hard veins, to soften that hardness and shape it to his will.

> J'ay desiré cent fois me transformer, et d'estre
> Un esprit invisible, afin de me cacher
> Au fond de vostre coeur, pour l'humeur rechercher
> Qui vous fait contre moy si cruelle apparoistre.
>
> Si j'estois dedans vous, au moins je serois maistre
> De l'humeur qui vous fait contre l'Amour pecher,
> Et si n'auriez ny pouls ny nerfs dessous la chair,
> Que je ne recherchasse à fin de vous cognoistre.
>
> Je sçaurois, maugré vous et vos complexions,
> Toutes vos volontez et vos conditions,
> Et chasserois si bien la froideur de vos veines,
>
> Que les flames d'Amour vous y allumeriez.
> Puis quand je les voirrois de son feu toutes pleines,
> Je me referois homme, et lors vous m'aimeriez.

> A hundred times I've longed to be transformed
>   to invisible sprite, within your heart to lie
>   deep hidden, and there to hunt the humor down
>   that makes you show yourself so harsh to me.
>
> Were I within you, I at least would master
>   the humor that makes you so sin against love:
>   no pulse nor nerves beneath the skin would stay
>   unhunted, so that I might come to know you.
>
> In spite of you and all your whims I'd learn
>   your every desire, your every state of mind,
>   and I would drive the coldness from your veins

so well that they would light with flames of love.
And when I saw them all so filled with fire,
man I'd make myself again, and you would love me.

Ronsard, The Loves of Marie

This is no more than a gracious fantasy of penetration; it is theater for the shape-changer, at last made wisp by his lady's hardness. If Michelangelo would carve the heart, Ronsard would pass beneath the skin to adjust the somatic mechanism and set the fires of lust. Both share the impotent fantasy of power: "Were I within you, I at least would [be] master," master of her contrary humor, and thus master of all the vulnerability that would follow her kindled desire. He aims to know her, heart and body. Yet such knowledge can be achieved only through this act of speculative violation. He comes to the edge of a contradiction, wishing to compel a love that can be love only when freely given. He must reemerge to receive this love that he himself has made; he must become man again and stand as the object of her desire in order to cancel the pain of the encounter with stone. But the poem can go no further; its lines are used up, and it dare not speculate on the discomforting gift—the other that is no longer other but a mere construction of his own intent. Even in perfect success the art runs contrary to the desired effect.

Assault

cum me saevus amor prensat sursumque capillis

when savage love yanked me up by the hair

Petronius

Ibase la niña
noche de San Juan
a coger los aires
al fresco del mar.
Miraba los remos
que remando van
cubiertos de flores,
flores de azahar.
Salió un caballero
por el arenal,
dijérale amores
cortés y galán.

Respondió la esquiva,
quísola abrazar,
con temor que tiene
huyendo se va.
Salióle al camino
otro por burlar,
las hermosas manos
le quieren tomar.
Entre estos desvíos
perdidos se han
sus ricos zarcillos;
vanlos a buscar.
"¡Dejadme llorar
orillas del mar!"
"¡Por aquí, por allí los vi,
por aquí deben de estar!"

Lloraba la niña,
no los puede hallar
danse para ellos,
quiérenla engañar.
"¡Dejadme llorar orillas
orillas del mar!"
"¡Por aquí, por allí los vi,
por aquí deben de estar!"
"Tomad niña el oro
y no lloréis más,
que todas las niñas
nacen en tomar,
que las que no toman
después llorarán
el no haber tomado
en su verde edad."

A girl went out
one St. John's Eve
for the cool, fresh air
in the open by the sea.
And she watched the oars
that there went rowing,
oars all covered with flowers,
flowers of the orange.

Out stepped a gentleman,
out upon the shore,
and spoke to her of love

in smooth and gallant words.
She put him off with her reply;
he took her in his arms,
but fear it was took hold of her,
and off she ran away.

Out then stepped another man
to tease her in her way,
and tried to take her
by her lovely, lovely hands.
Dodging to escape them,
she lost along the way
her precious earrings,
and they pretend to look for them.

"Just leave me here to cry
by the shores of the sea!"
"But here they are!" "I see them there!"
"No, here's where they must be!"

The girl was weeping,
couldn't find them
the men set out to look around,
trying to deceive her.
"Just leave me here to cry
by the shores of the sea!"

"But here they are!" "I see them there!"
"No, here's where they must be!"

"Take this gold, girl,
cry no more,
for all the girls that ever were
were born from taking;
those that don't take
someday will cry
that they never took
in youth's green age."

Lope de Vega

We are stone; we "ydly sit" and watch the play unmoved. Yet sometimes the rules of the play may be broken: woman/stone is battered; and we, in our walled galleries, squirm, knowing that the violation is not of any real woman but a violation of us, a forced penetration of the safe wall between us and the song. The distance of art is present only if the poem plays by the rules.

We have been told that poetry creates its own separate place, where words may play freely and not be bound to the values of our common world. Poetry has license: it is nothing more than the great game of all possibility within a frame, and whatever happens in its world should be isolated from our habitual moral judgment. Most poetry guards its license by claiming some easy ethic, hoping in this way to distract the moral sensibility from its darker workings.

It is true that in poetry there is a certain setting apart, more in some poems than in others, but always such reserved poetic space has significance only through its relation to the more common space of this world. Romantic critics dreamed of "arabesque," an art of purely arbitrary and meaningless play, the sweet liberty of insignificance; yet even such extreme hopes are interesting only as the most desperate recoil from a repressive and unfree outer world. Adorno meant something like this when he said that "Art is the social antithesis of society." In one world acts are "in effect" but are repressed; in the art world certain acts are allowed to appear precisely because they are ineffectual. Beneath the game of words may be a brutality that the boundaries of play just barely hold in check. We are never certain whether it is a brutishness in our everyday world that poetry plays against, or a brutishness repressed in our everyday world that poetry allows to emerge. And there is a pain in this display of our savagery: we cannot comfortably reprove or repress or deny the intensity of the interest that instantly summons up our virtuous social countermotions.

Sometimes poetry allows its dangerous doubleness of play to rise to the surface; after seducing us to believe that all is safe and lovely here, it lets the mask slip. "Take," says the man, playing with words, inviting her to take possession of a commodity and urging her to a sexual taking. His wordplay tells a truth, but a raw truth of power in the world's relations, a truth we do not want to hear as we watch this young girl by the seashore, terrified and humiliated, perhaps just raped.

The poem begins by gently stroking our hair: "Gode sire, pray ich thee, come and daunce wit me, in Irlande." It begins by playing love games and poetry games. But the poem was only deceiving us; the game turns dark, and rather than playing, we find ourselves being played with. The stroking hand suddenly takes a handful of our hair, yanks hard, forces our eyes to look into a grinning face. And at that moment its smiling lips repeat the old words of poetry, the song of love and seduction: "Gather ye rosebuds while ye may." But the words are sour now, no less true perhaps, but a truth of brute power.

The song is from one of Lope de Vega's dramas, and it starts out as a folk song, with a young girl going out to the seashore on Saint John's Eve. The gentleman who suddenly appears, the *caballero,* also belongs to the world of folk song; we are promised romance and sexual encounter that ends with the girl sad and abandoned. The gentleman speaks to her, as we know he must, with "smooth and gallant" words, which are the words of courtship and poetry's stylized mask.

This is the moment of choice, and in the world of poetry there is always choice. The man proposes something, the woman decides.

> Fair young maid all in the garden;
> Strange young man passes her by,
> Says: fair maid, will you marry me?
> This then, sir, was her reply . . .

In the world of poetry there are few commanding parents, hardly any rapes, and rarely indecision: desire flares up and in a few lines is consummated or deflected against stone. Unlike in this quotidian world, in poetry's world there is the appearance of a core of freedom.

The girl chooses to be coy; she evades him, and he makes to "take her up all in his arms." We are still in the easy world of the love song, but we are on its margins: beneath the dance of love words and gestures, and ready to supplant words whether they succeed or fail, is force. He wants to take hold of her, to take sexual possession in a sense that blurs into the physical possession of an object. With their games of freedom and choice, words try to hide or defer physical force, as the word ceremonies of courtly love tried to cover over male power in social relations. But garment is only garment when there is a naked body beneath.

The lilting rhythms of song continue, but the event breaks away from the common anticipations of the song world, whose manner now becomes ironic and incongruous. This is the crisis, the moment of decision. The girl responds outside of the rules of poetic encounter: she neither surrenders to passion nor blocks his passion with the language of stone—she runs. She responds with fear, and well she should, seeing the fact of force that lies beneath the lying words. The beast of prey scents fear. When a second *caballero* steps out to block her escape, the illusions of the conventional love song are shattered and the poem has gone astray.

"Young girl" and "gentleman" are anonymous types, but the poetic illusion of the erotic encounter requires singularity: a particular man desiring one particular woman or a particular woman desiring one particular man. Only in a particular election is there any promise of relation beyond the moment of mating. What is masked here is a series of takings, brute assertions of desire and power that reduce man and woman to replaceable body shapes. The appearance of the second anonymous *caballero* strips away the mask and shows us a world where men and women are mere representatives of their genders, where any and all will take any and all.

Now those "smooth and gallant" lies of love and romantic persuasion are replaced by another kind of lying language, a mocking language that exults in its power to lie. The game has become cruelly playful: "'But here they are!' 'I see them there!' / 'No, here's where they must be!'" She cannot flee the game and is powerless to make them go away. Their language mocks the poetic pretense of doing service to one's lady.

She loses her earrings or another conventionally precious thing, the jewel of her virginity. If, as we suspect, it is indeed her virginity that has been lost, then their mocking pretense of helping her find what has been lost is a new level in the devaluation of poetic language, the dead metaphor ("loss" of virginity) exploded by their laughing "search." But here, as in the closing, there is also the unpleasant truth that this loss is no real loss, only an illusion.

An exchange is offered. She has been humiliated, her body reduced to an object and something precious taken from her. Acknowledging now that there was someone at home in the body, the men feel they must repay what they caused her to lose: maidenhead as thing, honor as thing, woman as thing, her status as other person temporarily stolen from her. If force turns the world around it into object, the rules of commodity exchange attempt to give a restraining law to a world of objects, all potentially subject to brute force. They offer her gold, one precious thing for another. And for the third time the men play with words, now playing on *tomar,* "take." "Take this gold, girl." Having reduced her to object, they would complete her corruption, teach her to participate in a world where all is economy, where sex is taking and possession.

They tell her the truth of force now, a truth of which poetry is not supposed to remind us or her: that her very being comes from a taking—a man taking a woman, perhaps mutual taking, perhaps violent and forced taking, perhaps a taking worked out as an exchange of gold, or status, or security. Nature is indifferent to whether her parents danced and sang love songs or did not. And without that taking she would not be here to be taken. She is not a particular person: she is a member of the animal species, a category—"girl"—and like all girls and *caballeros,* born of taking. Consent and reciprocal desire are a fragile ceremony by which we try to win some illusion of freedom from brute and unfree nature. But the end remains the same and we come back at last to nature.

Having been reduced to an object and made to witness the truth of force, she has choice restored to her: to be merely an object for the taking in the fallen world of power or to participate in it, to accept an economy of exchange and take for herself—take the gold, take men, take pleasure in the taking, to become hardened.

Finally they sing to her the oldest words of the seduction poem: take now while you're young, because once you're older, you will have no chance to take; the commodity will have no value, rotten fruit. The commonplaces of the love song come back to close and frame the poem. If we were to read only the beginning and the end, we would never know how it goes astray. But having gone astray with it, we find those light conventional words of the love game twisted and ugly. Once the mask of sweet poetry is dropped and we see the face beneath, those smooth surfaces come to mean something else.

Before the straw dogs are presented at the sacrifice, they are set in bamboo coffers covered over with finely patterned embroideries. The Impersonator of the Dead and the Priest who Addresses the Dead fast and practice abstentions in order to bring them to the sacrifice. But once the presentation is over, people walking by will step on their heads and spines, and straw-gatherers will pick up the pieces and burn them.

Master Chuang Chou, "Heaven's Cycles"

Heaven and Earth have no sympathy:
they treat all things like straw dogs.

Lao-tzu

Comic Interlude

In which brute Nature assails the impenetrable surfaces of monk/stone.

From dawn to dusk before the eaves
    rain increases the flowers,
here eighty monks of the southland
    sup on parboiled sesame:
now fixed in meditation, when
    will they emerge again,
unaware that nesting swallows have
    crapped on their cassocks?

Ch'in Hsi (eighth century),
"Written on the Cell of the Monk Ming-hui"

The Buddhist monk is also an artist with intent: his goal is to transcend, through meditation, the cycles of birth and death, to press beyond effective nature. He is sculptor, and his body in meditation, the
sculpture. As the powerful goddess Venus turned carved ivory into
soft flesh, the monk would turn soft flesh into sculpted stone. A shell
will remain, with no one at home inside: all is emptiness.

But spring is an aggressive season: lush, sexual, with everything
bursting into life. And swallows are the spring's agents, nesting in the
rafters, eating, defecating, procreating, producing prodigious flocks
of swallowlings. In front of the monastery eaves the trees are all in
flower, with the rain feeding that fecundity, their sensuous colors the
brighter for their wetness. And here inside are eighty monks, aspiring
to anonymity in their bald heads and cassocks, lined up in rows as
they eat their austere vegetarian meal. The first couplet sets up a
choice between two worlds, one outside and one inside, one abun-
dant, sexual, brightly colored, growing, the other disciplined, neuter,
and austere. Yet there are secret unities between the two worlds: when
the poets describe Buddhist monks, they usually speak of them in
their monkish functions, rather than in this embarrassing concession
to their animal natures—eating.

Chinese poetry lives by balanced pairings: each process initiated
awaits its consequences. Eating too has its outcome, even an austere
meal of sesame—good bird food. This might be a thought in the mind
of our bored poet (who has come from the outside world to pay the
monk Ming-hui a visit) as he watches these good monks eat their
meals and then go into the fixed stillness of devotional meditation.
Perhaps he imagines a natural process within the blank shells of bodies, the sesame working its way through their digestive tracts. If he
wonders when they will emerge from meditation's stillness, one mo-

tive of his query is surely the visitor's impatience, but another may come from reflection on those internal calls of nature to which meditation should render the body indifferent. For the swallows in the rafters, the body's processing of seed is swift and unmysterious— plop, again and again on their motionless cassocks.

The fact that the poet notices this in the words of a poem may recall a primordial principle of poetry: the Latin adage *ubi dolor ubi digitus*—"one needs must scratch where it itches" (Robert Burton's translation). Words of poems are also the outcome of a natural process, following in their own oblique way from something that concerns the poet, catches the attention, provokes; and by the places where he must scratch, we see where the poet itches. There is indeed a strangeness here to provoke a poet who comes from the secular world and confronts these humans that sit so still upon the margins of another world, not only forbidden to scratch (literally and figuratively) but aspiring to transcend even the itch.

Like the poet the swallows make the crossing between worlds, coming from sensuous springtime into the ascetic space of the monastery, and making still more physical contact with the monastic robes. Such secular intrusion would be a befouling even without the more solid deposits. In some sense springtime and its swallows are the victors in this encounter, reducing the monks to objects of ridicule. But nature's agents have not captured the attention of monks so easily as the attention of the poet. Beneath the fouled surface of cassock and skin a Buddhist truth is equally triumphant: the monks are genuinely "unaware"; the impassable boundary between the worlds is preserved, and the "liquid siftings" of nature's mockery cannot touch them. Nature dances all around them, trying to catch their attention, trying to get through the surface of monk/stone. The poet watches undecided, laughing with nature's laughter, yet puzzled at their stony indifference.

The poem is a puff, and the boundaries between its comic emptiness and Buddhism's serious emptiness may be impossible to discover. Humor exposes the emptiness beneath all value and intensities (including austerity), and exposes it more swiftly than the long discipline of meditation. Humor is assault and assault's deflection, breaking the bubble of just indignation and minor embarrassments, such as come from swallows in the rafters. Humor even evacuates the irritation of the neglected guest, visitor from a springtime world. There may be something ridiculous in the dances we do on both sides of the barrier, one hiding, the other knocking, trying to get through.

Counterstatement: Force Withheld

> How hard it is to propose something for another person's judgment without corrupting that judgment by the manner of the proposal. If a person says, "I find it beautiful," or "I find it unclear," or some other similar statement, he disposes the imagination of the other to make the same judgment or provokes it to a contrary judgment. It is better to say nothing at all and then the other will make his judgment according to how it is, which is to say according to how it is then and according to the other circumstances in which it is given, but of which the person making the proposal is not the cause. At the very least he will not have interfered, unless of course his silence also has its effect, according to the interpretation that the person making the judgment will give such silence by his whim, or according to what he supposes from the movements, the expression on the face, or the tone of voice—insofar as he is a physiognomist—so hard it is not to displace a judgment from its natural position, or even more, how little there is in judgments that is secure and stable.
>
> Pascal, *Pensées*[7]

We detect a quiet anxiety in his discovery of this obvious truth: there is a desire to withdraw that realizes, at each stage of the withdrawal, how impossible it is, how the case proposed for judgment cannot be disentangled from circumstance and relation, even from the very act of proposal. Even if, after posing the question, the questioner were to suddenly disappear from the face of the earth, that too would exert its pressure on the other's judgment, and strongly too. Judgment is "soft"—nothing secure or stable in it—and takes its shape in a circumstantial encounter between two creatures. "To propose something for another person's judgment": they stand face to face. Corruption is already present in the soft and corruptible flesh. But like Michelangelo, Pascal does not recognize the power that the other exerts on him; he senses only the force of his presence on the other. He is fastidious and uncomfortable with his power; he wants to draw back, to disengage, to hide his force. He is driven to silence. Then he recognizes the impurity even of silence, how circumstance creeps in— the chilly wind of a November morning, the other's hurry to make an appointment, the distraction of the leaves whirling around their feet.

Worse still, he realizes that his very silence is a heavy force that presses on the decision of the other, who scrutinizes the look on his face, the motion of his hands for clues about his motives or opinions.

Something like an attempt at exculpation is present here: at least I have not actively interfered. He makes his face stony, hard, impassive; he tries to fade away. He has utter confidence in his power of active influence; his restraint is only the shadow of such confidence. The use of his power would corrupt, but in trying to renounce it he finds it strengthened and still active.

In the unrecognized pride of such confidence in his own power, he scarcely notices how that power is undone in the encounter. The factors he observes are strangely indeterminate: his gift of an opinion would enter into the other's judgment, but he can't say how, whether compelling assent or contradiction. And how the other might read his silence, or the fidgeting hands, or his rigid expressionless face—who can tell? The judgment can never be free of relation to the other, but neither can it be foreseen and managed in any certain way. Nothing firm or stable here: the meeting is always soft and pliant, a shifting surface where two mammals come into contact, the relation of flesh close to flesh.

What he flees from here is rhetoric, the science of human pride, the absurd faith that he can manipulate the other with words. Perhaps he half sees the error that lies beneath both the willful attempt and the renunciation. What can influence be when the person who wishes to influence (or not to influence) is more clearly determined by this particular desire than the other person, on whom he presumes to work, can be determined by the influencing words? The only certainty remaining is that each is changed in and by the relation: there is no cause and no effect, because each putative cause for one person is at the same time the effect of the other. Nothing stable or firm here.

Someone comes up to you. His voice is at first urgent, excited. He has made a discovery and wants your opinion. You listen. As you think about the question, he keeps his face straight and says nothing, caring so much about what you will say that he fears his care will press on you, that you won't say what you really think. You cannot help noticing that he draws back. What does it mean, what is there in the words that can be sifted out from the face and the quickly moving lips that cold November morning? There must have been something in it because what he said comes back to you at odd times, in new circumstances—but even then trailing something of the way he first said it, and how it struck you at the time, and your impatience to get away then, hurrying to an appointment, and the cold wind in your face. But every time it comes back to you—even now as you wonder what there was in it apart from the circumstance of being addressed, then and in such weather—it is elicited by some new circumstance and is impossible to unravel from the situation that called it forth.

There may be in words something like meaning, but it isn't really terribly important in itself—it is only a way to collect circumstances for this moment, this encounter, this relation.

And those poems: you didn't really care about their meaning, nor were they merely aesthetic objects, however hard they may have tried to present themselves to you that way, silent and holding their faces hard and expressionless. What mattered was the way the words were able to catch you up, take you, *tomar*. When they caught you, you may have resisted, tried to run away, or rushed to meet desire with desire; or perhaps you hid behind a stony surface and pretended not to notice as the words danced around you, trying to catch your attention. There was something like a person on the other side of those words. Meaning, art—mere excuses to clothe an embarrassing pleasure in the insistent intimacy of words.

Address

The chapter on Rilke in the late Paul de Man's *Allegories of Reading* is one of the most strangely compelling of his critical essays. De Man is disturbed by the seductiveness of Rilke's poetry, the way so many readers surrender to it and allow Rilke's voice to be their own, the poetry's alluring invitation to intimacy and the bad faith that seems to lurk behind its call. De Man is in a hurry to get on with his business, which is delineating the rhetorical mechanisms that bear such a problematic relation to the heart's transparency. But he recognizes he must first confront the mystery of the seductiveness itself, acknowledging the territory where the poetry of these poems is usually found, however much he hopes to shift it to safer ground.

Whether readers give Rilke their wholehearted faith or twist free of his clutches by demystifying the poetry in a precise demonstration of its bad faith, they are caught up in an intense and unusual relation to this poet. Even as De Man climbs to firmer territory outside that dangerous relation, he acknowledges the origin of his motion as a reaction against the more gullible responses of others. The very intensity of his austerity makes him, paradoxically, the most intimate reader, and his resistance to the blandishments of the poetry indicates the full shape of its seductive power. He wants, like Pascal, to leave the Other alone, to let Rilke's poetry show itself apart from the corrupting presence of any personal relation it forces upon us. That may not be possible. There may be nothing apart from such a relation or nothing that can be disentangled from it. We have nowhere to stand from which we can offer a neutral judgment on the question posed for our judgment or speak of "bad faith." There is only our disappointed love, and seduction is nothing more than the name we give to illusions of power—either to illusions of our own power or to illusions so attractive that they put us in jeopardy, creating distrust of the other's motives and producing countermotion.

Such desires and dangers of relation are often very close to the surface in Rilke's poetry. We see at once why we go along with him, why meaning, beauty, truth, art, rhetoric, and language are all utterly immaterial. There is nothing stable and firm enough in this poet to make bad faith even possible.

> Du, Nachbar Gott, wenn ich dich manches mal
> in langer Nacht mit hartem Klopfen störe,—
> so ists, weil ich dich selten atmen höre
> und weiss: Du bist allein im Saal.
> Un wenn du etwas brauchst, ist keiner da,
> um deinem Tasten einen Trank zu reichen:
> ich horche immer. Gib ein kleines Zeichen.
> Ich bin ganz nah.
>
> Nur eine schmale Wand ist zwischen uns,
> durch Zufall; denn es könnte sein:
> ein Rufen deines oder meines Munds—
> und sie bricht ein
> ganz ohne Lärm und Laut.
>
> Aus deinen Bildern ist sie aufgebaut.
>
> Und deine Bilder stehn vor dir wie Namen.
> Und wenn einmal das Licht in mir entbrennt,
> mit welchem meine Tiefe dich erkennt,
> vergeudet sichs als Glanz auf ihren Rahmen.
>
> Und meine Sinne, welche schnell erlahmen,
> sind ohne Heimat und von dir getrennt.

You, neighbor God, if too often I
in the long night disturb you
with sharp pounding at your door, it's only
because I hear you breathe so rarely
and know: you're all alone inside.
If you needed anything, no one's there,
to offer you a drink for your thirst:
I'm always ready for your call. Just give
a little sign. I'm close by.

Only a thin wall lies between us,
and that, by chance; it would be possible:
a shout from your mouth or mine,
and it would break down,
noiselessly and without a fuss.

It is built of your images.

Your images stand in front of you like names.
If once the light flames up in me,
with which my depths recognize you,
it spends itself as glow upon their frames.

And my senses, so quickly crippled,
are homeless and cut off from you.

Rilke, from The Book of Hours

It begins with the language of intimate address, setting out at the beginning, as poems always do, the ground on which the poem will happen, where we are and where the poet is. He begins by excusing himself, with a pretense of solicitude so contrary to all our assumptions about the relation between God and man that it is transparent, a figure no less literary than Michelangelo calling his lady's heart the sculptor's uncarved marble block.

Within that transparent pretense we are allowed to hear a shyness and reticence. Unable to ask for God's attention on his own behalf, he draws the courage to knock by the deception or self-deception of acting on behalf of the other, solicitude toward God. Is this perhaps the mirror image of the bad faith that is found in Rilke's work: the appearance of being interested in us, when in fact he is interested only in having us pay attention to him? Or is it his admission of such inversions and the mark of the forces that drive them, taking him beyond the possibility of bad faith? Even hiding in its deceptive solicitude the voice is timid, apologetic. But in the ability to overcome its

reticence and address God, we read the power of its need. The loneliness of the speaker becomes "you're all alone inside," and the request "Just give a little sign" hardly conceals his own need for reassurance underneath the motive he claims: to see if God is all right,
if he needs anything.

He permits us to see through the words to their motives and contin-
gencies. Like a dramatist, he offers us transparent deceptions that do
not deceive, a naked body visible beneath sheer veils. By such "seeing
through" we are invited to intimacy, which requires this permission
to penetrate opaque and concealing surfaces presented to the rest of
the world. The pretense and surface are necessary; without clothing
the act of stripping is impossible.

The form of address—words given as a surface to be penetrated—
is made an explicit concern in the middle of the poem: the wall that
can be destroyed so easily, a wall that is in place only *durch Zufall,*
by chance. The barrier between self and other is unnatural, unneces-
sary, and fragile (though we know it must be present for the joy of
breaking through it). That promise too is a desire. The wall's surfaces
are *Bilder,* images, paintings, artwork—surfaces without depth; the
poem invokes depths, someone on the other side of the wall. Those
images are renamed as "names," words which seem to take the place
of God's presence and are also the words of the poem.

By the end the veils have almost fallen away. The reversal is complete; he admits his own solitude and need, that he has been "homeless and cut off," the senses crippled to dullness by the barrier. The
request to help God becomes a request for God's help. There is another poem in *The Book of Hours* that begins solicitously: "Was wirst
du tun, Gott, wenn ich sterbe?" (What will you do, God, if I die?)
and ends "Was wirst du tun, Gott? Ich bin bange" (What will you do,
God? I am afraid). The pretense breaks down, the clothes are removed, but he still calls out without reply. Pygmalion's statue does
not move.

Swerve: Disillusion

As I read Rilke's poem, I am so caught up in the intensity of his address that I feel it is directed to me alone. I ignore the crowds that
stand around me in the pit; I forget that it is a public performance.
Then I notice all the others, each one feeling included in the intimacy
of address just as I do. I have been taken in, betrayed. I announce

angrily that this is not what it pretends to be—it is only a public performance, given for all to read. And the tone of my announcement betrays a special distrust, reacting against the way in which this poem has tried to entangle me with promises of particular interest in my case.

We hear him make excuses, propose pretenses, come up with hypothetical interpretations as he speaks to the wall. Yet simply because we recognize how such discourse is formed does not mean that it fails. Of course, we cannot accept it at the level on which it offers itself, but then do we ever accept any discourse as it offers itself? It has confessed its deception or self-deception in the poem; it has freely shown us the first structure of concealment and depth; and if we discover other intimacies and depths, we are only continuing the invited intimacy. Or we may feel that we have been manipulated, trifled with; we recoil, demystify, show the invitation to intimacy as a mechanism of seduction, expose its promiscuity. But this also is relation; we have been no less caught by it.

Why does he try so intently to seduce us to an intimacy? We already know. It is because we matter to him, we, his readers. There is a hunger here for an individual intimacy with all; he is both God and Don Juan. The poem is addressed to us, not to God. No one publishes a poem to God. Its readership would be too limited. Moreover, God does not need to read: surfaces and depths do not exist for him.

The truth is that even if we see the manipulations of the would-be seducer, and even if the seducer believes in the efficacy of his manipulations, the energy invested in the act reveals the seducer's need for us. Rilke's address to God here is the ghost of his address to us. We, in our turn, respond to that need; we hunger for the promise of private intimacy. The poet displays two solitudes trying to cross a barrier of words, and we find ourselves in God's place on the other side of the wall, perhaps disturbed by the pretense in his intrusion into our solitude, perhaps not. In either case he is our neighbor.

There is nothing here but a dance of relation: desire, division, and the fear of betrayal. In other poems of Rilke we do find something more substantial in the intimacy shared, like two lovers talking; what they talk about is only a shape around which the exchange of words can dance. But in this poem the stage is bare except for the two dancers in their shifting roles. It does what it is about: it compels relation. It is simian poetry: scratching, stroking, cuddling, poking.

An author who writes in his own person has the advantage of being who or what he pleases. He is no certain man, nor has any certain or genuine character; but suits himself on every occasion to the fancy of his reader, whom, as the fashion is nowadays, he constantly caresses and cajoles. All turns upon their two persons. And as in an amour or commerce of love-letters, so here the author has the privilege, dressing and sprucing himself up, whilst he is making diligent court, and working upon the humour of the party to whom he addresses.

Anthony Cooper, Earl of Shaftesbury,
Characteristics of Men, Manners, Opinions, Times (1711)

Of the Sleep and Dreams of a Man Restricted to the Sense of Smell: Man/Stone

Let us say then that a poem is a play of relation through a wall of stone. There is no place to stand outside the relation; apart from this nobody is at home. Each pretense of distance or reserve (Baudelaire's soul on its crystal cliff, as before him the beloved dances, naked in her jewels) is mere countermotion, some hard-won glory of negative intensity. At the limit of such negative intensity it is possible to postulate a blank isolation, the shell of hardest stone. What a person might be or dream within the stone can be reached only by a calculus; there will always remain some infinitesimal space to separate our research into solitude from solitude's final perfection. And within that space words are still possible.

> "Here I am, then, alone on earth . . ."
>
> I would have loved human beings in spite of themselves. Only by ceasing to be human were they able to hide themselves from my affection. So there they are, then, strangers, unknown, now at last nothing to me because they wanted it. But as for me, once detached from them and from everything, what am I in my own right? There is the thing that remains for me to find out. Unfortunately this examination must be preceded by a glance at my situation. This is an idea through which I must necessarily pass in order to reach myself from them.
>
> Rousseau, "Reveries of a Solitary Walker"

"Here I am, then, alone on earth," "Me voici donc seul sur la terre." "Then," *donc,* is the term of summation, as if drawing a conclusion in some ongoing process of reflection. This is the speculative moment of closing the final aperture in the shell of stone. Yet in its rhetoric of address the event of closure recalls the blank history from which it now withdraws.

The word of summation is set against the location of the sentence, the first in the book, where it serves as a calculated gesture to catch the reader's attention and establish the gound for the literary encounter. This is the character who walks onstage at the beginning of the play, speaking as if we had just come in upon the middle of some ongoing discourse.

"Here I am, then": although the voice locates itself in perfect solitude, it addresses and invites inspection. It is still somehow caught up in relation—the courtship display of an animal presenting itself for sniffing, ogling, giving itself up to be desired: "here I am." Yet: "here I am then alone on earth." It is the theatrical declaration of a virginal seclusion, a public intimacy, like Rilke's—but in this case the cry for our attention is truly oxymoronic rather than simply oblique. He signals the game of soliloquy, which speaks to be heard while pretending to be alone; and it carries the implicit promise of all soliloquy, that truth will emerge out of solitude, liberated from the pressure of others' attention. In this soliloquy we find that Rousseau's voice speaks precisely on the question of what such a truth discovered in isolation might be—even though to speak it returns him to the very world of relation from which he would extricate himself.

Even this minimal display is stage-managed; each showing forth is also a concealment. Mind's unproblematic motions have no need for declaration, much less for ostentation. However, the theater of one's "true" condition will always be a double act, an act of suppressing a contradiction whose negative force is in direct proportion to the force of the assertion.

Such is the nature of all display of self, especially display in language; the suppressed term always wins its way back to the surface, however indirect the form of its return. For Rousseau, the more forcefully the voice proclaims its solitude, the more deeply it is engaged in relation to others. This pair of terms is mutually sustaining, and it glows with the energy of assertion and suppression.

The return of the suppressed term to the surface destabilizes the semiotic order, which must function by unproblematic exclusions. Words used in this way can never "mean" anything; they can only continue, interpreting and elaborating, trying either to cover over the suppressed term or to control it by giving it a place within some stable structure. Yet the very need for continuation only strengthens the opposition and intensifies the instability. Even when the discourse wearies and terminates, as all human discourse must, we keep returning to it—rereading, or setting out to tell the story just one more time.

Such words, which are the words of poetry and of some other things as well, do indeed tell the truth, but never the truth we wished to tell or pretended to tell. More disturbing, they do not even tell the kind of truth that language is supposed to tell. It would disturb us only a little if the suppressed term were finally victorious and annihilated the surface term from all consideration. Such was Freud's great hope: that by a victory of inversion the contest could be silenced.

Yet Freud came closest to describing this process of words when he described the laws that inform our dreams, how all logical relations—exclusion and inclusion, conditionality and causation—become in dream the items of an inventory: "there is this and this and this." He called this an element of "dreamwork," trying in his own words to forget where the real "work" must occur: organizing these antithetical vectors and aggregates of care, which constitute the heart's inventory, into language's assertions of subordination, determination, and exclusion.

When we encounter ordinary assertions of the heart's truth, the least reflection, honestly pursued, reveals to us the full stock of the heart's junkshop, alive in figures of contradiction. He looks out on the audience and announces earnestly: "Here I am then alone on earth."

Such pairings and aggregations of terms are no pure indeterminacy. We might even call these sets a "language," but they would be a different order of language, a language that exists prior to the decision between yes and no, a language of care, constituted of only the questions. As in the model of what we commonly call language, the language of care is articulated by exclusions—in this case, not by the suppression of terms but by disinterest and things overlooked or forgotten. Indeed, as the terms of the language of care are bound intensely together, they allow us to forget the world of other words around them more perfectly than words in the carefree common language.

This language of care must become articulate in the surface language of the waking exegete, the language of decision—which is made unstable, and in trying to achieve stability often ends in inver-

sion. Let us say that in the language of care Rousseau offers us "relation to others" and "absolute solitude"; the exegete in reverie may
say: "I am with others and not alone," or "I am alone and not with
others," or perhaps "I used to be with others, but now I am alone,"
or then "My relations to others made me choose to be alone." He can
give us the complete conjugation of solitude and relation to others, as
he does throughout the rest of the first "Walk." The particular state-
ments and sequence of assertions made by the exegete in reverie do
have interest for us, but their continuation, their variability, and their
loud insistence all refer us back to the point of pain, which exists
before this surface language and for which this surface language exists. In the articulation something determinate in mind is communicated through language, but it eludes meaning and all that can be
found "in" language.

"I would have loved men in spite of themselves." Having begun in
contradiction, he now begins to weave the interpretations that will
keep the tensely opposed terms separate. He conjugates relations—
"would have loved," a condition(al), relation to others as an unfulfilled possibility, reasserting the opening solitude as actual. In this act
of interpretation additional terms are drawn into the primary set of
relation to others: love and hate, deserving and not deserving. "I
would have loved them": there is desire, pleasure and pain, guilt and
self-exculpation. "Only by ceasing to be human have they been able
to hide themselves from my affection." The others negated themselves; they wished it. It is told as a story of thwarted love and the
solitude of rejection.

We must not forget that we are being addressed—however twisted
the vectors of address may have become. Does he include us, who
now read him, in his complaint? Are we blamed, and in being blamed,
are we supposed to feel shame at the history of our indifference toward him? Are we to go to him and beg him to allow us to come into
being again, or are we hard? Here too is the figure of contradiction:
in being consigned to nothingness, we are also being called back
to him.

He manages the act of address in order to open up a space for us.
From the opening "me voici donc," "here I am, then," we come to
"les voilà donc," "so there they are"; and by putting them "over
there," he makes it possible for us to separate ourselves from them, to
be excluded from his exclusion, and, unless we harden ourselves
against him, to be together with him, alone on earth. By placing the

blame squarely on them over there, he assures us that he does not want to be apart from all others. Perhaps he suspects that we will suspect him of misanthropy, that we will read some suppressed hatred and contempt in his protestations of love. He speculatively sees himself through our eyes, sees more clearly than we an image of hatred against others in his core. He must reassure us that it is not so: "I would have loved them," he says.

He writhes in his words, at every moment seeing himself being seen, hearing himself being heard. He feels naked in the eyes of the world, where others "hide themselves." Unwittingly and by indifference the beloved has caressed a deep wound in bare flesh: there is only intense pain, but the pleasure of the caress remains as a possibility missed. Both elements linger after the brush of pain, equally strong and mutually fortifying, the memory of injury and of pleasure missed: "j'aurais aimé," I would have loved.

He postulates a figure of release. He imagines how it would be to be encased entirely in stone, in the perfect isolation of Condillac's conscious statue. "But as for me, once detached from them and from everything, what am I in my own right?" It is the merest hypothesis; still they remain as shadowy presences all around him, tormenting him, forcing him to keep on speaking.

> Rumor.
> Aunque no quede más que el rumor.
>
> Aroma.
> Aunque no quede más que el aroma.
>
> Pero arranca de mí el recuerdo
> y el color de las viejas horas.
>
> Dolor.
> Frente al mágico y vivo dolor.
>
> Batalla.
> En la auténtica y sucia batalla.
>
> ¡Pero quita la gente invisible
> que rodea perenne mi casa!
>
> Murmuring.
> Even if only murmuring is left.
>
> Scent.
> Even if only scent is left.

But rip the memory out of me
and the color of old hours.

Pain.
Facing the pain, magic and alive.

Struggle.
In the genuine and nasty struggle.

Just get rid of the invisible people
that are always walking around my house!

Lorca, "A Statue's Yearning"

Alternate Route from Rilke's Chamber:
The Crumbling of the Figured Wall

"Only a thin wall lies between us . . . It is built of your images." We will imagine a different ending to the story of stone. Through death or human forgetfulness the person has withdrawn entirely behind the hard facade; all that remain are fading images on the flat surfaces.

A T'ang poet sees a painting by an earlier master. He would like to speak its praise through the commonplaces of poetry on painting and marvel how the artwork comes alive, like Pygmalion's statue: it is endowed with some animate force that transcends pale verisimilitude and the trompe l'oeil, breaking from its plane into the viewer's world. But if the statue is chipped and missing parts, or the painting is fading, dirty, crumbling, its material groundwork is exposed. Like a mortal person, the work of art suddenly acquires a history—a shining successful past, a decayed present, and occasion to reflect on the disparity. Nevertheless, the poet may also notice that despite the fading, crumbling, or other material changes that cannot be ignored, the essential art is still present and, strangely, in no way diminished. The poet may even wonder exactly where the art lies in such a work of art—does the crumbling of a wing or the graying of a painted feather touch what is essential to the art?

The poet discovers that the material work of art is mortal; he discovers that the essential art does not decompose with the material, but that it is all the same embedded in the material and must disappear with the material painting—at least from this world. Add to this knot of paradox the further complication that the subject of such a fading painting might be a group of cranes, immortal birds of immortal beings; and further consider that if these painted cranes are the mural of a master such as Hsüeh Chi, we expect them to come alive, fly off the wall, and truly become immortal birds—we have heard many such tales of painted cranes. We have a difficult situation, and one proper for the master poet of difficult situations, Tu Fu.

> Eleven cranes by the master Hsüeh Chi, all
> faithful copies of true Ch'ing-t'ien birds:
> from long time their painted colors are almost gone,
> but, graying, still they stand above the common dust.
> Some ascending, some dropping down, each
>   with its own intent, aloof
> in dignity like the noblest men; and I
> honor the distances on which
>   the force of their desire is set—
> not merely some freshness of the pigment.
> Unstraining they cross ten thousand miles,
> wandering as a flock, by souls' secret accord;
> they wind off to far places, postures in flight
>   like white phoenixes,
> and make no society with the common oriole.
>
> Before this high hall had collapsed, they
> always consoled the welcome visitor;
> now exposed to weather on an outside wall,
> they end with wind and rain hard upon them.
>
> High in rose clouds are found the true birds,
> disdaining to drink from muddied pools below,
> and through the dark spaces they go where they will,
> free of all restraints, where none can tame them.
>
> "Cranes Painted by Hsüeh Chi on the Back Wall
> of the County Office in T'ung-ch'üan"

Hsüeh Chi (649–713), who once left this trace of his passage through T'ung-ch'üan in exile, had been one of the great literary men and painters of the generation of Tu Fu's grandfather. His literary works, no longer popular, had passed out of circulation, and only his paintings were preserved; now these too are fading. Hsüeh Chi had a particular affinity for and mastery of painting cranes, immortal birds that embodied a freedom from the constant anxiety, pain, and humiliation of the common world. These birds were no less the figuration of Hsüeh Chi's desire than was Pygmalion's woman of ivory. Tu Fu, who might also find in such birds the embodiment of his own desires, comes upon them too late, when they are already crumbling. They never flew away.

Tu Fu begins by counting—eleven cranes, all faithful portraits (*hsieh-chen*, literally "to sketch the true") of the Ch'ing-t'ien cranes. We might be willing to pass this by as a glancing allusion to immortal cranes (disregarding the perplexing problem of how one paints the perfect portrait of a legendary bird). Tu Fu is precise about the number and insists that all portray Ch'ing-t'ien cranes, but the legend to which Tu Fu alludes is equally precise: there were only two cranes that lived by Chu-mu Creek in Ch'ing-t'ien, under the care of immortal beings; every year the pair would hatch a brood that would fly away while the parent cranes remained, trapped in that single place. There are too many cranes in the painting, even with a year's brood. We might wonder why, of all the legendary cranes of the Chinese tradition, these should be the Ch'ing-t'ien cranes. Perhaps it is not the number but their entrapment that makes these birds of art like the Ch'ing-t'ien cranes: tamed birds of immortal keepers, or these painted birds held in place by the master's hand, their minds set hopelessly on distant heights to which they are unable to escape. And through the course of the poem we find that these cranes of the mural, like the Ch'ing-t'ien cranes, are set against other cranes that fly away, freed of all restraints, not to be tamed.

The paired terms are clear: art's fixity set against the movement of living things, their softening to life; constraint set against unbounded freedom; and strangely here, the mortal art work set against the immortality of what is represented or of the art apart from the work, the art that recedes into invisibility behind the crumbling surface of the wall. Tu Fu is much concerned with calling our attention to what is *chen*, "true": the "true birds," *chen-ku* (literally, "true bones") in the upper heavens beyond the eyes of poets and painters, which belong with "true humans," *chen-jen*, the term for immortal beings.

The cranes of the painting may be the perfect portraits of immortal birds, but we are strongly reminded of the perishable materials in which these birds are fixed. The bright colors of the painting are fading away: *ts'ang-jan*, a "graying" that links the process of aging with the dulling of bright color. Nevertheless they still "stand above the common dust," *ch'u-ch'en*, a term for excellence that becomes literal here as the birds still show out through the dirt on the wall, still rise above the dust of this mortal world to pure immortal heights. Here too is the governing contradiction of the poem: the ruin of the material painting and the permanence of both the creature and the work of art that is embedded in impermanent material.

In great paintings the creature painted has an autonomy apart from the fixed stance that the painter gives it: it has its own desires and intent that leave behind human desires and the artistic intentions that produced it. A painted hawk will strain against the flat plane of the painting, struggling to get loose, to strike its prey, to *be* a hawk. These cranes have that commonplace autonomy of great painting, and something that goes mysteriously beyond any mere autonomy of art that fights the prison of the painting; the cranes are aloof, indifferent to the fixity of the painting and its material decay. Their minds are set on distant heights.

The painted cranes may take no note of the fact that they are empirically dissolving; but we and the poet cannot match their glorious unconcern, and we must note the contrast between the lingering spirit and their material condition. There is a fascination with such nobility in harsh circumstances, the ancient Confucian principle of "firmness in adversity," painted cranes whose spirits are a vector elsewhere, even while their forms fade on a common material wall. At this moment Tu Fu realizes that wherever the true art lies in this material painting, it is not in the material. It goes beyond "some freshness of the pigment."

> Some ascending, some dropping down, each
>   with its own intent, aloof
> in dignity like the noblest men; and I
> honor the distances on which
>   the force of their desire is set—
> not merely some freshness of the pigment.

One departure and fading away seems to correspond to another departure, flight from this dusty material world. Whether these paired departures occur in Tu Fu's imagination or in some illusion of perspective, the cranes seem to be leaving us now, receding into some nonmaterial space behind the painting's surface, winding off ten thousand miles with ease. This flight is without strain, a movement of spirit, as they vanish to join birds never seen, white phoenixes, departing from the plane of the painting that holds them close to common birds.

The birds are gone—in spirit—but the disintegrating paintings are still here. We consider the stark, material facts. The building's roof has fallen; the mural is exposed. Instead of departing immortals, we see a thing trapped in time, with a history. The paintings are found on the wall of an office building in a minor county in west China. Once their aloofness reminded imperial officials, sent to these out-lands in exile, of the insignificance of events in this dusty world. The pigments were fresh then; both the representation and the consola-tion were clear. Now the roof has fallen in; something of the paintings seems very mortal. This dirty testimony to the power of the dirty world makes the consolation more difficult.

The fading birds are *hsieh-chen,* faithful copies; the birds up there in the dark, invisible heights of the heavens are *chen-ku,* the "true" birds. The true birds are not the Ch'ing-t'ien originals that were tamed and bound to one place, a muddied ford like Chu-mu Creek. And the true birds are not the copies on this decaying wall. The fading copies are of this world and still visible; the true birds are out of sight, in the darkness of the heavens or perhaps within the darkness that is overtaking the mural, graying and fading.

Hsüeh Chi came into these outlands an exile. He left the figures of his desire on the hard surface of the wall of the county office building. Unlike the work of Pygmalion and like that of the ordinary sculptors and painters of our dusty world, the painting never came alive; he continued to paint his cranes again and again, trapped in repetititon. For decades afterward these cranes remained bright, shapes to snare the hopes of every wandering official who passed, who dreamed that these cranes, like the cranes of legend, would fly off their wall and carry the weary person away with them. And now Tu Fu passes by the ruins to see the most perplexing realization of the artwork, the crumbling of the hard wall that traps them and their escape from this world backward into nonmaterial spaces, the "distances on which the force of their desire is set."

When Midir won his chess game from Eochaid the king, he claimed the kiss from Etain that had been the game's stake. At that moment he and Etain were transformed into a pair of swans that flew out through the smoke-hole of the king's hall and returned to the Great Land.

4 Replacement

The rites are done now
    drums beat together,
The wands are passed on,
    new dancers take our place.
Fairest maidens' songs.
    slowly sung and softly,
In spring the orchids come,
    chrysanthemums in fall,
Forever and unceasing from
    the first and on forever.

          "The Rites for the Souls,"
                coda for the
          "Nine Shaman Songs,"
       fourth to third century B.C.

The rites remain the same, with the same songs and the same dances, but one set of dancers yields place to the next, each handing on the performer's wand still warm from withdrawing hands. The exchange of place, so simply accomplished, calls forth this ritual song to confirm the moment of transfer; the song celebrates and frames the moment within larger cycles of continuous natural change and exchange. We recognize instantly what melancholy underlies the song's celebration of nature's permanence and the rite's. The act of passing on the dancer's wand reminds participant and observer alike that the person who dances is not the dance and is less than the dance: the human being who fills the dancer's role is no more than the organic stuff that fills the lovely form of the seasonal flower.

At the moment of replacement, it is customary to invoke the permanence of the ritual role, setting it apart from the individuals who change places. Such an invocation is a law to compel change of place in face of resistance and hesitation: there is the pain of loss of place in the one who withdraws, and uneasiness in the newcomer, who finds no comfort in these dancing robes so lately made famous. The melancholy resonance of the song lies in the singers' acquiescence to the tenuousness of any individual's claim on a place and acquiescence to the necessity of its surrender.

A song that invokes such necessity weighs in the balance against open possibility and a contest of uncertain outcome; in the same way a song that assigns the two persons fixed roles in a ceremonial exchange weighs in the balance against a fiercely private relation between separate individuals. In their hearts the person withdrawing and the person newly come contest this place with motions of mutual love, envy, intimidation, and emulation. Then, in the very rite whose performance they contest, this song is required of them, in which they are forced to sing the cyclical permanence of the rite and their joint willingness to play their parts within its repetitive mechanisms. The contest of individuals is repressed, its traces surviving only as a resonance of melancholy even as, in their professionalism, the individuals perform the smooth gestures of transfer.

The event of replacement binds forerunner and newcomer together: the identity of each now is understood in relation to the other. The forerunner survives in the awed and envious memory of the newcomer and in the memories of those who have seen both and compare; the newcomer always practices the art in the forerunner's shadow and knows that by replacing the forerunner, he or she too is destined to be someday replaced.

This matrix of oppositions is basic to our kind: changing place and seizing place, yielding place and contesting place. These forms of internal opposition are themselves jointly opposed by a rule of anonymous necessity, a smooth rhythm that carries on indifferent to private will and desire. To be an attentive audience for such rites, we must remember that no isolated term in this matrix can appear without calling forth all its intricately related contraries. In the ritual song of acquiescence we hear the pain of loss in the one who withdraws and the newcomer's exultant claim of right; in the newcomer's gloating we hear his uneasiness about enduring comparison with the forerunner and realizing that he has accepted the contract for his own eventual replacement. Each statement of humility calls forth secret pride; each statement of pride calls forth self-doubt. As with the performers, so too with their words: each word that holds a place before the audience recalls both the struggle and the working of the law by which it came to be there.

The assertions of our ordinary language and of our gestures work by actively holding a place and holding back their contraries, which hover at the edge of our awareness. If we pay close attention, we can recognize them dimly gathered in the shadows. But in a special kind of language or act, such as the ritual coda above, replacement becomes the explicit concern and is figured on the surface. It is a true coda, not internal to the ritual cycle but rather set outside as a frame, enclosing the cycle and assuring its circularity in order to make the continuation possible. It speaks for the moment of crisis in the exchange of place, summoning the person who has been hidden within the role into the performance as a performer. Among our secular words, which have replaced the old ritual language, the work of the ritual coda (the unmasking of role and replacement) belongs to literary art, and most strongly to poetry.

Poetry is an intricate art of replacement, occurring through every level of a poem. In poetry all things are touched by the powerful forces at work in this relation. On the most subtle and basic level, such words admit that they have come from elsewhere to occupy the places they hold—apparently having displaced other words, or those more portentous and shadowy forerunners, meanings and oblique intentions, which have withdrawn and can no longer be found. We know they have been carefully chosen to fill these places so strange to them, but what they replaced is unimaginable.

In poetry we see clear evidence of replacement in these words that behave so much like newcomers, insistently declaring the perfection with which they occupy their places, while in every way revealing their discomfort—twisted and wrenched from their habitual roles in the common language, each singing its part too loudly and, in a lovely way, off-key. In the fractured choreography of their syntax, in their metaphors, their overemphasized silences and stresses, there is a peculiar grandeur gained from their very awkwardness. Their perfection is strenuous, a hard-won appearance of ease. Like all newcomers they call attention to their individual presences in the places they occupy.

In order to be brought into the foreground of the poem, replacement and usurpation are repeated on the larger scale: new lines evoke older lines, only to take their places; new poems replace older poems; and poets willfully usurp their great predecessors, contesting each old excellence. We readers, in our turn, take the poet's places, reproduce their words in our voices, and make those words signify what we will. No one is at rest in poetry: we know that the words and the positions framed by words have been taken from elsewhere and are open for the taking.

The very possibility of such taking depends on poetry's law of property. Elsewhere words are the pure means of the moment's intent and dissolve in air: they are used up. That we say what another might have said before escapes our notice. There is a fine line that separates saying something that someone else happens to have said before and quoting another person. Quotation creates a complex relation between the new speaker and the absent forerunner who has left his or her mark on these particular words. The law of ownership, given first by poetry, becomes generalized copyright in the modern world. Through poetry individuals can lay claim to particular words (the rule of "quotation"), just as the words are discovered to have "proper" senses. Both property and propriety—theft and the right of free gift, or words' assuming "improper" places—have interest only when the possibility of transfer arises. Like the recipient of the dancer's wand in the ritual coda, we are authorized to accept these words for our use, but asked to pay homage to their true and absent owner. Poetry forces the event of replacement upon our attention; it institutionalizes possession, legacy, legitimate use, and theft.

To replace something requires that this "something" be displaced: voluntarily withdrawn, eliminated, lost. Each place is hereditary, and it can be held only by the death of the forerunner—thus the Chinese emperor conventionally referred to himself as "the orphan." Yet the forerunner still seems, by sheer priority, to retain some essential right over the place. The newcomer always recognizes himself potentially as a usurper, and in showing the trace of such self-recognition, he is so recognized by others. As a usurper he has force, but the force has an element of discomfort that never leaves him entirely at home in the place he holds. Thus he makes his claim insistently, asserts his suitability for this place in every detail, demands our assent.

This place of which we speak may be no more than a fiction created from the tension that occurs in the event of replacement: it is a memory, an imprint and form that survive the forerunner who has departed. All forerunners—persons, things, or words replaced—may take on the aura of a mythical, primordial forerunner, who held the place without knowing it, without even knowing that it was a place—in those first days person and role, the word and the thing were perfect unities.[1] The very concept of role and function came about through the first displacement and replacement: a shape of space, a hollowness, robes left behind that still hold the imprint of the forerunner's contours.

When the latecomer "takes the place," the fit is always somehow wrong; points of tightness and large gaps remind us and the new-

comer of the difference between himself or herself and the place occupied. From replacement follow mortality and history: by coming
from outside to occupy this place, the newcomer knows that he, she,
or it can and will ultimately lose the place. Individuals discover themselves in a tragic structure of lineage. Place has become separable
from the person who fills it and can never be secure. The newcomer
tries to make the place his own, to gather its contours around him in
hopes of either passing for the forerunner or changing the contours
in order to pass on the burden of his own shape to the next newcomer. We watch: now that person and role have been divided, there
is a performance that may be closely marked and judged.

Perhaps there never was any forerunner—only a lineage of uncomfortable latecomers like ourselves whose faces have always been
pinched wearing the forerunner's archaic mask. There never was anyone for whom the function was proper and thus not merely function.
We are all impostors, impersonators of the dead who never existed.
No word was ever used in its proper sense (since propriety is only the
postulate of impropriety). We are usurpers of Adam and Eve's language in a Darwinian age who draw on a capital of metaphor that
miraculously grows because of a misplaced faith in some original in-
vestment.

> After the Fall we may suppose, that *Adam* and *Eve* extended their
> Language to new Objects and Ideas, and especially to those which
> were attended with Pain; and this they might do sometimes by in-
> venting new Words, sometimes by giving new Senses to old ones.
> However, their language would still continue narrow, because they
> had only one another to converse with, and could not extend their
> Knowledge to any great Variety of Things; also because their Foun-
> dation was narrow. For the Growth and Variations of a Language
> somewhat resemble the Increase of Money at Interest upon Interest.
>
> David Hartley, *Observations on Man, His Frame,*
> *His Duty, and His Expectations* (1749)

The truth of the speculation that the forerunner never existed does
not matter; any consolation afforded by such speculation holds no
power for us, unless somehow we were to make it our own myth. The
great lie of the forerunner and the husks of his or her abandoned
functions serve as the truths we live by. All that really matters is the
discomfort, the poorly fitting clothing. No parent is ever at home

being a parent; he or she is only so from the eyes of the child. No role is neutral; our own performances grasp in vain at or grate upon the performances of others whose places, either in imagination or in fact, we have taken.

Yet let us not pretend too much reluctance. Each usurper takes the emptied seat greedily, enjoying a hold over the place of another. Through this act the newcomer becomes fully human, discovering an identity in the very awkwardness of the fit and the struggle with the received contours. Mastery is never complete: there always remains some part of some province that will not submit, where one hears the peasants grumbling and recalling the good old days under former rulers. Because the final goal is to fit the old space perfectly while remaining oneself, the result is always unease, desperation, and ultimate failure—nagging whispers that must be drowned out with loud counterclaims of comfort and success. But our defeat is given with the system.

Nothing is stable: once replacement and substitution are set in motion, layers upon layers of multiple substitutions, displacements, coverings are formed. Nor is it possible to trace back through the layers to some primal forerunner for which everything else is a token; all we have are "clews," filaments leading in every direction, each promising to lead us out of the labyrinth. The best comfort we can hope for is to stop at certain moments to celebrate the illusion of exit, when everyone and everything seems to be in its proper place. Shakespearean comedy presses toward the final unmasking, in which all the characters at last show themselves as they really are—at least until the actors go offstage, remove their makeup and costumes, and drop their false voices, revealing the innocent young lovers to be tired and aging men and women who won these roles because, far better than innocent youth, they could inhabit such roles with all the persuasiveness of desire for what has been lost.

Empty Bed: Joys in the Fin

In the "old poem" the woman stood at the window and issued the invitation:

> Once long ago I sang in the barroom,
> Now I'm the wife of a traveling man.
> He travels for pleasure and never comes home now,
> A lonely bed can't be kept empty for long.

The poet was wise to stop there. If the song had permitted the man watching from the garden to accept the invitation and to take the place in the empty bed, he would have found only discomfort as the consequence of his yearning for comfort and place: adulterer and usurper, perpetually haunted by the knowledge that in taking this place, his own place would then be open for the taking, either by the forerunner returning or by the next lover.

Yet poetry does reach for the place of another, just as it dreams of the offering of place, the invitation. Drama is the great game of ill-fitting roles, in which both dramatist and actor play at being Other. They understand perfectly the true nature of the act: there is some character whom they may represent well or poorly, and the first condition of their success if the capacity to make us forget that the dramatist is inventing the words and that the actor is merely playing a part. If we interrogate them offstage, they report to us a belief that the character as presented never existed in our world, but the report is only for the sake of conventional mores; they know that their art gains grandeur only as an act of illicit impersonation.

The lyric poet impersonates himself as he would be seen, and claims to be that person, an act so threatening that its most common result is a tense pose or a defensive, professional neutrality. Far more than with the dramatic actor, we apprehend neither pose nor a hypothetical person who poses, but rather the active relation between image and desire, the complex and shadowed event of posing. This is an oddly reflexive act of occupying an alien place as oneself, hoping to be recognized and accepted in that role by an audience of one or many. But the audience perceives the tense hope that animates the role and not merely its schematic surface.

To produce a role for oneself and then to occupy it is a deed of private desire, inevitably set in opposition to the community, which reserves to itself the authority to define and assign place. The voices of communal courtship in folk lyric are largely comfortable with the generic role: the lover can speak for himself through repeatable words that are the common possession of the community. But when the lover creates himself in words as an individual, he is stepping outside the authorized words of courtship; his individuality is trespass beyond and deviation from the norm. It should therefore not be surprising that the individual love lyric has often been in close complicity with countercultures of adultery: actively in Rome, medieval Japan, and Provence, speculatively in the European love lyric after Dante.[2] In lyric poetry the structure of replacement echoes and redoubles itself. The lyric poet who aspires to occupy an alien place does so in several senses—and often aspires to occupy a bed that the community assigns to another. The role of particular beloved must be invented against and "in the place of" the role of spouse. But do not misunderstand the poem's function in this counterculture: though the poem may masquerade as sexual persuasion and mere means to fleshy ends, it is, in fact, nothing more than the dreaming replacement for such ends, pragmatically successful only if it encounters another dreamer who usurps the poet's fantasy as his or her own.

The poetic construction of self and the claim of ownership over particular words make possible all manner of usurpation and impersonation: it is a Pandora's box of fantasy. The beloved, reading the poem, may incorporate the poetic lover into his or her own fantasy; the poet too may not only impersonate himself but may also usurp the thoughts (and often the voice) of the beloved and dream her desires in intricate dramas of substitution.

Chang Chien-feng of Hsü-chou, the former state minister, had a much loved concubine named P'an-p'an, an excellent singer, fine dancer, and a woman possessing every grace and charm. When I was a young secretary, I was traveling in the area of Hsü-chou, and Chang Chien-feng held a party for me. We were getting a bit drunk, and Chang brought out P'an-p'an to add to my pleasure. And it was pleasure indeed. Afterward I gave her a poem with the lines:

> Sweet in her tipsiness, out of control,
> the breeze ruffling peony blossoms.

Experiencing the pleasure of her company only once, I left. I had heard nothing about her for the past dozen years until yesterday Chang Chung-su visited me and recited some of his new poems. Among these were three poems entitled "The Tower of the Swallows" whose words had a paticular warmth and beauty. When I asked him the curcumstances behind their composition, I found out they had been written for P'an-p'an. My visitor, Chang Chung-su, had been serving with the army at Wu-ning for a number of years and was well-informed about what had happened to P'an-p'an. He told me that after Chang Chien-feng's death, the body had been taken to Lo-yang for burial. The Changs had an estate in nearby P'eng-ch'eng, and on that estate was a small tower named "The Swallows." Mindful of the love she and Chang Chien-feng had shared, P'an-p'an refused to remarry, but instead took up residence, all alone, in this tower for more than ten years. She is still there

today. I much admired Chang Chung-su's new songs and thought
fondly back on my previous meeting with P'an-p'an. Out of all this
I wrote the following three quatrains on the same theme [of which
the first is given here]:

> Her windows fill with bright moonlight,
>   her curtains fill with frost;
> her blankets cold, the lamplight dying—
>   the hand runs over the bed where she lies.
> In the Tower of the Swallows
>   this night of moonlight and frost,
> as autumn comes, the nights grow longer
>   for one person, all alone.

Po Chü-yi

The year was 815 or 816. On hearing the poems of Chang Chung-
su, with their title "Tower of the Swallows," Po Chü-yi was touched
with curiosity and wanted to know the circumstances behind their
composition, or, more literally, "what they came from" (ch'i-yu).
There was something in these poems—some specific detail or perhaps
the precisely local title, "Tower of the Swallows"—that caught Po's
attention and lead him to search out the particular circumstance that
explained the motives behind the poems.

Po Chü-yi's preface answers our anticipated curiosity just as Chang
Chung-su answered his own. Po traces the origins of his own poems
on P'an-p'an, incorporating his question to Chang Chung-su and
Chang's reply. This exegetical move is the essence of the hermeneutics
taught by Confucius, how to read all actions (including acts of words)
in the world: first to see "how it is" (ch'i so-yi), as Po first observed
that Chang Chung-su's poems possessed "a particular warmth and
beauty"; then to understand such qualities by considering "what they
came from" (ch'i so-yu), their origins in circumstance—this was precisely Po Chü-yi's second question. But there is a third and final clause
in Confucius's instruction, the most difficult and elusive clause: ch'a
ch'i so-an, "reflect on the conditions in which the person would be at
rest"—where is the secret desire whose fulfillment would bring the
doer or speaker peace of mind? All significant words and acts are
vectors of disequilibrium that locate lost equilibrium in the speaker
or actor.

As for P'an-p'an, we see clearly "how it is" for her now: a self-
imposed loneliness in the Tower of the Swallows, named for those

most domestic birds whose legendary fecundity mocks the solitary barrenness of her present life. We also see "what it came from," the chain of events that bring her to these present circumstances, which in turn become the origins of Chang Chung-su's quatrains, and those in turn the origin of Po's own quatrains. But finally, in the putative situation of the quatrains, we can see the supposition that, in order for P'an-p'an to be "at rest," the self-respect attained through chaste solitude is insufficient. The only peace of mind that Po Chü-yi's poem can foresee for her would lie in the impossible restitution of the dead.

These poems are not P'an-p'an speaking for herself, but the voices of two men speaking for her, taking her place; and in the restlenssness of the desires attributed to her, we can read the restlessness of their own desires. We see "how it is" for Po Chü-yi too: wistful memories of an evening of pleasure twelve years ago, and the glow of his lingering desire shed around this pity for her solitude. He lets us read "what it comes from," the past circumstances from which these feelings follow. And we can guess his unspoken hope, the speculative possibility in which he would find rest. In only one way could this secret desire of his be reconciled with her secret desire: if he could stand in for the dead, as once before in Hsü-chou he had stood in the place of Chang Chien-feng.

One drunken evening twelve years ago, P'an-p'an was brought out to "add to the pleasure," and the experience of that pleasure came only once. Then, too, he wrote his fantasy of her desire, her control slipping away in sexual drunkenness; perhaps there was pleasure for her too in sharing his fantasy of her desire. "Sweet in her tipsiness, out of control, the breeze ruffling peony blossoms." We cannot know whether his remembered pleasure was a real sexual encounter or only a suspension of desire in sexual banter and its performance in song and dance, which left its imprint on the poet. But it was an intimacy. Po Chü-yi, the outsider, was allowed to stand where Chang Chien-feng alone had a right to stand, to view her and write the image of his desire in a poem. And he occupied the place by Chang Chien-feng's own authorization.

Now, by her own choice, P'an-p'an honors her emotional contract with Chang Chien-feng. She keeps herself under his permanently silent authority rather than place herself under some new male power: she is free to marry, but she will not. She is sober now, and in control. Only Chang Chien-feng had the right to fill that empty space in her bed—or, just perhaps, his authorized proxy.

A wistful eroticism runs through Po Chü-yi's poem as he imagines her hungry solitude, an empty space he might fill, a cold wakefulness that he might be able to transform to warmth and sleep where both would be "at rest." In the same way Po's poetic vision of P'an-p'an's desire, whose pedigree is given in the preface, replaces Chang Chung-su's unauthorized poetic fantasies. On the most basic level, these poems of perpetually unfulfilled desire take the place of action, of his physical body in the empty place in P'an-p'an's bed in P'eng-ch'eng far away. Wherever there is one act of replacement, there are many.

Po Chü-yi could not go to P'eng-ch'eng. A hungry body was left there waiting. Let two and a half centuries pass to the year 1078, when another poet does come to P'eng-ch'eng and occupies the place that Po Chü-yi never managed to reach: the later poet spends the night in the "Tower of the Swallows." He has, unfortunately, come too late for the physical P'an-p'an, and he too writes a song to take the place of his unfulfilled desire, a song that likewise takes the place of Po Chü-yi's well-known poem and becomes the lyric ever afterward associated with the story of P'an-p'an. Po Chü-yi's poem and preface are reduced to a footnote. This latecomer styles himself "Eastern Slope," Tung-p'o, recalling a famous "eastern slope" of which Po Chü-yi wrote (though later ages will always think of this later poet as Su Tung-p'o rather than Su Shih, his proper name; and they will hardly remember the forerunner Po Chü-yi). Su Tung-p'o is the Chinese tradition's master usurper; he plays his many borrowed roles loudly and always asserts his ease and self-realization, claiming that he is not playing a role but merely being himself.

> I spent the night in P'eng-ch'eng's "Tower of the Swallows" and dreamed of P'an-p'an. I then wrote these lyrics to the melody "Meeting Forever."

> Bright moonlight like frost,
> a good breeze like the water,
> the clear, cool scene unbounded.
> A fish leaps up in the winding bay,
> round pads of lotus spill their dew:
> in this stillness no one sees or hears.
> The drum of the watch booms—midnight—
> a single leaf crackles
> in the dark as my dream of clouds breaks apart;
>   I awake with a start

and through night's vast shadow
  there is no way to reach her again.
Now up, I walk all through the small garden.

At world's edge, weary traveler,
through these mountains, my road of return,
my eyes and mind gazing toward home
  as far as sight will go.
Empty now, Tower of Swallows—
its lovely woman, now where?—
empty, enclosing only swallows.
Present and past are as in a dream
and from that dream will we waken ever?
Nothing but pleasure past, and new bitterness.
Yet in times to come when they stand before
  the scene of the night around Yellow Tower,
the sighs that then come will be for me.

As he has taken the place of another, he knows that his own place will be taken; and in the final lines of the song, Su Tung-p'o moves to preempt usurping futurity. If others someday come to stand on Yellow Tower, where Su himself once lived, and think back on him, they will know that Su has already put himself in their place and has imagined all their imaginings. Through the two stanzas he presents himself as both subject and object of remembrance. In this small drama of substitution Su Tung-p'o writes all the roles for himself: he stands with those who remember with desire, and at the same time assumes the role of the one remembered with desire, P'an-p'an.

But for the moment Su Tung-p'o spends the night in the Tower of the Swallows and dreams an erotic dream, called in Chinese "a dream of clouds" (surface words that take the place of and cloud over forbidden sexual words). If such a dream is brought to the point of cloudburst, it will disperse fertile liquids everywhere. But Su achieves only cloudburst *interruptus,* the dreaming body's sexual momentum led astray by the thundering rumble of the watch drum, and in the intense silence that follows, by the crackle of a dry leaf scudding across the pavement. It may be that "he who wants to present ecstasy on stage . . . should give it to a man asleep"; but sleeping poets keep their silence, and all poetic ecstasy can be given only in anticipation or in loss.[3]

Each sexual encounter must have its matchmaker, or pimp, someone who introduces the woman and claims authority over her, providing the newcomer with legitimacy or the thrill of usurpation. For Su Tung-p'o this role is filled by Po Chü-yi, whose preface and poems introduce the self-cloistered P'an-p'an to the world and publish her desirability, in the tension between her renunciation of sexual relations and her lingering desire. The old claimant to the place must withdraw; Po Chü-yi performs this service by dying and leaving a space for Su Tung-p'o to fill, just as space had been left for Po himself by the death of Chang Chien-feng. The nature of the substitution has changed. The T'ang poet, Po Chü-yi, had wanted to replace someone who had an empirical claim over the woman; his forerunner is Chang Chien-feng, a lord of immense political power. Su Tung-p'o, the Sung poet, wants to usurp the place of an earlier poet; he plunders fantasies.

Once, long ago in the past, there had been an experience of pleasure in her company. Successive poets reach back toward that moment but never quite attain it. Something always separates or interrupts the conclusion; and in that space of interruption the poem occurs, taking the place of completion.

Po Chü-yi at least retained an elementary tact and diffidence. The recurrence of his old desire for P'an-p'an, in his poetic fantasy of her loneliness and hungry body, was left politely unstated. He did not try to leap across that space of separation, to brashly usurp Chang Chien-feng's place that P'an-p'an had chosen to leave unfilled. But Su Tung-p'o takes the license of dream—"all of us are like the savage when we dream"[4]—to move across that space, or even more arrogantly, to have P'an-p'an move across the space toward him. He would possess sexually and spectrally the lost body, whose beauty now exists only as a report lodged permanently in old poems. The past is a fabric of words that has taken the place of what truly was. Keats too stood in for the lover in the text:

> Pale were the sweet lips I saw,
> Pale were the lips I kiss'd, and fair the form
> I floated with, about the melancholy storm.
>
> Keats, "A Dream, after Reading Dante's
> Episode of Paolo and Francesca"

Outside forces block the completion of the sexual dream, as they always will, and in the frustrated aftermath these song lyrics are written, new words to seize the place of old poems of desire. Pieces of Po Chü-yi's quatrains return in Su Tung-p'o's song: fragmented, deeply embedded in their new settings, so usurped that for the next nine centuries all will recognize those words as Su's own. "Bright moonlight like frost," a commonplace simile snatched from Po Chü-yi's poem, where "Her windows fill with bright moonlight, her curtains fill with frost"; but it is welded to a more daring and memorable comparison that figuratively immerses the poet-viewer in his own poetic construct: "a good breeze like the water." Then follows the triumphant line in which Su tacitly proclaims his occupation of the forbidden place. He need not, like Po Chü-yi, merely imagine the woman enclosed within the tower; he lets us know that he stands there in her chamber, looking out. All dividing enclosure is broken into an unbounded scene that has no past or present, the same sight filling the eyes of the woman then and the poet now: "the clear, cool scene unbounded."

There is a ground of continuity in which present and past are indistinguishable to the senses, a scene of elemental metamorphoses in which the woman long dead can meet the present man in a moist sexual dream. Upon this ground appear forms of interruption: a fish leaping up and back into the water with a splash, a round lotus pad filling with dew until the weight makes it unstable and it spills its load back into the waters, which are the figure of the wind. The lotus (*lien*) was a venerable homophonic pun on sexual passion (*lien*), and the flower itself was a common figure of a woman's sex, as the dew was the common figure of the sexual fluids of men and women, now spilled back into the waters that are the breeze across the face.

The opening scene occurs in poetic rather than narrative space. Only in the following lines does Su wake, becoming witness to an emptiness where "in this stillness no one sees or hears." The opening does not belong to the poet's waking eyes or to the eyes of dream. It is a condition that can exist only in poetry, where ancient beauties and modern poets, past poems and present poems come together. Yet as the poem recapitulates the narrative in its introduction, this opening scene takes the place of the dream and the dream's unrealized consummation, liquids spilled, the jolt of interruption, a drifting stillness broken by sudden sounds.

The act fails; words replace consummation, and in the celebration of failure the words succeed in taking the place of all predecessors and all those who will come after. But it is a dubious ("fishy") consolation. We were awash in dream and in a wind like water; the flood suddenly withdraws, leaving fragments and half things:

As *Nilus* sudden ebbing, here
Doth leave a scale, and a scale there,
And somewhere else perhaps a Fin,
Which by his stay had Fishes been:
So Dreams, which overflowing be,
Departing leave Half things, which we
For their Imperfectness can call
But Joyes i'th'Fin, or in the Scale.
If when her Teares I haste to kiss,
They dry up, and deceive my Bliss,
May I not say the Waters sink,
And Cheat my Thirst when I would drink?
If when her Breasts I go to press,
Insteed of them I grasp her Dress,
May I not say the Apples then
Are set down, and snatch'd up agen?
Sleep was not thus Death's Brother meant;
'Twas made an Ease, no Punishment.
As then that's finish'd by the Sun,
While *Nile* did only leave begun,
My Fancy shall run o'er Sleeps Themes,
And so make up the Web of Dreams:
In vain fleet shades, ye do Contest:
Awak'd how e'er I'l think the rest.

William Cartwright (1611–1643),
"A Dream Broke"

The poem is neither the interrupted ecstasy of dream nor the fancy that rashly promises to complete dream's broken web. As Spenser says: "Such labour like the Spyders web I fynd, / Whose fruitless work is broken with least wynd." The poem lacks dream's frail perfection and fancy's partial license. It is an imperfect replacement for ecstasy, pointing to one interrupted ecstasy receding into the past or its completion anticipated somehow in the future: it is mere stopgap. The fish leaps, splashing in the bay, and the poet is left with "joys in the fin," the fragments of dead things whose reanimation he may only imagine. Like the ritual coda the poem is not the actual performance, but the joint between performances: it does not touch the edenic body, the breast-apples, but imagines or remembers or anticipates the touch. Most important, in imagining, remembering, or anticipating, the poem knows that it is only the shadow of a shadow and nothing real. Its words are lovely and flawed substitutes for action, in the world or even in the mind; and if the words are to have value, that value must be invented or won from action.

Words/Deeds

Eisoptron: the mirror is the most ancient and one of the most enduring metaphors for the workings of poetry. The clear mirror, polished bronze or silvered glass, seems to catch the image most perfectly and pass it on. In this way the mirror becomes the metaphorical mimesis of mimesis. But like all acts of mimesis, the metaphor of the mirror itself lulls us into overlooking essential evasions or obvious distortions of perspective in an image that we hope to take as truth's undistorted reflection.

The mirror of mimesis gives us back the image of human actions, or of nature, or of the heart. It is true that the mirror promiscuously reproduces whatever comes into its angle of light. Such unflinching willingness to reflect what comes before it permits us to overlook the fact that this mirror is made for one purpose only: to show each of us the one image in the world we cannot otherwise see—our own face seeing.

We would like to believe that a work of art is indeed a mirror which shows us the world in such a way that we can "reflect" on it and discover the patterns that govern its bewildering shapes. But perhaps the mirror of art gives us instead only the image of the perceiver, whether that perceiver be the artist or ourselves:

> If it is so, that in hard stone
> one likens every other's image to oneself,
> ashen and often pale I make it,
> just as I am made by her.
> And thus I ever take model from me,
> intending it be she.
>
> Michelangelo

It is the mirror that shows us the Other whom we had never before seen. This is what happened to Narcissus as he gazed into the pool and discovered the rarest, most beautiful beloved. If we "hold a mirror up to nature," it blocks our view: we see only our own eyes seeing.

But let us be polite and pretend—as this ancient metaphor for mimesis would persuade us—that the mirror reveals to us absolutely everything except our own selves looking. Painting and sculpture give the perfect reflection of visible forms, while poetry passes on the image of more elusive realities: "we know to mirror lovely deeds in one way only," says Pindar.

It was probably in 467 B.C. that Pindar wrote a choral ode to celebrate the victory of young Sogenes of Aegina, winner of the boys' pentathlon in the Nemean Games. After beginning with conventional praise of the city and its youthful champion, Pindar turned to one of his favorite topics, the power of art to keep the glory of victory from dark forgetfulness.

> If good fortune come to any act, it runs upon
> the wellsprings, with sweet thoughts, of
> Muses' creeks; for great acts of prowess have
> much darkness if song is lacking;
> we know to mirror lovely deeds in one way only:
> if by remembrance, with her shining crown,
> a ransom is found for suffering
> in words of song heard far and wide.

> Skilled sailors know the storm-wind
> that will surely blow
> on the third day, nor does hope for gain
> mar the doing; rich man, poor man
> together reach the margin that is death. But I believe
> that Odysseus' story was more than what he endured
> —because of Homer's fine words:

> for on those lies and on their wingéd craftiness
> there is some holy force; his skilled misleading
> cheats with its tale; and there is a blindness
> in the hearts of all men alike. For had they seen
> the truth, never would staunch Ajax,
> enraged about the armor, have driven home
> the smooth sword into his breast.

Through fine twists and turns the passage comes at last to the story of Ajax, who, as the greatest living warrior of the Greeks, laid claim to the arms of Achilles after that hero's death. But Odysseus disputed Ajax's claim, and by fine, beguiling words managed to persuade the assembly to award the arms to him. Ajax, made mad by the goddess, was at last driven to suicide. He withdrew from the contest, leaving the field to Odysseus (who was surely the sort of man who would abandon his shield in battle, then later boast how he had escaped with his life).

Pindar opens the passage softly, with beguiling words and a promise of permanence: "If good fortune come to any act . . ." The physical contest of the games is over and the excitement of victory is already receding. For a brief moment the boy Sogenes and his family had been the focus of all, drawing admiration and envy; now the eyes of the admiring community are already beginning to turn away, back to their daily tasks. The poet reminds the victor that these glorious deeds and his hard-won success in the games are only momentary and will go into "much darkness if song is lacking." He offers protection: mirroring song is labor's recompense and a balm for the victor's growing realization of victory's frailty. In the poem the boy's deeds will be remembered and honored.

The poet speaks here as a professional. His art—the composition of choral odes for victors in the games—is a skill to be sold, though the sale must be figured in the distorting image of a spontaneous gift. The poem belongs to a system of exchange: words for deeds (or more precisely, for the hunger to have one's deeds seen and recognized), financial rewards for words. But the poet is a good businessman and will take all: "nor does hope for gain mar the doing." The usurper's grasp is matched by his insecurity; the declaration of the value of his art is also a defense of his livelihood. Even in 467 B.C. poetry somehow required defense, a public exposition of its value. But this strange defense goes astray and tells the truth about its lies. Through the course of the passage, the perfect mirror, held up spontaneously in response to lovely deeds, imperceptibly moves to reflect secret pride in the raw force of this art of words, which can bring a great hero to destruction by the beguiling and holy power of its untruth. The poet stands exultant over his opponent.

A poem is supposed to mirror completed action, but instead replaces it. It is a distorting mirror, lulling its audience with the illusion of simultaneous reflection while slipping into the place of deeds now lost from view. Just as the reflection in a real mirror vanishes with the act, so the metaphor of the mirror quickly disappears, outlived by celebration of the duration of commemorative song. The place of the mirror is taken by *klutos,* renown, that which is heard far and wide. In the poem, repeated and passed on, *klutos* lasts, but without its origins, its wellspring" in action. It is free to twist its reports and tell pleasing lies.

There is a threatening darkness: death and forgetfulness. Against such danger, one ventures like a sailor hoping for gain, traveling far and wide. In the same way the poet's words, carriers of *klutos,* go wandering. But the pivot of the poet's wandering words is *pleon,* "more." The *logos,* the "word" and "story" of Odysseus, lasts longer, has "more" duration than that most famous wanderer, Odysseus, or his deeds; and the *logos* travels even farther than Odysseus' famous travels. Suddenly those remarkable actions—of a victor in the Nemean games or even of long-suffering Odysseus—are diminished in face of the distorting majesty of song, which is immortal to their mortality and makes them seem greater than they were (here it confesses that these words of fame have indeed taken the place of actual deeds).

Human beings, you see, are blind to words' sweet lies: they take them as true, even as the perfect mirror of deeds. The marvels of the *Odyssey* are untruths, greater in every way than the actual sufferings of Odysseus. Suddenly twisting again, Pindar recalls one of those beguiling stories about Odysseus, a particular story that gives a double meaning to the statement that Odysseus' story or words (*logos*) were "more than what he endured." In this second and dominant sense the line refers to Odysseus' claim of his own greater merit before the assembled lords of the Greeks when he contested with Ajax for the armor of Achilles. The question of that moment was which man was to take the place of Achilles, the man of deeds or the man of words, whose lesser deeds were magnified by the distorting majesty of artful words. It was by words that Odysseus won those arms, charming the blind hearts of men, men unable to see the greater merit of Ajax, who had truly performed "great acts of prowess," but who lacked Odysseus' gift of speech. When the blind hearts of men refused to award Achilles' armor to Ajax, that hero went out into the night and, blinded by the goddess, slew a herd of animals, believing them to be human. Then Ajax, freed from his blindness, saw the truth of his actions and killed himself with his own sword. Only later, when Odysseus again met him in the underworld, did Ajax become eloquent, and then his eloquence was in his silence.

We have a knot here of true seeing and blindness, of truth and deception, fine words linked with immortality and silent deeds linked to death and general mortality. As the thread of the song twists itself into this knot, we recognize that the poet's sense of his own vocation has somehow gotten out of control; the comforting commonplace of the opening, that song is recompense for glorious deeds, has undergone a strange mutation as the man of words is set in competition with the man of action and overcomes him.

We can only wonder what Pindar is saying to the Nemean victor.

He sings beguiling words on behalf of the Nemean victor and his "great acts of prowess"; and in those words he tells how Homer's beguiling words of Odysseus' beguiling words were greater than his actual deeds, and how by using such words Odysseus won for himself the reward for "great acts of prowess," sending the inarticulate man of action into humiliation and self-destruction. We follow a mutation from poetry as the mirror of deeds, to poetry that is "more" than deeds, to poetry that contests with deeds and overcomes them, destroying the doer and sending him into "much darkness."

This is no common contest in which the old champion is finally overthrown by the newcomer, the artful usurper. It is a contest in which the victor by words can find no easy joy in his victory; the usurper's ultimate self-defeat is given with the form of the relation. He must display his success, for without public confirmation his own victory is lost, gone into darkness. To do so, the warrior of beguiling words must restore sight to the blind herd of men; he must boast of his own distortions and must show that Ajax was the true hero, the greater opponent overcome by craft. Yet in doing this he rekindles and spreads the *klutos,* the renown, of the very man whom he tried to "send into darkness."

Corridor: Suicide and Flower

In order to savor his own victory, Pindar is finally compelled to remind us of the dignity of the vanquished man of deeds. Triumph by words becomes at best equivocal, and at worst a hollow noise beside the grandeur of a hero's silence. To win a less dubious victory the poet must make the man of deeds speak; Ajax must be given his inferior measure of eloquence. To contest the issue between words and deeds entirely on the home ground of words unfortunately diminishes both: the man of deeds blusters, and the man of words proves his superiority only over rhetorical ineptness. Such utter humiliation of the man of deeds is proportional to the deep resentment and envy in the man of words. The poet unseats the hero and permits him no place of his own, either in life or death.

This is precisely what occurs when Ovid retells the story of Ajax in the thirteenth book of *Metamorphoses.* First there is a stylized debate between mind and muscle; Ajax speaks well for himself, but not so well as Ulysses (Odysseus), whose silver exposition wins the judgment and the arms of Achilles. Then Ovid gives Ajax the unkindest cut of all, reducing the humiliated hero to theatrical blustering, by which Ajax comes to a bad end in more ways than one.

> the huddle of princes was stirred, and
> the outcome showed what power
> lies in fineness of speech: an eloquent man bore off
> the arms of a strong one.
>
> He who so often endured alone
> Hector, the steel, fires
> and Jove, could not now endure
> this single outrage; and the pain
> conquered a man unconquered;
> he yanked out his sword, saying
> "This surely is mine! or does Ulysses
> demand it also for his own?
> This I must use against myself; although
> full often it has streamed
> with Trojan gore, now it will stream
> in the gashing of its lord,
> nor can any man but Ajax
> overcome Ajax."
>
> He spoke, and within a breast laid open
> to steel, receiving at last
> its first wound then, he hid
> the deadly sword,
> nor had the hand strength to draw
> the shaft implanted forth:
> gore itself propelled it out; and earth,
> reddened with his blood,
> engendered a purple flower
> from the green sod,
> the very flower that first was born
> of Hyacinth's wound.
> On its petals were written the letters
> shared alike by man
> and boy: the name of the one,
> outcry of the other.

The reader of this passage may justly object that one purple flower was quite adequate in consequence of Ajax's death and that such a verbal patch of purple is excessive. But this florid death scene in *Metamorphoses* ultimately comes to a botanical etiology.

Old legends lie behind the names of things; what the naive observer might think to be nature's mere object is discovered to have a depth of history. Sometimes there are too many legends for a particular thing. The markings on the petals of this flower have a crowded etiology. "AI" is marked on the petals, the world's first ambiguous text, admitting competing interpretations. Priority must go to Apollo's cry of lament, "Ai!," after he unintentionally slew Hyacinth with his discus; the god inscribed his perpetual grief on the petals of the flower to which he gave Hyacinth's name (though foreseeing that Hyacinth would later have to share the inscription with Ajax). Ovid begrudges the vanquished Ajax even full possession of his own flower. Ajax (Aias) is the newcomer; he also dies into this flower and, unable to take the flower's name (already assigned to Hyacinth by Apollo, god of poetry), he contests the ownership of the inscribed syllable, claiming the AI as the first syllable of his own name. The replacement of one mortal by another may be no more than the exchange of organic stuff that fills the beautiful form of the seasonal flower; but it is quite otherwise when both leave on its petals an ambiguous inscription to contest their ownership. Poor Ajax is left with only half a claim to only half his name.

It is a lovely and ambiguous myth: a name and a history reduced to inscription on a surface—page or petal. They undergo a metamorphosis into words that survive and are disseminated afar, words that are perhaps "more than what he endured"—yet the lies are too lovely for us to care about the truth. Then someone later-born comes and tries to take the inscription as his own, and the message becomes uncertain and undecided.

Such a myth might tempt someone to die into flower (or into anthology, a garland of "flowers of words") and to usurp the form, if not the syllable, of Hyacinth's and Ajax's fame (though, to avoid competition, the person must be careful to make his flower's name entirely his own). Such a fantasy of dissemination is a countermotion away from some fear: humiliation, death and forgetfulness, danger, a repulse from stone. The alternative is renown, *klutos*, which travels far and flees from actual labor and suffering into the renown of suffering. Such renown could be carried in a poem on the common page, an anthology piece.

Je veux pousser par la France ma peine,
Plustost qu'un trait ne vole au decocher:

Je veux de miel mes oreilles bouscher,
Pour n'ouir plus la voix de ma Sireine.

Je veux muer mes deux yeux en fonteine,
Mon coeur en feu, ma teste en un rocher,
Mes piés en tronc, pour jamais n'approcher
De sa beauté si fierement humaine.

Je veux changer mes pensers en oiseaux,
Mes doux soupirs en Zephyres nouveaux,
Qui par le monde eventeront ma pleinte.

Je veux du teint de ma palle couleur
Aus bords de Loir enfanter une fleur,
Qui de mon nom et de mon mal soit peinte.

I would send forth my pain through all of France,
   swifter than arrow shaft flies to the mark,
   with honey I would stuff my ears
   to hear no longer my Siren's voice.

I would shed my eyes into fountain,
   my heart into fire, my head in stone,
   my feet in tree trunk, and never draw near
   her loveliness, so haughtily human.

My thoughts I would change into birds
   and into fresh breezes, my gentle sighs,
   for a worldwide disclosure of lament.

And with my complexion's pallor I would
   beget a flower by the banks of Loire,
   painted with my name and with my woe.

Ronsard, First Book of Amours (1587), 16

Like Ajax's sword spurted from his body, Ronsard's pain shoots out like arrows in every direction. The fame of his suffering is disseminated through all France (and in another version of the poem, through the whole universe). He begins as Odysseus, fleeing the Sirens into far wanderings, and ends as Ajax and Hyacinth, dying into flower. His substantial parts are scattered into their counterparts in solid nature, until all that remains are airy thoughts, sighs, and finally, a complexion, the gossamer surface of skin that engenders the eponymous flower, returning to the banks of his native Loire to complete a homecoming like that of Odysseus.[5] This flower is the body's last replacement and remembers both the forerunner's name and the essence of his history. The two forerunners, Hyacinth and Ajax, contested the meaning of the inscribed syllable: as Ovid says, "the name of one, the outcry of the other," which is the phrasing to which Ronsard alludes in the last line. Ronsard will monopolize his flower; keeping the doubleness of meaning, he will claim both.

This metamorphosis into disseminated fame and flower seems an act of self-determination, a countermotion against helplessness before compulsion—the Siren's voice that brings desire, shipwreck, and death without inscription.[6]

This is a variation on the male myth of woman/stone, the figure of fear and desire: the Sirens sit on rock, and they cause a softening in the one who listens, a coming loose of that which is restrained.

> Whosoever shall,
> For want of knowledge mov'd, but hear the call
> Of any Siren, he will so despise
> Both wife and children, for their sorceries,
> That never home turns his affection's stream,
> Nor they take joy in him, nor he in them.
> The Sirens will so soften with their song
> (Shrill, and in sensual appetite so strong)
> His loose affections, that he gives them head.
>
> *Odyssey*, XII.58–66 (trans. Chapman)

Instead Ronsard "makes a name for himself" in the dark shadow of absorption. Yet this countermotion to figure himself in the mimesis of suffering is only the inverted reflection of his motion toward the compelling voice.

Contesting the Name

> In deine Reimart hoff ich mich zu finden.
>
> In the ways of your verse
> I hope to find myself.
>
> Goethe, "Imitation"

In approximately 1247 the followers of the Sufi poet Rumi finally succeeded in driving from Konya the wandering dervish Shamsi Tabriz, with whom the master had become spiritually infatuated. After the explusion, Rumi became disconsolate; and thenceforth, in the final, "signature verse" of all his poems, he signed himself "Shamsi

Tabriz" in place of his own pen name Rumi. Or he used some other of Shamsi Tabriz's various pen names.

Love, competition, envy, emulation: a matrix of contraries binds him to this person. His presence is overwhelming: the Other must be removed—either by unwitting disciples who think that their actions oppose the master's intent, or by being dead, displaced into the past. He then can step in to fill the vacant place; he becomes both himself and the Other.

In his old age, Goethe published the "East-West Divan" (1819), inspired by Joseph von Hammer-Purgstall's translations from the lyrics of the Persian poet Hafiz (ca. 1326–1390). It is a collection of poems like no other. They are not translations, though they borrow much from the translations of Hafiz's poetry. We would like to say complacently that they are written "in the spirit of Hafiz"; but many of the poems are so much *about* writing "in the spirit of Hafiz" that they become utterly alien to "the spirit of Hafiz." Goethe cannot permit himself simply to disappear into the place he has taken: he must contest the place, show that he has come from the outside and is taking it by his own power—however much such repeated claims call into question his right to it.

The poems are lyrics in many voices, speaking back and forth to one another in competition, love, and friendship. Goethe becomes a complete set of dramatis personae, sometimes marked in the headings of the poems and sometimes unmarked. He is Goethe speaking to Hafiz and Hafiz speaking to Goethe; he is Hatem, the conventional figure of the lover, speaking to his beloved Suleika, and Suleika speaking back to Hatem[7]; he is both the anonymous poet and his companion "cup-bearer," the *saki* of Persian poetry. He is all voices, half lyric poet, half dramatist, revealing the peculiar passion that lies at the core of both: the secret dramatist in lyric, who writes an Other as if it were himself, and the secret lyric poet in the dramatist, who writes himself as if he were some Other. Through all these voices there is another Goethe, who understands that in the sheer multiplicity of his metamorphoses he has somehow come loose from his moorings and been disseminated into scattered names and a babble of disparate voices.

He is the gleeful thief of names. After all, those names made so famous in Perisan poetry were only *Beinamen*, "assumed names," signatures of roles, qualities, and ways of being that were somehow already external to the person who went "by" such a name. These names had been given as gifts to the old poets or had been assumed by them through a willful act of self-interpretation. And now, like houses left vacant, these unoccupied names seem to be waiting for newcomers to lay claim to them and move in. The former owner, absent now, can be fictively called back and made to yield place gracefully.

In the poem entitled *Beiname*, "pen name" or "assumed name," Goethe calls back Mohammed Shams-eddin (Hafiz) by his "proper name" and interrogates him on how he came by this name Hafiz, "Preserver" or "Rememberer." Being a polite man, Hafiz answers Goethe politely, explaining to the newcomer that the people gave him this name because of his ability to "preserve" the verses of the Koran by memory—one might say that he made a name for himself by this capacity.

Hafiz was no usurper; he was a preserver of old words. But Goethe hungers for this now vacant name and wants to add it to his collection. He is the modern poet of historicism who has both "progressed" beyond past poetry and can subsume it.[8] He explains to Hafiz why this name should now be his:

> Hafis, drum, so will mir scheinen,
> Möcht ich dir nicht gerne weichen:
> Denn wenn wir die andre meinen,
> Werden wir den andern gleichen.
> Und so gleich ich dir vollkommen,
> Der ich unsrer heilgen Bücher
> Herrlich Bild an mich genommen,
> Wie auf jenes Tuch der Tücher
> Sich des Herren Bildnis drückte,
> Mich in stiller Brust erquickte,
> Trotz Verneinung, Hindrung, Raubens,
> Mit den heitren Bild des Glaubens.
>
> Then, Hafiz, it would seem to me
> I may not need to yield to you:
> For when we think as others do,
> we become like those others,
> thus perfectly like you am I,
> who have absorbed the glorious image
> of our own sacred books,
> as on that cloth of all cloths

the figure of the Lord was pressed
and revives in my calm breast,
in spite of denial, checks, and theft,
with the happy image of belief.

Unlike Hafiz, who received his name freely from others, Goethe claims it by right, and he justifies the appropriation on the grounds that his own memory of the Bible is the equal counterpart of Hafiz's scriptural learning. Not only does Goethe replace the Koran with his own sacred text, he also has no commitment whatsoever to this vaunted capacity for memory of the Bible. It is a mere stratagem of his desire, a means to get hold of the name. Once he has become "Hafiz," that knowledge of the Bible is utterly forgotten: he really wanted the forerunner's place, not simply to wear the forerunner's name and remain the person he already was. Once he is dressed in the other's name, this new Teutonic Hafiz speaks for a Koranic cosmos.

The forerunner always says just enough; the newcomer and usurper says too much. He offers examples, persuasions, elaborations, and proofs where silence would serve him best. Within such excess there is inevitably something that complicates the very case it is attempting to support. Unlike the great storehouse of Koranic words for which Hafiz received his name, the figure for the historicist's memory is Christ's image on the shroud: the uncertain afterimage (*Nachbildung*, "imitation") in textile and text, the imprint of death and absence that is open to doubt and interpretation, like the marking "AI" on the petals of the hyacinth. It is an image whose meaning must be questioned and whose interpretation requires an active affirmation of belief.

Put no faith in his faith. He had no allegiances; his faith was mere will and convenience. Goethe, a great botanist, would have willingly read the "AI" on the hyacinth's petals as nature's random strokes. Yet if it served the purposes of his desire he was capable of an imaginative act of faith. He would gladly have read these and other marks as the imprints of a dead forerunner. It was not that memory received the indelible impressions of the dead, but rather than, when he wanted to interpret those marks as such, he could give himself over to the role and claim belief, displacing all other possibilities into a frame of general doubt. Although he asks in the poem that we reject such doubt, he always says a word too much. In prohibiting doubt, he reminds us of doubt's shadowing presence. For the poet of historicism, self may be projected, then inhabited; the forerunner is a husk, open for habitation, that may be added to the collection.

He interprets the name, the old markings, and projects a vacant place and role; then he moves to occupy the place. He sets out on this journey as immigrant rather than tourist. He breaks with his prior past and begins a new era, a new calendar, like the one that dates from the hegira, Mohammed's flight from Mecca to Medina.

> Nord und West und Süd zersplittern,
> Throne bersten, Reiche zittern,
> Flüchte du, im reinen Osten
> Patriarchenluft zu kosten,
> Unter Lieben, Trinken, Singen,
> Soll dich Chisers Quell verjüngen.
>
> Dort, im Reinen und im Rechten,
> Will ich menschlichen Geschlechten
> In des Ursprungs Tiefe dringen,
> Wo sie noch von Gott empfingen
> Himmelslehr in Erdesprachen,
> Und sich nicht den Kopf zerbrachen.
>
> Wo sie Väter hoch verehrten,
> Jeden fremden Dienst verwehrten;
> Will mich freun der Jugendschranke:
> Glaube weit, eng der Gedanke,
> Wie das Wort so wichtig dort war,
> Weil es ein gesprochen Wort war.
>
> Will mich unter Hirten mischen,
> An Oasen mich erfrischen,
> Wenn mit Karawanen wandle,
> Schawl, Kaffee, und Moschus handle;
> Jeden Pfad will ich betreten
> Von der Wüste zu den Städten.
>
> Bösen Felsweg auf und nieder
> Trösten, Hafis, deine Lieder,
> Wenn der Führer mit Entzücken
> Von des Maultiers hohem Rücken
> Singt, die Sterne zu erwecken
> Und die Räuber zu erschrecken.
>
> Will in Bädern und in Schenken
> Heilger Hafis, dein gedenken,
> Wenn den Schleier Liebchen lüftet,
> Schüttelnd Ambralocken düftet.

Ja des Dichters Liebeflüstern
Mache selbst die Huris lüstern.

Wolltet ihr ihm dies beneiden,
Oder etwa gar verleiden,
Wisset nur, dass Dichterworte
Um des Paradieses Pforte
Immer leise klopfend schweben,
Sich erbittend ewges Leben.

North and West and South break open,
Thrones explode, empires tremble;
So flee then to the pure East
To taste the air of patriarchs.
You should, in love and drink and song,
At Khiser's fountain there grow young.

There in purity and right
I want to penetrate the depths
Of the origins of the human race,
Where from God they still receive
Heaven's wisdom in earthly speech
And don't need to break their heads over it;

Where they honor fathers highly
And ward off foreign servitude.
I want to taste the limits of youth:
When belief is broad and thought is narrow,
Since words are so important there
Because they are the spoken word.

I want to mix with herdsmen there,
Refresh myself at the oases,
As I wander with the caravans,
Trading in shawls, coffee, and musk;
I want to cover every path
From the wilderness to the cities.

Up and down hard mountain trails
Your songs give comfort, Hafiz,
As the leader in his rapture
From the high back of his mule
Sings to wake the stars
And frighten the bandits away.

Among the baths and taverns I want
To think of you, holy Hafiz,
As my beloved lifts her veil,
Her shaking tresses smell of ambrosia:

Yes, whispers of love from poets
Fill even houris with desire.

If you should envy him this
Or try to spoil it altogether,
Then understand that poets' words
Hover around the gates of paradise,
Always knocking lightly,
Making a claim on eternal life.

"Hegira" is the first poem of "East-West Divan." It is a declaration of the end of history and a return to a changeless world of origins. It is the historicist's version of the poetic myth of return to Eden, in which knowledge and innocence meet and are rejoined: the place of the ultimate forerunner is usurped.

Such a return involves delicious paradoxes that can never be resolved. Goethe freely chooses to belong to a world whose chief attraction is its determinancy; he would change and become part of that which is changeless. His identity has been a collection of roles, a perpetual metamorphosis that seeks to encompass all things. At last there remains only one condition he cannot attain, placed beyond his reach by the very form of his reaching: he can never become a unity, can never be one thing alone.

In the old marks on the page, the name of Hafiz the preserver, he reads an Islamic East whose stability and permanence define the place he desires to inhabit—one where he can be at home and at rest. But it lies just beyond him, separated by the thinnest line of impossibility. The metamorph can never be at home because he can always imagine how it would be to be at home. Goethe understands the paradox all too well. If he cannot resolve it, he can at least play around it. And in such play the paradox stays important and alive.

He begins his journey to this land of heart's desire under the guise of necessity: exploding violence on all sides leaves only the East as an open vector of flight. In his apocalyptic vision of Armageddon and Eden reborn, many places collapse into one place and a world fallen into history returns to timelessness. This is the oldest world and the youngest, a place where all contraries are true: a patriarchal world that will honor the old man Goethe, yet at the same time a world of rejuvenation in which the old man grows young. It is a world of innocence that is closely akin to stupidity, yet a world of great wisdom—a world not of the written but of the spoken word (or so he writes on reading the translations of Hafiz). It is a western fantasy of the East, the ultimate orientalism, in which all condescension is simultaneously a desperate longing for the Other. In that Other all contradictory extremes exist: youth and old age, sophistication and naivete, sensuality and decent restriction.[9]

The usurper and immigrant is fascinated by boundaries, whose crossing alone provides the pleasures of becoming other. He catalogues limitations, restrictions, and coverings: old age and mortality, law and custom, the weight of the past. But this world is "unbounded," and every limitation is somehow transgressed and dissolved. The urge to cross the boundary line is an erotic one: the veil covers and inhibits, but only to add force to the moment when it is lifted. And its lifting is achieved by the power of poetry:

> As my beloved lifts her veil,
> Her shaking tresses smell of ambrosia:
> Yes, whispers of love from poets
> Fill even the houris with desire.

The verses are Hafiz's and his own, coming from the lips of one who is both the new man and the old man, both Goethe and Hafiz, the preserver of old words of power. The words carry him past the veil to paradise where the houris live, reunifying the contraries of Eden and the sexual world of the Fall.

By turning back, Goethe makes a circle of history; and in the infinity of this circle he achieves what is "Unbounded," *Unbegrenzt:*

> Dass du nicht enden kannst, das macht dich gross,
> Und dass du nie beginnst, das ist dein Los.
> Dein Lied ist drehend wie das Sterngewölbe,
> Anfang und Ende immerfort dasselbe,
> Und was die Mitte bringt ist offenbar
> Das was zu Ende bleibt und anfangs war.
>
> Du bist der Freuden echte Dichterquelle,
> Und ungezählt entfliesst dir Well auf Welle.
> Zum Küssen stets bereiter Mund,
> Ein Brustgesang der lieblich fliesset,
> Zum Trinken stets gereizter Schlund,
> Ein gutes Herz das sich ergiesset.
>
> Und mag die ganze Welt versinken,
> Hafis, mit dir, mit dir allein

Will ich wetteifern! Lust und Pein
Sei uns, den Zwillingen, gemein!
Wie du zu lieben und zu trinken
Das soll mein Stolz, mein Leben sein.

Nun töne, Lied, mit eignem Feuer!
Denn du bist älter, du bist neuer.

You cannot end—that makes you great,
You never begin—that is your fate.
Your song revolves like the arch of stars,
Beginning and ending forever the same,
And what the middle brings is clearly what
Remains at the end and in beginning was.

You are true poet-fountain of joy,
And from you flows uncounted wave upon wave;
A mouth always ready for kissing,
A song in the breast that streams with love;
A throat ever itching for a drink,
A good heart that pours itself out.

And let the whole world sink under,
I would have you, Hâfiz, and you alone,
As my competitor. Let pleasure and pain
Be shared by us, the twins!
To love like you, to drink like you
Should be my pride, should be my life.

Ring out now, song, with fire of your own!
For you are older, and you are younger.

He enters into a relation that takes him out of linear history, out of a world of lineages in which the places of forerunners are effectively seized, thus opening the newcomer to his own eventual eviction. In the place of lineage is the twinning of self and other. Linear time is bent into a ring, which is the immortality of circular song.

So Tung-p'o took the place of his forerunner Po Chü-yi in a lineage that was pure family romance. Po was dead, and his poem disappeared into the song of the later poet. Goethe interprets the forerunner's name and preserves him as a twin with whom he is locked in eternal love and competition. Within the circle nothing is completed and lost; the other is transformed into an interpretation and projection.

This is the work of historicism: subsuming the voice of the Other into the play of interpretation. All variant relations coexist without requiring decision between them: he is the other, he is like the other, he is different from the other ("Ring out now, song, with a fire of your own!"). There is the affirmation of opposition, the movement to opposites, and the union of opposites: the Western poet becomes the Eastern poet, the modern poet becomes the early poet (and in another sense, the late and modern poet becomes the primordial poet), the old man returns to youth; and later, writing in the voice of Suleika, the male poet becomes the female poet. Despite his illusions of an intense relation to the forerunner or to the beloved, the poet can be all things and participate in all relations because there is no intractable Other to bind him to any particular relation or place: able to be all, he is no one.

Although he cannot escape it, Goethe understands clearly the consequences of this play of metamorphosis. The continuous departure from the person he had been, always shedding his old skin, ensures that he can never reach primordial stability, only some ultimate instability. The poet is a wind-shape who can lay only conditional claim to any name by "thinking as" the other. But no name and no thought and no word holds.

> Weiss denn der mit wem er geht und wandelt,
> Er, der immer nur im Wahnsinn handelt?
> Grenzenlos, von eigensinnngem Lieben,
> Wird er in die Oede fortgetrieben,
> Seiner Klagen Reim', in Sand geschrieben,
> Sind com Winde gleich verjagt;
> Er versteht nicht was er sagt,
> Was er sagt wird er nicht halten.

> Does he know then with whom he goes and he changes,
> being one who acts only and always in madness?
> Boundaryless, by single-minded love
> he is driven forth into wilderness,
> his rhymed laments, written in sand,
> are likewise blown away by wind.
> He understands not what he says,
> and will not hold to what he says.

> from "Indictment"

It was inevitable. The first act of replacement always leads to many others; it never brings the hoped-for satisfaction, and the poet is driven on continuously to repeat the act. Just as later-born Pygmalions can never produce the ultimately gratifying statue, the metamorph can never find the self in which he is at home and at rest. His soul becomes nomadic. He comes loose from his moorings and passes into continuous metamorphosis, pursuing a never-ending chain of desired forms of the Other, forms he longs to take for his own. There is a grim immortality in this process of continuous self-creation; it requires continuous self-destruction, a path littered with abandoned husks of the self.

At the core of all such acts of usurping the place of another, we find shame, self-hatred, and a limitless capacity for violence against self. Close at hand is some terrible threat: death at the hands of an enemy, or a sentence of execution from the community, or suicide. But rather than allow the body's destruction, the poet destroys the self who inhabited it.[10] Threatened by the blade and disgrace, and having lost his shield, Archilochos used words to create the new man:

> For my part,
> I was saved, so what do I care
> about the shield—let it go.
> I'll buy another just as good.

One of the oldest acts of self-definition for Western lyric poetry is the replacement of epic motifs of war with the lyric themes of love and drinking. The refusal of epic violence begins, perhaps, with Archilochos' flight from the battlefield; the second of the *Anacreonta* calls for Homer's lyre, but a more inebriate tune. But the most telling moment is to be found in the ninth poem of the *Anacreonta,* in which the singer begins: "I want, I want to run mad." He continues with other examples of running mad until he comes to the case of Ajax, running mad with the sword received from Hector, the sword with which Ajax killed himself. Encountering this terminal similitude, the lyric poet swerves immediately into an act of replacement, claiming for himself something else in hand: "but I have cup / and wreath."

Yet the new role is never stable, never satisfying; and he hungers for stability and satisfaction. He willingly casts off his present form to take the place of yet another, and repeats the act throughout the work of words. Yet each act of taking a new place is a violence against self, a suicide of ego, "kamikaze man," reincarnating himself in new words and in renown, *klutos,* that goes far. Always in these words he deflects the blow away from the body, deflects the sword against Ajax used against himself.

> Of these two thousand I's and we's I wonder, which one am I?
>   Give ear to my babble, do not lay your hand on my mouth.
> Since I have gone out of control, do not put glass on my path, for
>   if you do I will stamp and break all that I find.
> Because every moment my heart is confused with your fantasy, if
>   you are joyous I am joyful, if you are sorrowing I am sorrowful.
>
> You are the original—what person am I? A mirror in your hand;
>   whatever you show, that I become, I am a well-proved mirror.
>
> The grace of Salah-i Dil u Din shone in the midst of my heart; he is
>   the heart's candle in the world; who am I? His bowl.

Rumi, Ghazal[11]

> Die Inschrift aber hat nichts hinter sich,
> Sie ist sie selbst, und muss dir alles sagen,
> Was hinterdrein mit redlichem Behagen,
> Du gerne sagst: Ich sag' es! Ich!
>
> But inscription has nothing behind it,
> It is itself, and must tell you all
> that much later, with sincere satisfaction
> you gladly say: I say it! I!

Goethe, from "Good-Luck Tokens"

Toward Metaphor

The story is told in the *History of the Tsin Dynasty* how Shih Ch'ung (249–300 A.D.) had a beautiful concubine named Green Pearl, who was desired by the powerful Sun Hsiu, an ally of the Lord Protector. Sun Hsiu sent a messenger to Shih Ch'ung to demand Green Pearl as a "gift." At the time Shih Ch'ung was in his villa at Golden Valley, high on a cool terrace overlooking a clear stream, with his women gathered around him. When the messenger delivered Sun Hsiu's demand, Shih Ch'ung brought forth every one of his concubines and maidservants before him; all smelled of orchid and musk and were robed in gauze and mesh. Shih Ch'ung said, "Choose." And the messenger said, "Your attendants are lovely indeed; but I have received an order to take only Green Pearl, and I don't know which one she is." Immediately Shih Ch'ung said, "I love Green Pearl; you cannot have her." The messenger tried in vain to persuade him, reminding him of the consequences of refusal, but still Shih Ch'ung would not give her up. On hearing of Shih Ch'ung's refusal, Sun Hsiu was enraged and urged the Lord Protector to have Shih arrested. Shih and his friends heard rumors of the plans being laid against him and set in motion a desperate counterplot to unseat the Lord Protector. The plot was discovered. When the soldiers came for him, Shih Ch'ung was feasting high in a tower; seeing the soldiers at his gate, he understood immediately what had happened and said to Green Pearl, "It was for your sake that it has come to this." Green Pearl wept and answered, "Then I shall die now before you," and threw herself from the tower.

Shih Ch'ung and all his family, his mother, his elder brother, his wife and children, were taken by the troops of the Lord Protector and executed.

The man has a family name, Shih, and the given name Ch'ung, "lofty," an auspicious quality that he is enjoined to fulfill; "Green Pearl" is a bonded concubine and has only the name of a precious object, a treasure. As she could be possessed, so also she could be traded away as the price of Shih Ch'ung's political security. But Shih Ch'ung refuses the exchange: he tells the messenger that he loves her, using the word *ai,* which suggests not desire or care for her as another person, but that he treasures her so much that he "begrudges" (also *ai*) losing her to another. Shih Ch'ung gambles to keep possession of his bondservant, prized for her value as sexual object; he risks boldly and loses.

Her value as an object is very high indeed, almost passing beyond the possible worth of any thing. At the end Green Pearl chooses to read Shih Ch'ung's high appraisal of her value as an opportunity. By committing suicide, she renounces the safety of her status as possession (to be confiscated by Sun Hsiu after the arrest, along with Shih Ch'ung's other household effects) and seizes for herself, if only for a brief moment as she falls from the tower, the status of human being. By her own choice she enters the deadly economy of feudal relations, based on the acceptance and repayment of obligations. Green Pearl declares herself to be the good retainer, and like many good but poor retainers in early Chinese stories, she pays her debt with the currency of her life. A human being suddenly appears behind the surface of lovely object; the body that falls from the tower is a person, not a thing.

In the first half of the ninth century, the poet Tu Mu visited the site of Shih Ch'ung's villa in Golden Valley and there recalled this woman who seized humanity for herself by destroying the precious object that was her body. Like P'an-p'an in the Tower of the Swallows, she entered history, which is restricted to human beings, by a free act of denial, something inflicted on herself. The men who came later seemed always to want to "repossess" her, to make her an object again, and in doing so to reanimate her. Su Tung-p'o broke down P'an-p'an's vows of chastity, if only spectrally. And Tu Mu in Golden Valley transformed the crushed and fallen body into the detritus of a garden scene.

> What happened in seasons of splendor
>   scatters in fragrant dust:
> the flowing waters lack all feeling,
>   plants turn to spring as they will;
> the sun sets and east wind's offense
>   makes the birds cry out in pain:
> where falling flowers resemble still
>   the person who leapt from the tower.
>
>   Tu Mu, "Golden Valley Garden"

Further Replacement: Death by Poetry, Death by Fiction

Now we must tell the dark embellishment worked upon P'an-p'an. Poetic replacement is often a gesture of continuation, a story that is left in suspension; by not going on to the end it makes going on possible. So P'an-p'an's decision to maintain her solitude was, for Po Chü-yi, a possibility, an empty bed. Po's fantasy of her desire rekindled his own desire and a dreaming resistance to her withdrawal. For others that dangerous opening had to be closed.

In later anecdotes they retold the story, and in the retelling expanded it, changed the wording, and added an ending to make it a proper story. Indeed they gave it an ending in more senses than one. And, as anecdotes often do, the embellishments twisted the circumstances to transform the story of P'an-p'an into a new version of an older story.

The older story will sound familiar, for it is based on the still older story of Green Pearl. A poet of the turn of the eighth century, Ch'iao Chih-chih, had a beloved concubine by the name of Emerald-Green Jade. The story goes that Emerald-Green Jade was taken from Ch'iao by a powerful kinsman of the Empress Wu. Then Ch'iao wrote a lovely poem on Green Pearl's loyal suicide and sent it secretly to Emerald-Green Jade, who, shamed by the precedent, tied the poem to her sash and drowned

Tradition provides a moribund set of metaphors for the woman as thing: she is a flower, and the sensual pleasures in her company are a full flowering, a season of splendor. The Chinese text allows us to hold in suspension the interpretation of the opening line as an ancient story or a present scene of late spring and fallen blossoms.[12] "Fragrant dust" is both the crushed detritus of petals and the remains of a lovely woman. Seasonal recurrence perpetuates sad stories of passion and passion's end, and in this endless reenactment of the drama of falling flowers nature demonstrates its insensitivity to pain. Nature reads no storybooks, has no corrective memory, and lacks those finer sentiments that teach us tact in the face of pain. Nature possesses nothing and indifferently yields things up to the possession of human beings; these things neither know they are possessed nor care.

There is something terribly wrong with Tu Mu's act of figuration in this poem. Various botanical items of the late spring scene take the place of the precarious heights, falling body, and broken body of the story, but the substitution reminds us only of the distance and difference between the person and the things of nature. Although the poet

---

herself in a well. When the body was recovered, the poem was found. The enraged imperial kinsman soon brought about the death of Ch'iao Chih-chih, even as Shih Ch'ung had been killed by Sun Hsiu.

Old stories are retold in new stories, and often in the retelling problems are solved. "It was for your sake that it has come to this." Shih Ch'ung's words did not compel Green Pearl's death; he told her her value, and she acted for herself. In the new anecdote the power to give death is transferred to the man, who uses poetry to shame Emerald-Green Jade into suicide. For the storyteller the poem is merely a means to narrative ends. The next retelling of death by poetry (or death by fiction's framing of poetry) will kill the woman and save the man.

In the embellished version of the P'an-p'an story the three poems recited by Chang Chung-su are understood as being not *about* P'an-p'an but *by* P'an-p'an (and three mediocre quatrains are included for which Po's quatrains can serve as response). The added ending is based on a misreading of Po's third quatrain:

This spring there was a traveler
    returning from Lo-yang,
who there had visited the tomb
    of Chang Chien-feng;
when told the poplars there had grown

insists that spring's east wind distresses the birds by blowing the flowers down from the trees, we know that such attribution of human response is only an act of art, a poetic figuring of their insouciant warbling.

Everything earlier in the poem is a mere antechamber for the simile in the final line—the explicit comparison of the falling flowers to Green Pearl's suicide, toppling from the tower. If Green Pearl had been simply an ancient beauty who died of natural causes, we would feel far less discomfort in her comparison to the broken petals of the late spring scene; it would be a commonplace, the loss of one lovely object taking the place of the loss of another. But to replace that woman, who showed her humanity by an act of violence against self, with these delicately tumbling blossoms is an act of poetic violence: its dissonance exposes the uncrossable gap between woman and flower, the true human being who dies without replacement and nature's unimaginative repetitiousness. These lovely but mindless latecomers cannot fill the place of the forerunner, however lovely she may have been; to put them in her place only recalls what has

---

      big enough for columns,
   how could the rouged beauty keep
      herself from turning to ash?

Po's preface and first poem were left hanging in desire. Although Po's third quatrain is not a very good poem, it brought the sequence to an acknowledgment of P'an-p'an's loyalty to Chang Chien-feng. On hearing how large the trees planted by Chang's grave have grown, P'an-p'an becomes aware of the time that has passed since Chang's death. This so fills her with grief that she wishes to die, having so long outlived him.

But for those who made stories out of poems, this third quatrain was not an admiring supposition about her sentiments, but rather Po Chü-yi's suggestion that she should kill herself. The rhetorical question becomes a literal question. They continued the story: On receiving Po's quatrains, P'an-p'an was deeply shamed and angered. She complained that Po Chü-yi had profoundly misunderstood her intentions and that she had refrained from suicide only to keep Chang Chien-feng's name from being stained by scandal. After composing yet one more quatrain to vindicate her honor, she stopped eating and died soon after.

Thus the story subsumed and swallowed up the poems. The story goes on to terminate the suspension and close the space of desire that the poems had opened up.

been lost. These metaphors are figures of absence, stopgaps.

Or perhaps this metaphor is used to hold open a gap that is in danger of closure. The gap can be crossed all too easily. There is a grim empirical metamorphosis that links forerunner and latecomer, woman and flower beneath the soil. The body becomes thing and dust. Fallen here, she can indeed be transformed into these falling flowers that dumbly mimic the act she freely chose and to which she gave meaning.

Body is earth, territory of violent metamorphosis and substitution. We are all in peril of becoming thing. The grotesque gap between our humanity and this thing—the body killed, damaged, wounded—is held open by metaphors. These metaphors stay alive and may sustain the person's life by violent usurpation or ludicrous imposture, shoving aside more sluggish words that once were themselves metaphors, but which have died and decayed into the complacent names of things. When life's blood leaks out of the gap, it is the occasion for hysterical wit, with metaphors contesting the place of body, which is metamorphosing into stuff.

> What a thrill—
> My thumb instead of an onion.
> The top quite gone
> Except for a sort of hinge
>
> Of skin,
> A flap like a hat,
> Dead white.
> Then that red plush.
>
> Little pilgrim,
> The Indian's axed your scalp.
> Your turkey wattle
> Carpet rolls
>
> Straight from the heart.
> I step on it,
> Clutching my bottle
> Of pink fizz.
>
> A celebration, this is,
> Out of a gap
> A million soldiers run,
> Redcoats, every one.

Whose side are they on?
O my
Homunculus, I am ill.
I have taken a pill to kill

The thin
Papery feeling.
Saboteur,
Kamikaze man—

The stain on your
Gauze Ku Klux Klan
Babushka
Darkens and tarnishes and when

The balled
Pulp of your heart
Confronts its small
Mill of silence

How you jump—
Trepanned veteran,
Dirty girl,
Thumb stump.

Sylvia Plath, "Cut"[13]

In this carnival of metaphor the wit of substitution becomes the violent defense of words against physical violence to the self, against being transformed into thing. In Sylvia Plath's poetry the body is always in danger of being made thing; through words she fights it back to life. The poem is Archilochos' second shield, a shield of words, filling a gap or cut through which we are threatened with metamorphosis into matter. Had he been able to use words,

never would staunch Ajax,
enraged about the armor, have driven home
the smooth sword into his breast.

The cut she wants to make is directed outward, to the quotidian onion; but it slips and turns on the body that wields the knife. Somehow the thumb, the homunculus, is her Isaac that has taken the place of the onion, the ram.

The flowing blood becomes a flow of metaphors that attempt to animate the self made matter, but in their awkward striving to fill the place of the cut and the flowing blood they call attention to the desperate need to make the replacement. "Taste is the capacity to judge an object or a manner of representation through satisfaction or dissatisfaction, but without any interest in it whatsoever. The object of such a satisfaction is called 'beautiful.'" In the *Critique of Judgment* Kant requires distance, an absence of personal interest or care as the central condition of an aesthetic judgment. An "aesthetic object" will be subjected to a lovingly curious and disinterested examination:

> the top quite gone
> except for a sort of hinge
> of skin . . .

When the object of bemused contemplation is one's own wounded body, words may try to cover but do not fully conceal the depth of interest. The poet reaches to the freedom of play in metaphor, but each metaphor is stained by the desperate distance of that reach; their freedom is no more than the negation of a deeper unfreedom (the material body that bleeds). These metaphors play like the play of "leisure time" in late capitalist society, where the human being is so much a function of the structure of work that all other time is understood only as the desperate negation of work. The complex fictions of autonomous choice are stained by the unfreedom that motivates them.

The cut and its metaphors operate on the margins of the self, and through the poem the metaphors gradually lose the war ("Whose side are they on?") to displace the body's wound into other: first "a flap like a hat," but the wound sinks deeper and deeper, the thumb becomes a homunculus, a scalped pilgrim, and finally, the war over, a "trepanned veteran," now witless and no longer able to fight back with metaphors, reduced to the unmetaphorical acknowledgment of the completed cut: "thumb stump."

She does battle with her metaphors (somehow managing to mix Freudian images of castration with the history of violence in America) and with her poem, her "papery feeling" that is killed by the numbing pill; it is also a process of covering over—a bandage that replaces the "hat" of skin with the hood of the Klansman and the east European babushka, perhaps of the Jew that is the Klansman's victim. But still the blood leaks out, stains and tarnishes, tells the truth beneath the covering, "straight from the heart."

Her metaphors, her words, don't hold. New ones always emerge to take the place of the old ones, none of which is secure in that place.

They try each to hold the place lightly, playfully, as art; they try to hide the wound. But the condition of their play is pain.

> To fill a Gap
> Insert the Thing that caused it—
> Block it up
> With Other—and 'twill yawn the more—
> You cannot solder an Abyss
> With Air.
>
> Emily Dickinson[14]

Metamorphosis

The body betrays us; it is under threat of metamorphosis into matter. The eyes focus on a break in the envelope of skin; the body leaks out. The poet offers to name these changes, to reanimate matter and to replace nature's unimaginative metamorphoses with a free language of otherness. The self that plays with such fantastic names is no more stable than the body; it is nothing more than a place, an envelope of invisible space within a system of habitual relations. So long as the self holds its place in the familiar system, it is stable, cozy in enduring its oppression. It possesses customary names for its site, and the orbit of its changes is reliable. The self is shaped by its community. This is well known. Put the self in a new system, and it will usually adjust, complacently execute whatever horror the new community approves and shape itself to whatever oppression the community demands as the price of place. If, by some deviant history, the self resists its assigned place, the community will press on it until it bends or is destroyed.

There remains only one fierce rival to the public assignment of

---

A Brief and Unfair Execration on the Novel

The novel is the art form of the totalizing and ultimately totalitarian community. The genre receives its English name because of its capacity to assimilate all dangerous encounters with novelty into the form's profound commitment to the ordinary. Like the state, it makes use of constant repetition and custom to habituate us to any horror. It is the mimesis of the community's power to subjugate all particulars, to assign them to their "proper place" and to a relative value within the context place: this is some absolute focus of attention, desire, and fear—infatuation or obsession. In such errant intensities the self slips its moorings within the habitual system and becomes concentrated upon some singular "one." The multiple relations that held it bound to a secure place dissolve and are exposed as mere wisps; the soul takes up an orbit around one fixed, unyielding point. This in itself is not poetry, but it is the region in which poetry takes place. In this region a compelling vision of the particular is discovered to be more important than the whole which includes it.

It was not for the lure of petty sexual transgression that the love lyric appeared in association with adultery in various cultures. Such a poem permits no claims on the self apart from the focus of attention and desire: the lover is socially "mad." [15] Like Archilochos, the lover threatens the integrity of social whole by calling to each individual, whispering to each to throw down his shield and follow the most outrageous desire, which is given body in the poem.

The concentration on the singular one is sustained by its stubborn resistance to the lover's regard, an opacity and imperviousness to which we gave the emblems of woman/stone and man/stone. The

---

of the whole. All exclusive engagement with a particular other, a particular thing, a particular relation is contextualized as "obsession." Even though the novel is fascinated by obsession, its business is to put it in its place. As Bakhtin says, the novel "dialogizes" and becomes a play of many voices; but in doing so the genre aims to subsume these voices, just as historicism subsumes the past. The novel demonstrates that there is no erupting threat to the system that cannot at last be made cozy and put in the "proper" perspective. Of course, what remains of an outside voice after the novel has devoured it is only a husk; something was squeezed out in the embrace of fictional solidarity. In that docile community of voices any claim to multiplicity is a lie.

What the novel can never subsume is poetry's very limitation, its one-sidedness. We keep turning to the poem; we cannot get through; there is something there that commands our attention, something that refuses to be swallowed up in a system of relations, origins, and consequences. The novelistic project is, by sheer continuation, the defeat of such rebellious attention: it wears the heart down. At its core every true novel is another *Aeneid,* lessoning us on submission to the necessity of the grand design; only the weak, like Dido, are so bound that they commit suicide. Each terror and each passion becomes mere episode.

lover demands what cannot be demanded: to be loved. And when the beloved resists, the lover feels wronged. "He was wronged; from this he deduces a claim to right and must at the same time reject it, for what he desires can only be given in freedom." [16] The lover cannot compel the beloved to freely return his love, yet he will not yield up the liberty of desire in face of mere impossibility—such foolish liberty having been exactly what was gained in breaking free of the community's enslaving perspectives. Impossibility produces metamorphosis, chains of conditions proposed and transformations of self to break through the barrier.

Infatuation suspends the laws that hold the communal self in place. Within this focus upon one there can be no true mutual definition (though such mutuality is always the hope; if fulfilled its bliss and silence would have no room for poetry). But the beloved is stone, fixed, does not change shape; the desire to transform the other meets resistance and recoils upon the lover, who then enters into a state of uncontrolled metamorphosis. Poetry plays with metamorphosis and the desperate attempt to find a form from which there can be contact with the beloved and mutual definition. The lover seeks to become

---

This execration is not directed merely to the novel in its more traditional form. However aberrant the total vision of a contemporary novel may be, however radical and experimental, the structural operations still serve the state in the same way, integrating and subsuming; such works are revolutionary on the model of the Khmer Rouge and the National Socialists, exulting in the raw power of the totalized community to compel any particular to participate in whatever horror the community declares to be its norm. (I exempt from my charges a handful of poet-novelists like Kafka and Robbe-Grillet, who understand the true aims of the genre, its forced conformity, and expose those aims, mocking the very possibility of perspective and integration achieved by novelistically "going on.")

Rebel against its work. Open a novel and read only one paragraph; read it many times; refuse to "go on." At some other time open it elsewhere and read another paragraph at random. Eventually you will understand that the paragraphs are more important than the whole, which wants to swallow them up and diminish them. By reading only those paragraphs you are violating a taboo about understanding the novel; you are taking something "out of context." Remember, it's only a book: you can read it as you please.

other, to inhabit the speculative shape of the beloved's desire. In this way attempts to exercise will upon another inevitably lead to a re-shaping of oneself.

There is no question that love (or, more properly, the desire to be loved) produces metamorphoses: people in love dress in strange clothes, their voices take on strange accents, and they make menda-cious claims about themselves as they try to become the person who they imagine might be loved. And they seem little disturbed at the consequences of winning love by such imposture.

The metamorph is trapped in the paradox of compelling the be-loved's free choice. This compulsion operates through imaginary vio-lence: violence against the self, or a speculative intrusion into the other, or a violence worked upon her. So Michelangelo intended to sculpt the beloved's heart, and Ronsard wanted to become an "invis-ible sprite" that would enter his lady's body, change her disposition toward him, then exit to become human again and accept the riches of her love, freely given. Such a world of errant affections is played out in *A Midsummer Night's Dream*, where metamorphosis and ex-ternal compulsion become uneasily entwined with the free election that should bring the only valid fulfillment of desire.

The impossibility of liberated desire finds its only recourse in words. There is a common motif in Renaissance poetry in which the poet declares his desire to be transformed into some other thing—an insect, an animal, a piece of clothing—in order to be received against his lady's flesh, to pass the barrier of indifferent stone and attain touch. Even in antiquity the lover might seek to penetrate the barrier around the beloved by becoming her thing:

> I would be a mirror
> so always you might look on me;
> I would be your shift
> so you would wear me always;
> I would like to be the water
> so I could wash your skin;
> woman, I'd be the myrrh
> to anoint you;
> and the band for your breast,
> and the pearl for your throat,
> and I would become a slipper
> if only you would step onto me.
>
> *Anacreonta*

Were the poet to achieve the proposed metamorphoses into slipper, shift, or stomacher, he would be sadly unable to offer commentary on the quality of his satisfaction. At other times the poet's proposed metamorphoses may be those of Ovid's gods and goddesses, wittily demeaning their godheads to reach some unapproachable man or woman desired.

> Je voudroy bien richement jaunissant
> En pluye d'or goute à goute descendre
> Dans le giron de ma belle Cassandre,
> Lors qu'en ses yeux le somne va glissant.
>
> Puis je voudrois en toreau blanchissant
> Me transformer pour sur mon dos la prendre,
> Quand en Avril par l'herbe la plus tendre
> Elle va fleur mille fleurs ravissant.
>
> Je voudroy bien pour alleger ma peine,
> Estre un Narcisse et elle une fontaine,
> Pour m'y plonger une nuict à sejour:
>
> Et si voudroy que ceste nuict encore
> Fust eternelle, et que jamais l'Aurore
> Pour m'esveiller ne r'allumast le jour.

> I dearly would wish to turn lushly yellow,
> to shower in drops of a golden rain
> into the lap of fair Cassandra
> as sleep softly slips into her eyes;
>
> would wish then to whiten and be transformed
> into bull to bear her away on back,
> as she through the tenderest April grass goes,
> flower that ravishes thousands of flowers.
>
> To lighten my pain I wish dearly
> to be a Narcissus, and her the pool,
> wherein to plunge myself to rest one night
>
> and further I'd wish that this night be
> forever, and that dawn would never
> waken me by its rekindling day.

Ronsard, First Book of Amours, 20

The woman is obstinate stone. Because she will not soften or freely change, the lover can will only his own metamorphoses. Such acts of will are empirically impotent; they can exist only in the words that declare desire.

At first her resistance provokes violence, an act of force against the beloved, a dream of taking her unawares and against her will, on the model of two ancient rapes perpetrated by Zeus. In the proposed metamorphoses the human becomes a union of contradictory extremes: the most powerful of gods and the subhuman. He would turn yellow and liquefy, taking his beloved in an impregnating golden rain, as Zeus took Danaë locked in her iron tower. Then he would become Zeus the bull, carrying off Europa on his back. Yet these violences are mere liberties of words. Neither is what he truly wants; each is superseded by some further fantastic change.

None of this is remarkable. What is remarkable is the inversion of the transformations, the exchange of places with the beloved (which was the secret premise of his earlier sonnet in which he sought to enter the beloved as "invisible sprite"). As he works on her with words she becomes self as well as other. At first we see the exchange of qualities: he will liquefy into a golden rain, but later Cassandra becomes the pool in which he drowns. And if he proposes ravishing Cassandra, she is already "ravishing" a thousand flowers, herself a flower to be ravished by a lover who becomes Narcissus, himself passing through death and transfiguration into flower.

These exchanges occur in the strange metamorphosis of the third wish—as in a good fairy tale, the third wish always brings ultimate bliss or destruction. It is a dark desire, suicidal, violence against other transposed into violence against self and, more strangely, a desire for other transposed into desire for self: Cassandra will be the mirroring pool into which he casts himself, taking the place of Narcissus, passionately in love with his own reflection. He dies into flower. We should not forget that Narcissus is doomed to this peculiar fate because of his own hardness of heart toward the nymph Echo, who was doomed to repeat every sound she heard, a mirror of sound. Lover and beloved exchange places in this liquid darkness in which no further mirroring can occur. He proposes to sleep forever in her dark water, as before he came to her in a golden shower at the moment when sleep was slipping into her eyes. Here there will be neither mirror nor self nor other—a hope signed with the ancient wish of the aubade, that dawn never come.

Yet the final metamorphosis and liquid merging, in which the whole surface of the body is touch, must remain forever imperfect. Memory survives in the flower by the water's margin, flower that can never be itself, but only a replacement. It will always be wept over, even in a lethean world of otherwise universal forgetfulness.

Straying through great forests, and under
unkind light, among the reeds and poppies,
whose heads nod with weight, among silent lakes
without wave-fall, shores without murmur,
whose banks fade in the hazy light,
flowers wept for, once names
of young men and kings.

Ausonius

Parable

Feelings too strong may seem instead
    like little feeling at all;
all I know is that here with our winecups
    no smile will come;
but the wax candle has a heart's core,
    and pities that we must part:
in place of the humans it sheds tears
    until the sky grows light.

Tu Mu, "Parting"

They sit through the night, blank face staring into blank face as the candle burns away. Each looks into the facing blankness, trying to read it. They are able neither to come together by exchanged expression nor to break off the intensity of the mutual gaze and go their separate ways.

On its surface the poem is a parable of metaphor. The human affections, pressed to a certain intensity, withdraw behind surfaces of concealment—opposites, indifference, false trails. Yet those concealing surfaces are never a perfect blankness; they carry some oblique evidence of what is withheld, perhaps a too strident gaiety or a declaration of passion made a bit too loudly, or, as here, lips quivering faintly toward a reassuring smile, then at once sinking back into a dull absence of expression.

It is not that our signs and surfaces do not tell the truth; it is simply that the language of their truth-telling is far finer than we commonly acknowledge. It encodes the precision, the motions, and the intensity of the affections through its particular acts of concealment. We all know how to read these, and we prove our mastery of such doubled signs by a corresponding concealment in our reports, a claim to have read only the surfaces. A shared language of concealment no longer conceals, yet still it is very different from some edenic language where truth lies on a surface without depth. It is true that we all hide together, but from whom?

The pressure that produces an act of concealment creates a counterpressure. What is repressed seems to reemerge externally in the world of things, a realm of surfaces where objects are what they claim to be. The candle is such a thing, and it receives the image of the concealed affections. In the doubleness of language human feelings, lost behind the wall of the face, make their way to the surface. The candle has a *hsin,* a "wick" which is also a "heart," that rises out of the encasing wax and shows itself, burning. It melts away what hides it and is itself at the same time consumed. It takes the place of the human beings, who sit hidden behind their faces, and it feels sympathy for them (is its sympathy with the pain of their coming separation or with the fact that they cannot show their pain?). In their place it softens, melts, and sheds waxen tears throughout the night.

This displacement of feeling into the substitute thing is given as an idea for reflection; it does not command belief. Displacement and replacement are exposed as poetic acts, acts of wit. They are explicit, on the surface, just as the opening line pretends to be explicit about what is concealed: "feelings too strong."

If we read the poem by its own rules of concealment, we recognize the oblique traces of something beneath its surface assurance. There is uncertainty in trying to read the blank face of the other, and anxiety about how the other is reading the poet's own blank face. These uncertainties are repressed by the need for mutual reassurance about the presence of a concealed depth of feeling. On this level too the candle receives the pressure of the concealed affections, not as a weeping face but as the ambiguous evidence of blocked desire and the stasis of their mutual uncertainty: its burning binds their mutual gaze "until the sky grows light." If the truth of feeling were communicated through their faces or lips, or if they found there was no feeling at all and went their ways, it could be extinguished, but it continues, consuming itself, as they try desperately, driven by an intensity of care, to read the face on the other side.

Epilogue

... when a particular art is complete, it produces a kind of another little art in a toy, which possesses a trace of everything in it.

Plotinus, *Ennead,* 3.8[17]

In the early days of the K'ai-yüan Reign (713–741), His Majesty Hsüan-tsung possessed a favorite horse named "Flowers of Jade." His Majesty desired to have this horse commemorated in a portrait, but none of his court painters ever managed to capture the true spirit of the creature. At last the emperor entrusted the task to the greatest of his artists, Ts'ao Pa. Many decades later in the far west the poet Tu Fu met Ts'ao Pa, now an old man drifting through the war-torn empire, his past achievements forgotten. Then Tu Fu recalled that unique moment when Ts'ao Pa painted "Flowers of Jade":

> Of his Late Majesty's horses-of-heaven
>   there was a dapple, Flowers of Jade.
> Painters massed like mountains around it;
>   no likeness was its match.
> On that day they led it forth
>   to the foot of the Crimson Stairs.
> It circled and stood by the palace gates;
>   steady winds blew from it.
> Royal command bade you, general,
>   to spread the white silk—
> Brooding art-thoughts struggled there,
>   between the plan and execution.
> It emerged in an instant—true dragon horse
>   from Heaven's nine tiers,
> Wiping aside, once and for all,
>   common horses of all time.
> This Flowers of Jade was hung there,
>   above the royal couch—
> The one by the couch, the one in the courtyard
>   each loftily faced the other.
> His Majesty smiled: he gave you gold,
>   as grooms and stableboys
> all stood there in despair.
>
> Tu Fu, from "Song of a Painting"

Like a photograph that steals the soul of its subject, the work of art can replace the living creature; it will take the name of the living horse and its place in His Majesty's affections. Everything centers on that moment when the living horse and the painted horse face one another, one hanging up by the royal couch and enjoying new favor, the other down in the courtyard. Two pairs of animate eyes seem to meet, both proud. Yet the scene is a lie. The art that seems so perfectly to mirror the creature's spirit, thus usurping the creature's place in the master's affections, has eyes that look but do not see; there is only the hard, unmoving surface, the toy. Encountering that mirror without depth, the living horse is finished, its vitality drained—as the despair of the grooms and stableboys shows. Where that vitality has gone is uncertain. Perhaps it has withdrawn into a third dimension of art behind the two-dimensional painting, giving force to the figure on the hard, ummoving surface; perhaps it is gone altogether.

> Duke Huan was reading in his hall. Wheelwright P'ien, who was cutting a wheel just outside the hall, put aside his hammer and chisel and went in. There he asked Duke Huan, "What do those books you are reading say?" The duke answered, "These are the words of the Sages." The wheelwright said, "Are the Sages still around?" And the duke answered, "They're dead." Then the wheelwright said, "Well, what you're reading then is no more than the dregs of the ancients." The duke: "When I, a prince, read, how is it that a wheelwright dares come and dispute with me? If you have an explanation, fine. If you don't have an explanation you die!" Then Wheelwright P'ien said, "I tend to look at it in terms of my own work: when you cut a wheel, if you go too slowly, it slides and doesn't stick fast; if you go too quickly, it jumps and doesn't go in. Neither too slowly nor too quickly—you achieve it in your hands, and those respond to the mind. I can't put it into words, but there is some fixed principle there. I can't teach it to my son, and my son can't get instruction in it from me. I've gone on this way for seventy years and have grown old in cutting wheels. The ancients have died and, along with them, that which cannot be transmitted. Therefore what you are reading is nothing more than the dregs of the ancients."
>
> Master Chuang Chou, "The Way of Heaven"

5 Nakedness/Fabric

Aphrodite responds to Hera's request for the means to charm hearts:

> Then from her breasts she removed
>   the finely figured sash,
> wherein had been worked
>   all manner of enchantments:
> passion was there, and desire,
>   and alluring, intimate words
> that steal away the wits
>   of even the wisest.
>
> This she put in Hera's hands and
>   addressing her by name:
> "Take then this figured sash,
>   with all fine things inworked;
> put it upon your chest, and I believe
>   that nothing unaccomplished
> will remain, whatever it is
>   you cherish most in heart."
>
> Iliad, XIV.214–221

Furthermore, there is in the art of poetry much that is sweet and formative for the soul of a young person, but no less is there that which may stir them up and lead them astray—unless in reading the young person happen to have the proper teacherly guidance . . .

> "passion is there, and desire,
>   and alluring, intimate words
> that will steal away the wits
>   of even the wisest."
>
> Plutarch, Moralia, "How a Young Person Should Attend to Poetry"

Three Antechambers of Unmindfulness

Of the first documented case of nakedness and its shocking consequences, along with the dangers and pleasures that attend unmindfulness.

> while *Adam* took no thought,
> Eating his fill, nor *Eve* to iterate
> Her former trespass fear'd, the more to soothe
> Him with her lov'd societie, that now
> As with new Wine intoxicated both
> They swim in mirth, and fansie that they feel
> Divinitie within them breeding wings
> Wherewith to scorn the Earth: but that false Fruit
> Farr other operation first displaid,
> Carnal desire enflaming, hee on *Eve*
> Began to cast lascivious Eyes, she him
> As wantonly repaid; in Lust they burne:
> Till *Adam* thus 'gan *Eve* to dalliance move.
>   *Eve,* now I see thou art exact of taste,
> And elegant, of Sapience no small part,
> Since to each meaning savour we apply,
> And Palate call judicious; I the praise
> Yield thee, so well this day thou hast purvey'd.
> Much pleasure we have lost, while we abstain'd
> From this delightful Fruit, nor known till now
> True relish, tasting; if such pleasure be
> In things to us forbidden, it might be wish'd,
> For this one Tree had bin forbidden ten.
> But come, so well refresh't, now let us play,
> As meet is, after such delicious Fare;
> For never did thy Beautie since the day
> I saw thee first and wedded thee, adorn'd
> With all perfections, so enflame my sense
> With ardor to enjoy thee, fairer now
> Than ever, bountie of this vertuous Tree.
>   So said he, and forebore not glance or toy
> Of amorous intent, well understood
> Of *Eve,* whose Eye darted contagious Fire.
> Her hand he seis'd, and to a shadie bank,
> Thick overhead with verdant roof imbower'd
> He led her nothing loath; Flours were the Couch,
> Pansies, and Violets, and Asphodel,
> And Hyacinth, Earths freshest softest lap.

> *Paradise Lost,* 9.1004–1041

The passage offers many delights, for its readers as well as for its protagonists. All Eden's dull bliss seems redeemed in this single moment of transgression. If the moral poet was compelled to darken that sweet moment with the history of its consequences, it is not altogether certain that such consequences, set in the balance, entirely outweigh the worth of the moment. Before this feast they had looked on one another with blind habitual eyes; now, for an instant, they have attained "lascivious Eyes." Love there had been before, but not this hungry gleam that will never again be fully sated by gentle companionship. The story insists that it was shame which afterward caused them to clothe over their nakedness; but this explanation is perhaps itself only covering to hide the naked truth—which is that the clothes were merely the paraphernalia with which to restage, again and again, the pleasure of this moment.

Already Adam, so reluctant before, is rushing ahead in his fancy to new and deliciously prohibited pleasures.

> if such pleasure be
> In things to us forbidden, it might be wish'd,
> For this one Tree had bin forbidden ten.

Adam has already grasped the essence of the future human social order: an abundance of tempting transgressions made possible by the sheer multiplication of prohibitions. "'Tis *amabilis insania, et mentis gratissumus error,* so pleasing, so delicious, that he cannot leave it." [1] And as Adam turns to praise Eve's "taste" and elegance, which is "of Sapience no small part," he invents the first language whose gracious compliment is mere covering for more bodily desires, its aim "Eve to dalliance move." The voice plays with compliments, then as if casually bares his purpose: "But come, so well refresh't, now let us play." The serious fruit, which had previously been so much the focus of their intent, is here treated as a mere preparatory refreshment for the pleasures of the main course.

Yet there is a small clause that adds an essential qualification to sin's delight:

> For never did thy Beautie since the day
> I saw thee first and wedded thee, adorn'd
> With all perfections, so enflame my sense
> with ardor to enjoy thee, fairer now
> Than ever, bountie of this vertuous Tree.

This sight of Eve's naked body is *not* the first seeing, but a reseeing or revision: the very first day he saw her was comparable to this moment, and this first trespass opens the possibility of return to origins—though "fairer now" because this return has been achieved by will's action and rebellious liberation from a timeless Eden of habitual blindness.

It should be observed that not until this moment of transgression could Adam truly remember how lovely Eve had first looked to him; he might have recalled the fact that she had looked particularly lovely when he first saw her, but only with the eating of the fruit and the first comparative recurrence was memory truly possible. This is the gift, the "bountie" of the tree.

The story was told over and over again in many versions and with many different actors: the emperor became infatuated with one woman, called by the kenning "she who overthrows states." She engrossed the emperor's attention, until the polity finally dissolved in the fierce focus of imperial desire. One version of the story recounts how the last emperor of the Northern Ch'i (ruled 570–576) became obsessed with the palace maid Hsiao-lien, "Little Love." Unable to remain far from her company, he abandoned his army at Tsin-yang, which, without his leadership, soon fell to the attacking forces of a rival kingdom, the Northern Chou.

The T'ang poet Li Shang-yin (813–858) epigrammatically recalled this sequence of events as a set of consequences so inevitable that they scarcely deserved narration. A history is concentrated in that single

Warning: To the Unwary Reader Who Might Mistake Me for a Milton Scholar

Of course I didn't tell you the whole story. But then, if you recall, I promised never to tell you the "whole story." Report has it that the rest of the tale is very different; and if Milton would ultimately have preferred avoiding any claim that "unfortunately the flesh is sad," still it would seem that, taken with excess relish, the flesh may have consequences that are indeed unfortunate. Although I do recommend the epic in all its parts, one scarcely needs to read the "whole story." The whole story will inevitably put this moment in its proper place, cast shadows on the feast, call its joys in the moment lust, remind us that clothes must at last be put on and that an excess of fruit leads to stomach problems, not to mention problems with authority. In short, I have given you the serpent's incomplete account. It is still a persuasive account and caught our ancestors' fancy once.

moment when the imperial eyes fixed upon her body; in her nakedness the thorns were already beginning to grow in the ruins of his
palaces.

> Overthrown by a single smile:
>   next, a state destroyed;
> why even bother to wait for the thorns,
>   only then sing the lament?
> That very night Little Love's bare body
>   lay stretched out before him,
> we had the news already: Chou's troops
>   had taken Tsin-yang.
>   "The Northern Ch'i"

In this tradition desire is no sin, but a terrible and dangerous error
of attention, a concentration on one body that distracts from good
management: it makes the person unmindful of those things on which
the community depends. It is a breach or lapse, a space of nakedness
that breaks the solidarity of the shield-line. The T'ang Emperor
Hsüan-tsung was said to have first used trickery in order to observe
Lady Yang at her bath; but he too became bound to that body rising
from water, ultimately bringing ruin on his empire and costing him
his throne. In one couplet the poet Po Chü-yi defined the danger of
Hsüan-tsung's passion:

> In the harem there were beauties,
>   three thousand there were in all;
> but the love that was due three thousand
>   was fixed on one body alone.

Compulsory polygamy was the attempt to control imperial passion
by a surfeit of bodies, to dilute the focus of desire with a flood of
flesh. It was a fragile solution.

Writing of Little Love and the Northern Ch'i emperor, Li Shang-
yin, like Milton, accepts his charge to speak as the historical moralist;
yet in one simple line he exposes the force of the event: That moment,
that night, that bared body.[2] As when Milton described feasting on
the fruit, here too poetry somehow compromises the ethical intent of
the narrative sources. The naked body focuses and engrosses attention; we realize what the poet wanted to tell us, that nothing now
could be done to oppose the intricate structure of disastrous consequences. But we also know what he could not help telling us: that, in

the presence of the body, those consequences are somehow no longer of paramount importance.

There was a time then the gods did not hold themselves apart from men.

> Dann feiern das Brautfest Menschen und Götter,
> Es feiern die Lebenden all,
> Und ausgeglichen
> Ist eine Weile das Schicksaal.

> They celebrated then the wedding feast, men and gods,
> all things living celebrated,
> and held there in balance
> was for a brief while fate.
>
> from Hölderlin, "The Rhine"

> Their custom was then, the heavenly ones,
> to visit, in all presence, unblemished homes
> of heroes and to show themselves
> in mortal meetings, then ere piety was scorned.
>
> from Catullus, 64

Such "mortal meetings," *mortalis coetus,* echo the sexual conjunction (*coetus*) which is the great purpose of this occasion, the coming to-gether of humans and gods for the wedding of Peleus and Thetis, the sea nymph. The showing forth of the gods can be likened to sexual display, the focus of awe and attraction; and the present wedding is the consequence of just such a display. Thetis, the immortal bride, had first revealed herself bare-breasted in the waves, surfacing with the other Nereids in order to observe the great ship *Argo* as it passed, setting off on its quest for the fleece of gold.

> As with prow-beak it furrowed windswept waters,
> and the waves, oar-spun, whitened with spume,
> from the sea's gleaming eddies emerged
> Nereids, who looked on the wonder with marvel.
> Then, if ever, eyes of mortal sailors saw
> Nymphs in the light, bodies naked to breasts,
> rising up from the gray oar-eddies.
> And at that moment Peleus, aroused, for Thetis
> conceived love.

Catullus tells the story of the nymph's exposure, the gods' assent to their mutual desire, and the happy union of man and immortal. He tells the story in the Greekish way, the Alexandrian fashion, densely wrought, allowing the tale to break open with spaces into which fine things may be inserted. But at the opening becomes a dark breach.

At Pharsalus the guests, humans and gods, gather for the wedding in Peleus' rich palace, where on the marriage bed is a *vestis,* a bed spread covered with embroidery. And in the embroidery is worked the figure of Ariadne, daughter of King Minos and sister to the Minotaur, Ariadne who saved Theseus from the labyrinth only to be deserted by him and left on the dark shore of Naxos. Figured in the bed spread, she stands on the shore, bare-breasted in the lapping waves.

Theseus is *immemor,* does not remember what he should, and his forgetfulness is fatally conjoined with fabric. He forgets, as all men do, his way out of the labyrinth, to be saved only by the "clew," the reminding thread supplied to him by Ariadne. And after leaving Ariadne on Naxos, he forgets to raise the white sail that will tell his father of his return alive from battle with the Minotaur; in his grief his father leaps from the rock to his death. Here, *immemor,* always unmindful, he forgets what he owes Ariadne, and her abandonment is figured in cloth, in the *vestis* on Peleus and Thetis' bed.

Within this fabric, on or under which man and immortal nymph will join in desire (*sese mortali ostendere coetu,* "to show herself in a mortal meeting"), is another showing, another nakedness, that of Ariadne on the shore:

> Not keeping the mesh tiara set on her blond head,
> nor leaving her chest, veiled in gossamer, covered,
> nor staying her milk-heavy breasts in their finely wrought sash:
> all these fell in turn from her body
> as at her feet the salt tides lapped.

What does the figured *vestis* tell the new bride Thetis, the nymph, as she comes to the wedding bed? Will she see her double here, the bare body emerging from the water, the focus of desire and then desire forgotten?—a caution, perhaps, of the limits of mortals who are *immemor,* losers of memory, unmindful. From the shore Ariadne speaks this warning:

> So long as a soul, desiring something, yearns fiercely
> for the attainment, it fears to swear nothing, nothing

reserved in its promises; but mind's hungry lust is
no sooner satisfied than it again fears nothing,
fears no consequence from what was said, has no care for oath-
  breaking.

The "lascivious Eyes" that flare with desire also grow forgetful and
sink back into the dull routine of Eden. Here is a lesson in fabric:
beneath the fabric is woman's body, Ariadne on the shore or Thetis in
the marriage bed, layer upon layer, the acts of covering and uncovering that are the work of mortal men who lie and love lies—not the
bare showing forth of the goddess. Peleus saw the nymph with naked
breasts emerging from water, showing herself as the immortals so
rarely do to mortal men. But Theseus was forgetful and blind (some
say this was Dionysius' doing) and did not see Ariadne's bare body
on the shore.

> From there, safe now and much to be praised, back
> he bent his pace, ruling his trail that would go astray
> by the fine filament, lest the building's indetectable
> straying frustrate his exit from the bends of the labyrinth.

Coda for Ariadne: Fig Leaves

There is a legend that after her desertion, Ariadne, cursing Theseus
from the shore, met Dionysios with his Bacchantes and joined them.
It may have been that in the distance she mistook Dionysios for Theseus returning, an error perhaps due to the particular focus of *her*
attention: Ariadne speaks:

> See Satyrs dance along
> In a confused Throng,
> Whiles Horns and Pipes rude noise
> Do mad their lusty Joyes,
> Roses his forehead Crown,
> And that recrowns the Flow'rs,
> Where he walks up and down
> He makes the desarts Bow'rs,
>   The Ivy, and the Grape
>   Hide, not adorn his Shape.
> And Green Leaves Cloath his waving Rod,
> 'Tis either *Theseus,* or some God.

>   from William Cartwright,
>   "Ariadne Deserted by Theseus"

A Second Coda, for Thetis

> Slim adolescence that a nymph has stripped,
> Peleus on Thetis stares.
> Her limbs are as delicate as an eyelid,
> Love has blinded him with tears;
> But Thetis' belly listens.
> Down the mountain's walls
> From where Pan's cavern is
> Intolerable music falls.
> Foul goat-herd, brutal arm appear,
> Belly, shoulder, bum,
> Flash fishlike; nymphs and satyrs
> Copulate in the foam.
>
> from Yeats, "News for the Delphic Oracle"[3]

Lessons in Fabric

> When a plan has sorted out the subject in the secret places of your mind, then let Poetry come to clothe your material with words. Inasmuch as she comes to serve, let her prepare herself to be apt for the service of her mistress; let her be on guard, lest either a head of touseled hair, or a body clothed with rags, or any minor details be displeasing.
>
> Geoffrey of Vinsauf, *The New Poetics* (ca. 1210)[4]

As poetry concerns itself with covering and uncovering, so poetry itself may seem to clothe some more fleshy substance, some body of naked intent. Garment is an old figure for poetry, and the figure is itself a drape, hiding what occurs in mind's "secret places." Vinsauf belonged to that party, now virtually extinct, that suspected that beneath all finery was a grimy and unappealing wench. The more perfectly groomed and covered her body, the better.

But fear of body's disappearance behind the clothes is more ancient still. Against such a fear the garment should contain spaces of its own undoing—folds that gape open, stays that are imperfectly tied. Body and body's impulses require "proof," as in these lines of instruction to a painter from the *Anacreonta:*

> let the rest of her garments
> hang with purple shawls,
> yet let a little flesh show
> through—body's proof.

Or, in the more familiar English transformation:

> A sweet disorder in the dress
> Kindles in clothes a wantonness;
> A lawn about the shoulders thrown
> Into a fine distraction,
> An erring lace, which here and there,
> Enthralls the crimson stomacher,
> A cuff neglectful, and thereby
> Ribands to flow confusedly,
> A winning wave, deserving note,
> In the tempestuous petticoat,
> A careless shoe-string, in whose tie
> I see a wild civility,
> Do more bewitch me than when art
> Is too precise in every part.
>
> Robert Herrick

Here is a well-groomed little poem, declaring grooming's perfection in the avoidance of perfection. Yet this gracious puff has somehow become a pedagogic set piece for reflecting on what a poem is, beyond the conceptual commonplaces of its paraphrase. That some centuries ago Robert Herrick found a certain degree of negligence in a woman's attire to be erotically stimulating is, quite frankly, not newsworthy. The observation that such stylized negligence has been a code of eroticism for virtually every well-clothed civilization can be communicated with greater economy and precision.

The poem restates a commonplace of fashion that was, by Herrick's time, already a commonplace of poetry. How then can we account for this poem's particular resilience? We suspect that, beneath the inertia of canon and anthology making, something of importance is being carried on here. Whatever that something might be, it is neither obvious nor so well hidden that it is lost entirely from view. Like a woman's body in clothing, it is something perpetually emergent, offering an equivocal lesson either of nature breaking free of restraint or of nature's outbreaks restrained.

For the aesthetic education in poetry, Herrick's small verse may be the counterpart of nude sculpture and painting in the visual arts. It is the perfect anthology piece, encouraging the reader to observe frill and form imperfectly concealing the body emergent. On the canvas of the painting, body in pigment covers cloth, which in turn covers nothing but a blank space on the common wall. But this body in poetry is covered by text and unraveling textile. Body and its twin coverings—art and fabric—need one another. Body needs clothing in order to appear (otherwise it would fade back into the unremarkable fauna of Eden); clothing without body is no longer clothing. If the arts of covering are "too precise," neither body nor clothes catches our attention.

This poetry of covering and uncovering tends to be imperative, hortatory, or at the very least, instructive. Male poets show a disconcerting propensity to instruct women on when and how to dress and undress, staging occasions of desire. We understand easily enough the compulsions that led Dr. Donne to legislate minutely his wife's disrobing; but an uncommanded bareness can be disturbing and may lead the poet to issue commands, however playful, to make the woman cover up. When the Neo-Latin poet Giovanni Pontano (1429–1503) speaks "To Hermione, to Cover up Her Breasts" (*Ad Hermionen, Ut Papillas Contegat*), her nakedness is displayed as much in the speculative act of covering as in the uncovering, and the call for decorum is still more lurid than Donne's order to strip. Ultimately, the poets want only the movement between clothing and nakedness—in either direction—movement between resistance and answering desire.

Even when such poems offer a report on general laws for instigating desire, as Herrick's poem does, they still bear the signature of the speaker's bodily intent. Yet Herrick's confident statement of desire's general law is set against the facts of the case: for desire tends to be stubbornly circumstantial and unanticipated; and although propitious conditions can be staged and desire can be invited, Eros makes his most fatal shots from ambush.

As Herrick gives us his precise physics of desire's causes, we understand that it is a commentary on the ancient controversy between nature and art, or between what lies within human control and what is compulsion. Nature and art are at issue here in the relation between body and clothing; but equally in question are desire and the control of desire *by means of* body and clothing. In every line of the poem we read conflicting claims of being in control and being out of control, and the contest is undecided.

If we try to locate Herrick's general law for the instigation of desire in relation to some hypothetical outbreak of the particular, we discover an array of possibilities, each of which sets a quite different relation between the poetic act and passion, art and nature. Suppose that the poem is a conclusion drawn from specific instances of desire that may have occurred in the silence that preceded the poem. This playful, witty voice, discovering the law that governs the battering particulars, has won a distance for itself: Yes, that's how it happened: it was a sweet disorder in the dress ... But let us suppose, on the contrary, that the poem is speculative fantasy, a longing for desire's eruption. The wit expresses pain inflicted by a world too perfectly dressed and a hunger for compulsion—for there is anxiety lest the body disappear altogether behind our civil decorum.[5] The voice in the poem claims to be open to enthrallment, yet its tone and carefully controlled procedures of exposition suggest a distance from which he is untouched and perhaps untouchable. We are unable to decide how to read that contradiction: a longing to be overcome by desire, nature's outbreak, or an attempt to win free of compulsion, nature's outbreaks restrained.

Or suppose that the poem's propositions are themselves a "too precise" art, an invitation to an Other and instructions on how to stage an occasion of desire. This final possibility is always present. The poem is educational; it directs young men where to look for suppressed evidence of womanly wildness, and at the same time instructs young women how to leave signatures of wildness at the edges of a surface of general control. The poem is, or wants to be, an example of a precise art of negligence, a well-placed hem where nature displays itself through the public surfaces that conceal it.

Here, perhaps, is the poem's work: the play with these dangerous forces, holding them in balance. The poet's voice maintains a fine equipoise between lust and witty distance. His tone tacitly claims that by understanding nature's workings he can go along with them without being carried away; yet his attention is too intensely drawn to the woman's body to be certain of his invulnerability. Neither able nor willing to belong wholly to either side in the contest, we invest ourselves in keeping both in play.

Strict sumptuary rules must be observed here. As Leo Spitzer nicely noted, Herrick's poem is no hymn to slovenliness; it requires general order to articulate and limit hints of emergent savagery. On the other hand, any attempt to repress nature altogether is not only unwelcome but also potentially self-deceiving, as wise men well knew:

But let not a man trust his victory over his nature, too far; for nature will lay buried a great time, and yet revive, upon the occasion or temptation.

Bacon, "Of Nature in Men"

For Nature will not be mocked. The prepossession against her can never be very lasting. Her decrees and instincts are powerful and her sentiments inbred. She has a strong part abroad, and as strong a one within ourselves; and when any slight is put upon her, she can soon turn the reproach and make large reprisals on the taste and judgment of her antagonists.

Anthony Cooper, Earl of Shaftesbury,
Characteristics of Men, Manners, Opinions, Times (1711)

Yet it is no less true, and perhaps far more disturbing, that we cannot simply *be* nature: Herrick proves incapable of declaring his utter enthrallment without an involuntary smirk and wink.

Equally unable to win free of nature or win back to nature, he dresses himself in words that are the exact counterpart of the woman's imagined attire. His carefully ordered exposition both names and matches the items of the wardrobe. Beginning with the overview and a general statement on the category of dress, he gives a blazon of the clothing (passing, as writers of blazons usually do, from top to bottom). But even as he itemizes, the systematic itinerary threatens to unravel: his eyes run to the margins of the clothing, looking for entrance.

Clothing is a shield-space and the poet maps it into parts in order to survey it for significant openings. It is on those margins that nature appears—the shoulder wraps, the stomacher (which covered the breasts), the cuffs, the petticoats appearing beneath the edge of the skirts, the shoestring—boundaries where clothing seems ready to pass over into flesh. It is a tidy rhetoric that skirts the edges of disorder, a witty play against hidden power: risk.

Every erring piece of clothing stimulates desire because it is evidence of something within, both the naked body of woman and the wildness in her heart. If we look attentively for imperfect suppression, all surfaces become signs of suppressed depths. This is no less true of the words of the poem. We are aware of the hunger behind the wit, nature allowed to appear by being covered and then discovered in bulges, hems, and tightness. The art becomes perfect in its imperfection, breaking down at the edges, seams pulling apart; at such moments it evokes nature that is both under control and out of control.

We love neither nature's innocence nor our fallenness, but the moment of the fruit. We love the contest—perhaps because in the contest both sides remain within our reach. This supreme art of imperfection has no allegiances to either nature or civil control: it will lend its force to either side in order to perpetuate indecision. Such an art of imperfection is always putting control and uncontrol at odds in words. It tells of a "fine distraction," offering evaluative and lacily precise judgment of a condition in which judgment breaks down. It insouciantly notes the stomacher pulled tight by laces "here and there," though the eyes are not drifting so casually as they seem to claim, but are rather drawn to the breasts, open places in the bulging cloth, and passage within. "Deserving note" / "tempestuous petticoat": the cool adjudication of merit, dispassionately calling attention to storms in satin. But most of all such an art is summed up in the oxymoronic "wild civility" embodied in the "tie," the binding up that is in danger of becoming undone, the "loose ends," the unraveling.

Coda

entrancing feelings stir with song,
her frail paces move with the wind:
a hairpin, hanging, falls as she dances,
sleeves in flight brush tresses toppling down.

Hsiao Kang (503–551), "The Dance"

The woman is soft, driven by nature's forces acting both outside her and from within. The formal art of the dance and its formal coiffure enact their own dissolution. Then in its own controlled and formal art the poem celebrates the victory of nature, or perhaps—there is indecision here—the dancer's artful performance of nature's victory, the slow building to frenzy and the final dishevelment.

There are reciprocal rhythms between the force of body and the force of art that conceals body. The artifice of song moves emotion, which in turn moves the body, a body in brightly colored clothing that seems to move with each gust like a falling flower. The intensification of motion disorders the dance and shakes loose the hairpin and the tresses of the tightly bound coiffure. Then the erotic intensity returns to the formal order of song and poem, with which the motion began. It is the celebration of some victory in the loving conflict between body and art—but we can never know to which side the victory belonged. If the great aristocrats of the Southern Court sigh with approval at this artful performance of passion, beneath it all is an impossible hunger to be the flower that dives into the spring wind.

Wasted Pain

When will it cease—this pain
   of gazing from heights and thoughts on distances?
Nothing dyes us so deeply as feeling:
there is the sadness at being apart, just now
   drawn out by a thousand tangled threads,
beyond which on the eastward path
willow catkins fly in their haze.
His mount neighs, going ever farther,
and in the unceasing dust of travelers in passage
where can I make out his prints?

On the pool duck and drake
   in the rippling waters
crossed north to south by a small skiff,
then after dusk the outer staircase rising
   diagonally up the painted tower
and once again the moonlight angled
   on curtain and window.
If deep in bitterness you think on it carefully:
better the blossoms of apricot and peach
that still know to run off with their lover,
   spring's east wind.

Chang Hsien (990–1078), lyrics to the melody
"A Clump of Flowers"

The Chinese art song was a late and stylized art. In it we often hear a weariness, a weariness with all the common things of both poetry and the world. After departing Eden's seasonless invariance, we enter a world of alternation and repetition, no less habitual than the routine of Eden but understood differently; we are now fully aware of being driven through these repetitive mechanisms. Worse still, within this world of recurrence, the writers of song lyrics found themselves repeating even the observation that the world and its poetry at last prove repetitive.

Almost a century before Chang Hsien's song, the emperor and songwriter Li Yü, the last of his line, had begun one of his most famous lyrics with such an observation on repetitive nature: "When will it be over—the flowers of spring, / moonlight in the fall?" Now Chang Hsien, in a line patterned exactly on his predecessor's, finds a similar repetitiousness in human responses: "When will it cease—this pain / of gazing from heights and thoughts on distances?"

Poets and lyricists like Chang Hsien had said it a thousand times before: that separations and other enduring dissatisfactions drive a person to climb high places and stare off into the distance. Perhaps because poets wrote so often of this gesture, poetry's readers, in their private depression and longing, would climb high places and stare; then, finding the observations of earlier poets confirmed in the general sensibility and behavior of their contemporaries, later poets continued to write of the same motions. If they felt uneasy at the repetition, they could vary the response in a hundred different ways: they might declare their refusal to climb up and gaze, or tell others not to do so; they might climb high places, look into the distance, and tell us they feel nothing but cold indifference; or they might even comment on how commonplace such climbing and gazing was. But every variation served only to reconfirm the normative act, until it seemed to have the status of some natural instinct in the human spirit, and the only thing remaining to say was "When will it cease?"—referring more to the depression and longing than to the stylized response. And that too came to be said again and again. Not only is nature repetitive, human situations and the emotions engaged by those situations are repetitive.

Oscar Wilde, mocking his contemporaries' tedious adulation of nature, proposed that art's inventiveness could redeem unimaginative nature. But a hundred years later we find his proposal reduced to art's lowest cliché; and we have discovered to our dismay that even novelty and the ideology of novelty can be wearisomely repetitive.

There is a general suspicion abroad that what is too familiar lacks force; while this may be true of novelty, it is unfortunately not true of human feeling. The most banal joys and miseries of the tribe are remarkably indifferent to our embarrassment at their banality. "Nothing dyes us so deeply as feeling." The word *nung*, translated as "dyes deeply," describes something strong and pervasive: the dark richness of a color, the strength of wine, the overpowering influence of a passion. The conventional persona of Chang Hsien's song, a woman longing for an absent man, not only claims to experience the feeling but is also aware of experiencing it and weary of it: there remains some undyed thread in the fabric of the heart from which she can offer comment on both the passion's commonness and its tiresome force.

Such art songs are small dramas of emotion, and yet the emotion dramatized is not the passion, in this case the love-longing that is the ostensible subject of the song. Rather the drama and the emotion lie in the more complex relation between the passion itself and that small space of self-awareness, undyed by the purity of the passion. The song does not speak of the passion but of her weariness of it, poetically and personally, and the peculiar fact that her weariness at being pressed through the banal mechanisms of desire in no way diminishes desire's force. Most of all, she is weary of her own weariness.

The emotion in play in this drama is a strong one, but it is a secondary, reflexive emotion, one of those errant companions of all powerful feeling. Such reflexive emotions follow from an awareness that one is, involuntarily, "within" the primary passion. These secondary emotions are called forth by emotion; they are no pale reflection of the primary, but so amplified that they often overwhelm the primary. And these perhaps are the only true sentiments of the self-conscious creatures that we are. From their strength we can infer the might of the primary passion, but we can never quite touch it. Take, for example, love for someone who gives no evidence of returning it: the lover may be furious at his or her inability to escape the attraction; or embarrassed at the foolishness of his or her behavior; or angry at the beloved for causing such pain; or perhaps, eventually, just weary to death of unsatisfied desire. We are creatures who never know the taste, only the savor.

These secondary, reflexive emotions are consequent to our consciousness of forces within the self and acting on the self over which we have no real control. We have only strategies: an attitude adopted or behavior willed whose result, through some tangential momentum in the collision of voluntary decision and the compulsion of passion, is never what was intended. Complicated variations of the reflexive emotions surround all primary passions, and although we understand them quite clearly, such understanding is not the knowledge that liberates. This was God's great joke on our ancestors, the gardeners; the fruit merely mounted understanding on an animal body and forced it to go along for the ride.

In the art song the primary passion is often lucid and invariant; the secondary, reflexive emotions are more elusive and shift in erratic orbits around the primary. We cannot observe and locate them with precision because we ride in their orbit. In Chang Hsien's song the momentum of the reflexive emotions is not longing but a weary exasperation, as body and heart are driven through the same old motions, all too familiar in the human psyche and in earlier song. The voice does not cry out from passion's force; it talks about the passion, as the passion turns the head, fixes the eyes, and walks the body. The voice is dismayed and offers the comparative judgment that passion's influence is "deepest" of all.

The old machine of poetic correspondences grinds into operation: the woman notes things in the outer world that are supposed to reflect and instigate feeling, tangles of insect floss and willow catkins inducing in their human counterpart the "tangled skeins" of emotion. Chang Hsien's female speaker checks off each of the expected items as the body paces her familiar rounds. The particular correspondences and gestures are strange to us now, the stylization of an age long ago and a different continent; but the reflexive emotions are still our own.

In his famous essay on the marionette theater the German Romantic Heinrich von Kleist praised the perfection of the puppet's movement in its unselfconsciousness; opposed to this he noted the subtle awkwardness of the human being, who is forever the observer of his own motions. However, there was a possibility that Kleist did not consider: that the puppet might be fully self-conscious, able to observe but utterly impotent to disrupt the perfection of its own dangling motions.

The way in which the singer's particular feelings and acts are absorbed into repetitive norm is further repeated in the very scenes she encounters, where everything that is individual seems to disappear into collective repetition:

> His mount neighs, going ever farther,
> and in the unceasing dust of travelers in passage
> where can I make out his prints?

The traveler disappears into the dust of all travelers; his tracks are lost in all tracks.

> "How should I know your true love,
>   That have met many a one
> As I came from the holy land,
>   That have come, that have gone?"

Incompletion and absence reduce both the passion and its object to mere categories; the reflexive emotions are generated in the space of resistance between the particular case and the anonymous category.

She is a Penelope, trapped in the performance of a rite of art, weaving and unweaving the same section of the tapestry: she plays the "garden scene," where insect floss and paired waterbirds stir longing; then she plays the "night scene," lying awake in her chamber watching the moonlight and wondering if the beloved is lying awake thinking of her. "And once again the moonlight angled on curtain and window": she is as regular in her performance of this scene as the moon in its cycles, and as regular as countless other lovers in songs before. "And once again": she knows this and is sick of it.

Until the final lines the woman simply reenacts the Chinese repertoire of love-longing—but in quotation marks, sung with a growing tension of resistance, a resistance we can share, despite the lack of resonance for us in the gestures and objects to which the resistance is attached. The world of repetition is given only so that we can learn to hate it in our bones, to breed that resistance which will produce a vision of escape; we will dream the destruction of all repetitions:

> If deep in bitterness you think on it carefully:
> better the blossoms of apricot and peach
> that still know to run off with their lover,
>   spring's east wind.

After playing the commonplace scenes of longing, the voice, recognizing her own bitterness, invokes an edenic moment as a lost possibility: "if . . . you think on it carefully," you will see what a weary waste this is; better to burn out like a flower in spring. The fallen world of repetition produces the reflexive emotions, and the reflexive emotions strain to accomplish their own destruction—to break free of knowing one's own impotence in passion and to *become* the passion, to cast off the watching rider in the heart. Such desire to annihilate self-consciousness well understands its self-destructiveness: the act would carry us past the margin of our humanity, to become not half nature's thing but entirely nature's thing. It would be a moment without future, liberated from the extended time of repetition—an instant of death, freedom, and sexual union.

Yet this desire to end time can occur only from within time. We can never forget the position from which she speaks, and the bitter vehemence of her vision comes from its impossibility. There is a space between the desire to leap and the leap itself; that space makes even this a reflexive emotion, as repetitious as the kingdom of repetition it longs to finally overthrow. For behind this final desire—to burn out like a flower—lies a lineage of earlier poems, going back to Li Ho (790–816), who wrote of flowers that "run off with their lover, spring's wind, without an engagement."[6] Here too the meaningless destruction of the flower becomes a free act of self-destruction in passion.

The dancer's motions whirl faster and faster until the sleeves brush the tightly bound tresses and they topple down. We cannot decide whether this was body breaking free of art or art's controlled choreography of the body's liberation. But even if it is only a staged outbreak, we still know what forces made it of interest (or pretended disinterest) in art, witnessed by our tense appreciation. And again we cannot decide whether those forces have somehow mastered the staging or have been mastered in the staging.

Undressing

The fig leaf, then, was a far greater manifestation of reason than that shown in the earlier stage of development. For the one shows merely a power to choose the extent to which to serve impulse; but the other—rendering an inclination more inward and constant by removing its object from the senses—already reflects consciousness of a certain degree of mastery of reason over impulse. *Refusal* was the feat which brought about the passage from merely sensual to spiritual attractions, from mere animal desire gradually to love, and along with this from the feeling of the merely agreeable to a taste for beauty, at first only for beauty in man but at length for beauty in nature as well.

Immanuel Kant, "Conjectural Beginning of Human History"[7]

For whatever is composed is under a veil . . . is poetry and poetry alone.

Boccaccio, *De Genealogia Deorum*, 14

May God let me live so long
as to have my hands under her robe.

Guillem, Comte de Peitau (1071–1127),
Canso, "From the Fresh
Season's Sweetness"

In poetry, clothing and the promise of nakedness are conjoined, nakedness appearing in the bulges and contours or at the margins and through the folds, or in dishevelments and stylish disrobings. This promised nakedness can claim to be anything to which we attach value: with a flourish it tells us that it is Meaning, or just a thought, or the concealed animal body, or the secrets of the heart; sometimes it was Other, sometimes self, sometimes we really couldn't tell which. If we are so foolish as to hasten the unwrapping, we will always be disappointed—whatever it was we hoped to find. The thing unwrapped is cruelly overlooked, or covered over again. Each of us is *immemor*, unmindful of and loser of memory for what was once desired. We had not wanted to face this, that the intensity of the lure was in the form of disclosure; whatever value there is in the simple edenic nakedness, it is paler than our expectations and quite otherwise from what we had dreamed. Yet the pleasure we anticipated had required faith that we wanted the thing itself and not merely the unwrapping. Without such faith the unwrapping is meaningless. It is a conundrum. Fortunately our hope and our desire for pleasure is such that we can always be taken by the lure just one more time, which is the business of poetry and all great art. All the while unwrapped things are left to gather dust on the shelves of our houses and in our hearts.

> but she had a passion for absent things—
>   a feeling that moves many—
> there is, among human beings, a most foolish kind who,
> ashamed of what lies close at hand, gaze into distances,
> seeking wind-born things in hopes never to be fulfilled.
>
>   Pindar, Pythian ode 3, 19–24

The "foolish kind" she represents may be the only kind.

Poetry tries to bring us back to the moment of eating the fruit: the end of the eager uncovering, after which there will be forgetfulness and re-covering. It is hard to hold us there; poetry stands between two forms of time, edenic invariance and the repetitiousness of our fallen world. Dull Eden offers only a bareness that is as invisible as the body too perfectly covered. On the other side, the final danger is the disappearance of the body and its poetry into the sumptuous vestment itself, a vestment that has forgotten that its purpose is to hide, thus allowing us to forget the body beneath. Here poetry dies into art-thing: clothes that can be stolen and worn by anyone.

> I made my song a coat
> Covered with embroideries

Out of old mythologies
From heel to throat.
But fools caught it,
Wore it in the world's eyes
As though they'd wrought it.
Song, let them take it,
For there's more enterprise
In walking naked.

Yeats, "A Coat"[8]

Yeats was a poet who always spoke of disclosing what was concealed, promising to lift the veil and show us what lay hidden at the
heart of things. At first he tried to display the beauty that he hoped
to find directly in the surface texture of the poem—not realizing that
such figured clothing could be stripped from the body and hung upon
a stick, its promise of disclosure fading into complacent design.

And now we see how much it mattered to him, how essential it was
that the poetic vestment be recognized as his and that his be the body
within. This was something he had never admitted before, perhaps
never fully understood, as he made promises to expose the "heart of
things." But if we had listened carefully to that earlier poetry, we
would have noticed a strenuous poise in his mastery over each of his
poetic masks. Now, when we go back, we can recognize the strain.

He tells us: "I made my song a coat." He wants us now to know
(suspecting that we had previously misunderstood) that he knew
what he was about when he made those poems, that he was in control, that he had not used those "old mythologies" in his earlier books
of poetry because he knew no other song; the design of his coat of
song had been of his own choosing and his own making. More important, he wants us to recognize precisely what that art was—a
coat—and what we were supposed to find within it—him.

Perhaps we had mistakenly believed that those lovely songs had no
"inside," that they were only art for beauty's sake—the pure object
of the embroiderer's craft, an embroidery to hang on a wall, a surface
to admire. He reminds us forcefully now that he was both the master
craftsman as well as what lay inside the masterwork of craft. He
made it and wore it for display, so that he would be seen, admired,
desired.

"From heel to throat"—he adds this line to complete the rhyme,
but such formal necessities often draw from poets something they had

held in reserve, something crucial that is more than they had intended to say. In fact, he knows quite well why we hadn't noticed him in that clothing coat: it covered him too perfectly. No body was visible, except the mouth that lay above the throat and beyond the boundaries of the garment, the mouth outside the body "inside," the mouth that wove the first song-coat and that now weaves the self-proclaimed emperor's new clothes of his nakedness.

> But fools caught it,
> Wore it in the world's eyes
> As though they'd wrought it.

For those of us who now listen he stakes his claim of ownership quite explicitly and calls what occurred a theft. We hear, even more clearly, what he had wanted his song to be: something from him and for him, a possession imprinted with his mastery over it. He intended it to be a possession of an unusual kind, one which would point unmistakably to him while keeping him concealed. But unfortunately it was shown to be a mere thing, without copyright, something that could be disjoined from the master's naked self. And because it was merely "art," it was a commodity that could be stolen. He has discovered that when someone else put on this same art, he, the art's maker, was in it no longer. He has noticed his body's absence; others have not.

He piles scorn on those others: "fools," he calls them, and "the world." They are the other poets and their audiences who saw only the embroidery and not what was inside—or perhaps saw all too clearly that such an art could belong to anyone. Years ago he used to tell us that he cared only about beauty, in its most general and universal sense; and indeed such beauty should be the common possession of anyone who knows where to find it. Wounded now by seeing his original garment worn in copies, he discovers that such universal beauty had not been his intention at all. He displayed those beautiful things of his own making only so that we would look at him.

He intimidates us with his scorn. We fervently hope that he does not include us among the fools in that grossly undifferentiated world. He pretends he was not addressing us at all:

> Song, let them take it,
> For there's more enterprise
> In walking naked.

Hurt by the crowd's misprision, he dresses himself in a mask of pride; he pretends not to notice us listening and addresses instead the "song." But we know that it is only his wounded pride that makes him turn away, as we know that this song, which he both delivers and addresses, tacitly invites us to separate ourselves from both the fools and the world. He and his song invite us to be among the select few who see him for what he is. There is no mistaking the intimacy of this invitation: to behold him naked. Somehow he has transformed an act of literary brigandage—being stripped of his garments—into a courageous act of disclosure and disrobing, with all the sexual overtones that accompany this call to be "known."

We acknowledge his success, not in going naked (which has a place in words only as a promise) but in finding a new garment of words that more perfectly shows the contours of the body within. No, we do not confuse person and pose; there is no such thing as a pose, only a complicated act of posing that is the motion of desire, wounds, anxieties. If others misunderstand, he will move and pose again, pointing to the previous shape he has left hanging empty in the air. Such active posing exposes in the very act of attempting to cover over; and here it is at its most complex, a posing lie of nakedness that still discloses nakedness. He dresses himself in a garment of pride that pretends not to notice that he is seen, and he drives us away with his scorn, knowing that his dismissive gesture of expulsion will draw us back to look. He is not naked; it is only a claim, but the claim is a flimsy garment that reveals the intensity of his desire to be known and seen behind this new coat of song.

Perfect nakedness in words is either false claim, illusory remembrance, or invitation. Nakedness is silence; although poetry, in its dissatisfaction, may yearn violently for silence, it cannot attain it. However gossamer that barrier, it is an absolute one. Were the barrier to be removed, the beloved would be both attained and lost, disappearing from sight and hearing into the strangely "perfect" (completed) sense of touch, in which touching of the other can never be separated from being oneself touched. There is no danger of such perfection in poetry: "the frantic abolition of all distances brings no nearness."⁹; and each furious vector discovers an obstruction or countermotion of equal strength.

> Off with those clothes, sweet, lie close
> with naked body twined with naked body:

let nothing lie between—even
the sheerest gauze you wear
seems to me
Wall of Babylon;
chest to chest, lips to lips: all else in silence
hidden. I hate
the unstopped tongue.

Paulos (sixth century), *Greek Anthology,* V. 252

It is a fine piece of late Greek wit: Paulos decorously refuses to report to others the perfection of touch; yet his decorum is attained not by any inner reserve but by a meeting of lips that imposes silence on both the lover and the beloved. As long as even the sheerest textile remains, the tongue is unstopped and the poem can continue, proclaiming desire and longing for its own termination.

He doesn't mean it. It is only a verse game. And we know that even if—and it is hard to imagine—this sophisticated late Greek were to have recited his epigram to some learned girl, the consequence would not have been passionate stripping, but a smile at his cleverness. The poem postpones and deflects passionate engagement rather than leaping to union.

Poetry's physics has its precise equations, which may prove to be the same equations that govern desire in the human heart: all declared momentum is held in stasis by an equal and opposite momentum somewhere else in the poem. Such stasis is no quiet point of stillness. It is a plane (as covering fabric is a plane) that trembles, bulges, and splits with the opposing powers held in balance. All movement of approach is held back by a movement apart, all movement apart is countermanded by desperate invitation. Yeats speaks in pride and scorn, yets begs us to look and love; Paulos invites us back to Eden, while corrupting Eden with a knowing smile.

He sees the beloved; in order to gaze at her he must hide his gazing from her. Then the beloved discovers his desire. She becomes aware of the eyes looking at her; he can no longer conceal his gaze. Now she veils herself.

Lassare il velo per sole o per ombra,
Donna, non vi vid'io
poi che in me conosceste il gran desio
ch'ogni altra voglia d'entr' al cor mi sgombra.

Mentr' io portava i be' pensier celati
ch'ànno la mente desiando morta,

vidivi di pietate ornare il volto;
ma poi ch'Amor di me vi fece accorta,
fuor i biondi capelli allor velati
et l'amoroso sguardo in sé raccolto.

    Quel ch'i' più desiava in voi m'è tolto,
sì mi governa il velo
che per mia morte et al caldo et al gielo
de' be' vostr'occhi il dolce lume adombra.

Your veil set aside, in sunlight or in shade,
I have not, Lady, seen you so
since you have learned my great desire
that empties all other wants from my heart.

So long as I bore these dear thoughts hidden—
and death they brought to mind in its desire—
I saw your face decked out with kindness;
but once love made you aware of me,
your blond tresses were henceforth veiled
and your loving gaze, withdrawn to itself.

    That which I most desired in you is taken from me,
so does that veil master me
to work my death, in weather warm and cold,
shadowing sweet light of your lovely eyes.

Petrarch, Rime, 11

The beauty of Petrarch's poetry is the purity with which it writes desire's most basic laws. The poem reveals the laws of looking and covering over; if such poetic revelation pragmatically entered into the human relation, it might tip the balance and break passion's stalemate. But the poet preserves stasis by passionately addressing the beloved and at the same time never intending that the poem be read by her.

He cannot cross that plane of veiling fabric to touch the beloved, but he can at least imagine the possibility of the poem entering the relation, changing it. He imagines weaving a fabric of words whose workings would mirror her incendiary veiling; she would look and be set ablaze. If this could be achieved, the pain of his blocked desire would also become her pain. Like Michelangelo's speculative sculpture of the beloved's heart, such a poem would be the artwork that compels desire in the other. We cannot be certain what would occur at such a moment, when her passion suddenly mirrored his own. Perhaps like Narcissus he would leap through the mirror's permeable surface into union and liquid perfection of touch. Or perhaps the physics of countermotion would remain in effect: looking and suddenly seeing a face that looks back with desire, Narcissus would draw away, leaving the reflection of passionate eyes indelibly trapped in the pool's surface, denied the sight of *their* beloved as just retribution for his pain. Or perhaps, most strangely, both will remain in mutual gazing, unable to touch, an oblique union in an identity of suffering:

Se'l pensier che mi strugge
com'è pungente et saldo
così vestisse d'un color conforme,
    forse tal m'arde et fugge
ch'avria parte del caldo
et desteriasi Amor là dov' or dorme;
    men solitaire l'orme
foran de' miei pie' lassi
per campagne et per colli,
men gli occhi ad ogn' or molli,
ardendo lei che come un ghiaccio stassi
et non lascia in me dramma
che non sia foco et fiamma.

    Però ch'Amor mi sforza
et di saver mi spoglia,
parlo in rime aspre et di dolcezza ignude . . .

If the thoughts that consume me—
so stinging they are and fixed—
were dressed in just the right colors,
perhaps the one who burns me and flees
would feel some share of this heat,
and love would wake where now it sleeps;
less lonely then would be
the tracks of my feet, weary with passage
through meadows and over hills,
and the eyes less constantly wet,
setting her ablaze who stands like ice,
yet leaves not a drop in me
that is not fire and flame.

    But Love's compulsion
strips me bare of skill,
and I speak in harsh verses,
    naked of sweetness . . .

Petrarch, *Rime,* 125

His thoughts overcome him with fire; if only he could dress them in just the right fabric of words, the beloved too would be set ablaze. It is a fantasy that bears no promise of peace, only release from loneliness in the sharing of pain. However, it is only speculative fantasy: his words are made harsh by his blocked desire, and they are not under the control that could dress them in compelling colors. Passion both motivates the fantasy of powerful words and makes its fulfillment impossible: he is trapped in reflexive emotions, anger and frustration. The art always "runs counter to the desired intent."

Let us tell the story of fabric another way. The beloved is Penelope, the chaste wife, who manages to remain decently clothed by continually weaving and unweaving fabric, holding the embroidered tale and the suitors in stasis. The fabric she weaves and unweaves is Laertes' winding sheet (his "funeral weed"). Its completion would be old love's termination and the admission of Odysseus' death—for he is a "traveling man" and "a lonely bed can't be kept empty for long."

> All she made hope, and promis'd ev'ry man,
> Sent for us ever, left love's show in nought,
> But in her heart conceal'd another thought.
> Besides, as curious in her craft, her loom
> She with a web charg'd, hard to overcome,
> And thus bespake us: "Youths, that seek my bed,
> Since my divine spouse rests among the dead,
> Hold on your suits but till I end, at most,
> This funeral weed, lest what is done be lost.
> Besides, I purpose, that when th'austere fate
> Of bitter death shall take into his state
> Laertes the heroë, it shall deck
> His royal corse, since I should suffer check
> In ill report of ev'ry common dame,
> If one so rich should show in death his shame."
> This speech she us'd; and this did soon persuade
> Our gentle minds. But this a work she made
> So hugely long, undoing still in night,
> By torches, all she did by day's broad light,
> That three years her deceit div'd past our view,
> And made us think that all she feign'd was true.

Odyssey, II.143–163 (trans. Chapman)

Penelope accomplishes her desires by both weaving and unweaving; but there are other weavers. The suitors, a rough Homeric lot who complain of her feigning, become courtly seducers in the Renaissance, hiding their desires under fine clothes and fine phrases: "taffeta words and silken terms precise," Berowne calls them in *Love's Labor's Lost*. Fabric not only covers—a poetic "suit" by which the lover can press his "suit"—but in its more gossamer and meshy forms, flesh-revealing, it is a net or web in which hearts become entangled, able neither to advance nor to withdraw.

> Penelope, for her Ulisses sake,
>> Deviz'd a Web her wooers to deceave;
>> In which the work that she all day did make,
>> The same at night she did againe unreave:
>
> Such subtill craft my Damzell both conceave,
>> Th'importune suit of my desire to shonne:
>> For all that I in many days do weave,
>> In one short houre I find by her undonne.
>
> So, when I thinke to end what I begonne,
>> I must begin and never bring to end:
>> For with one looke she spils that I long sponne;
>> And with one word my whole years work doth rend.
>
> Such labour like the Spyders web I fynd,
>> Whose fruitless work is broken with least wynd.
>
>> Spenser, *Amoretti*, 23, "How His Beloved Undoes
>> His Work as Penelope"

Acting "for her Ulisses sake," her word is a sudden gust that blows apart the spider's web of his suit. He figures himself as the would-be adulterer, vainly attempting to occupy an empty place and understanding the frailty of the net he weaves. These are no "strong toils of grace," like those with which Cleopatra took Anthony, but gossamer insect floss. He is the artist, one of those failed Pygmalions of this later age, trapped in the performance of his art and trapped in repetition: Penelope, the great unweaver, retains her power by never allowing him to complete the "suit," a perfection of art that would compel her desire.

Words and Glances

> Das Wort ist ein Fächer! Zwischen den Stäben
> Blicken ein Paar schöne Augen hervor.
> Der Fächer ist nur ein lieblicher Flor,

Er verdeckt mir zwar das Gesicht,
Aber das Mädchen verbirgt er nicht,
Weil das Schönste was sie besitzt,
Das Auge, mir ins Auge blitzt.

The word's a fan—between whose ribs
outward peers a pair of lovely eyes.
The fan's just a pretty spray of flowers
that does indeed cover the face;
but it doesn't hide the girl beneath,
since her loveliest part, the eye,
flashes in mine.

Goethe, from "Sign," *East-West Divan*

hee on *Eve*
Began to cast lascivious Eyes, she him
As wantonly repaid . . .

Paradise Lost

The covering has many names (or we confer on many things the honor of serving as covering): it is the word, which is in turn the fan, stage prop of ambiguous motives—desire feigning shyness, shyness hiding in the appearance of coyness. Then the fan becomes a "spray of flowers" (*Flor*), a bunch of leaves and blossoms that is an edenic fig leaf for the face. Someone else is there behind it, covered over; leaf and flower, or veiling fabric, or text intervenes. Then, in a gap, there is an eye, only an eye. This is the moment between our fallen world and Eden, the single point that holds the two worlds apart and creates an absolute division between them by reminding us of their difference: nakedness and concealment. This point that articulates both worlds is at the same time our only hope of crossing the border.

He may have been the voyeur, looking through the gap in the fabric and hoping to discover flesh. All of a sudden the person looking finds that he is seen in return. Eye meets mirroring eye, and there is a movement to mutual drowning, like Narcissus in the pool that is both self and beloved. Or both cover over again; her eye retreats behind the fabric of the fan; he looks away. No matter which choice was made— mutual drowning or deflection—the seeing lasted only a moment; afterward, darkness.

There is an old claim that poetry restores Eden to us (and when Goethe speaks of the "word," he means the poetic word, a *Beiname*, "assumed name," which like the fan reveals the beloved's eye through concealment). This perhaps means that in poetry we have that moment of recognition and desire—a moment not in itself uncomplicated by the fallen world, but still a realized vision of what such an escape from complication might be. Like a gracious and forgiving divinity, the poet stages for us such encounters with revisited Eden, as in the famous passage from Sidney's *Defence of Poesy:*

> Neither let it be deemed too saucy a comparison to balance the highest point of man's wit with the efficacy of nature; but rather give right honour to the heavenly Maker of that maker, who having made man to His own likeness, set him beyond and over all the works of that second nature: which in nothing he showeth so much as in poetry, when with the force of a divine breath he bringeth things forth surpassing her doings—with no small arguments to the credulous of that first accursed fall of Adam, since our erected wit maketh us know what perfection is, and yet our infected will keepeth us from reaching unto it.

But the meeting of eyes, which is the moment of exit from and return to the garden, must occur "through" the text, which is a veil. It is that we find most difficult to accept—the necessity of mediation, the intervention of text, garment, or interval. The text itself always tells us such sweet stories of the veil's removal and the finally satisfying unwrapping. The eyes look up from their reading and meet. This was always our dearest wish—to burn out like a flower. But strangely, we can encounter it only *in* a text, as when Francesca speaks in *Inferno:*

> Noi leggiavamo un giorno per diletto
>   di Lancialotto come amor lo strinse;
>   soli eravamo e sanza alcun sospetto.
> Per più fiate li occhi ci sospinse
>   quella lettura, e scolorocci il viso;
>   ma solo un punto fu quel chi ci vinse.
> Quando leggemmo il disiate riso
>   esser basciato da cotanto amante,
>   questi, che mai da me non fia diviso,
> la bocca mi basciò tutto tremante.
>   Galeotto fu'l libro e chi lo scrisse:
>   quel giorno più non vi leggemmo avante.
>
> We were reading one day for our pleasure
>   of Lancelot under love's compulsion;
>   alone we were and with no suspicion.

But many a time the reading forced our eyes
  to meet, our faces colored,
    yet in only one moment were we overcome
when we read how that yearned-for smile
  was kissed by such a lover,
    this man, who may never be parted from me
kissed my mouth so trembling.
  Galeotto was the book and the writer:
  we read no more that day.

Inferno, 5.127–138

Each of us, singly, keeps reading and learns how they, a long time ago and in another country, stopped reading. The eye meets ours for a moment, then goes on, covering over.[10] The fruit may be eaten, even shared, but something intervenes, veil and text, a note left for the beloved on the refrigerator:

This is Just to Say

I have eaten
the plums
that were in
the icebox

and which
you were probably
saving
for breakfast

Forgive me
they were delicious
so sweet
and so cold

  William Carlos Williams[11]

Adam has come first and eaten all the fruit. The pleasure that might have been shared is denied her, yet communicated through the text. She can almost taste his tasting—but only almost, flesh appearing through the words. The poem is an address, but an address of the strangest kind: the words are an apology but they also flaunt the pleasure denied her; they are a mediated substitute for that pleasure. And we, who glance at the note in passing as we previously listened at Dr. Donne's bedroom door, have a speculative experience of absent plums.

There are pits in the garden, signs that the beloved was here and now is gone; messages are left—communication but never meeting. We always try to draw closer, more veils are always removed, but the flesh is never reached—only an eye looking back: "All high poetry is infinite; it is as the first acorn, which contained all oaks potentially. Veil after veil may be undrawn, and the inmost naked beauty of the meaning never exposed." (Shelley, *Defence of Poetry*).

We can never quite reenact this moment in the myth of Eden (as Paolo and Francesca did—texts often tease us with the possibility). We try again and again, but fumble somewhere, somehow miss the ending. Each attempt must begin with eating the fruit, or at very least the desire and intention to eat.[12] Like Tantalus we are hungry enough to keep trying. Do not believe you can simply sit back and look at it: the apples of the still life painting are a reminder of hunger, not form. One must reach in order to undergo the inevitable failure that makes the ensuing contemplative distance a beautiful lie. "A poem should be palpable and mute / As a globed fruit," MacLeish tells us.[13] But you must attempt to taste. The poem may be as illegible in the fingers as an "old medallion," but it must be caressed.

> Y es como el que halla en un libro
> borradas algunas letras
> que per sólo estar borradas
> le de más gana de leerlas.

> And it's like, in a book, chancing on
> certain words scratched out—
> and simply because they are scratched out
> one has all the more hunger to read them.
>
> Calderón, "Hard to Watch over a
> House with Two Doors"

The moralists who have always buzzed around poetry were quite correct; in their hearts they heard the Sirens singing them to shipwreck. The promised pleasures are raw ones, though always failed, mediated, never quite consummated.

Fruit

> Knife of northern steel like water,
> salt from the southland, whiter than snow:

slender fingers rip apart a fresh orange.
Now warmth grows by the draped brocades,
from a beast-shaped censer smoke rises unbroken:
she sits, facing him, playing the flute.

And in a low voice asks where he'll spend the night:
"Night's drums have beaten on city walls;
it's slippery for horses, the frost is heavy—
best make your mind up not to go—
hardly anyone's out on the roads now."

Chou Pang-yen (1056–1121),
lyrics to the melody "Youth's Roving"

It is given to us as a possibility: sitting face to face, desiring and looking into eyes filled with desire. For both the man and the woman desire is held back, veiled, uneasy about the appearance of desire. Neither can quite come to the point of speaking that desire, yet the desire leaks out into things, vectors of attention, actions, evasive words.

We know that the song is directed to a man, if only because out of the tense silence as they face each other, the woman is compelled to initiate contact, to speak the words. Her words are veiled, but only in gossamer, a low voice marking her hesitancy. She reveals her own want hidden behind her concern for him—the inconvenience of returning now, the chill of the night, the slipperiness of the roads. Her concern has the transparency of Rilke's solicitude toward God. She does what poems do: sketches an outside world to reveal one within. In the same way the "interior" scene of the song is the outer surface of the human heart.

They had been melting toward this moment, the veiled invitation to stay. The room seemed to get warmer, the scent heavier, the flute music more intoxicating, as they sat face-to-face. Desire, stirred, is always hard to speak. The question is always whether the other is looking back with answering desire, if the two pairs of eyes will catch one another. He discovers the returning look peering through the veiled language of practical concerns. That evidence is the discovery of another human being: not mere surfaces, but surfaces and depths.

The fruit initiates the process. Even though we do not eat our oranges with salt, and even though China had no garden of Eden by which to scripturalize the eating of fruit, the act is not lost in the translation. History does not matter here. There is the coolness of the steel knife, the figures of water and snow, juices on fingers and lips, inviting amid the heaviness of the room's odor and warmth. The steel glints as the eyes glint, and the steel's light is water, just as a woman's look of desire in Chinese "ripples from the eyes." It is dark outside; within the room the smoke of incense hangs heavy; but at the center is a flash of light, white salt. There is a tearing open, an unpeeling, with odor and the anticipation of sweetness, then the music of the flute. Each primary sense is called to in turn, deferring only touch, which is postponed into the silence after the poem.

The orange is no aesthetic object, however much it focuses and restricts the attention as an aesthetic object should. Desire, concentrated and withheld, leaks out into gesture; it leaks out through the hands that surround and frame the "thing." The thing, fruit, is filled and ready to be opened. Its tough surface is gashed, and the knife cuts away to the shape within, like a sculptor discovering the naked body hidden in a block of marble. The hidden shape, slowly discovered to the senses, is both the consequence and the displacement of desire: it is Pygmalion's statue, meant to be consumed.

There is the thing and a work of opening carried out upon it—a cutting and apparent mutilation of a hard surface. It requires a breaking of barriers and of safe covering. This thing and her hands working upon it stand between them, drawing their attention and deferring the meeting of their bodies. But perhaps it is the only ground upon which they can meet—fruit and poetic word. It is a separate, clearly defined space through which hearts, held in stasis by equal measure of attraction and fear, can pass.

Epilogues

Epilogue I (False Exit): The Blazon of Mutilation

We entered the museum that day, and following our guidebooks, went down along the long rows of connecting chambers, examining the objects of art contained there. We were exhausted by bodies, the bare shapes of gods and goddesses given up for our passing scrutiny. We had been told that there were lessons for us here, and we sought to find in them some secret order that comprehended their differences, some museum order. We looked closely, comparing shape with shape, and we read all the inscriptions appended. As we gathered around each pedestal, we felt ourselves safe in our first person plural: our attention converged and our eyes focused on the thing. We were voyeurs who saw without being seen. And then, through the broken places of the stone, the god looked back.

> Wir kannten nicht sein unerhörtes Haupt,
> darin die Augenäpfel reiften. Aber
> sein Torso glüht noch wie ein Kandelaber,
> in dem sein Schauen, nur zurückgeschraubt,
>
> sich hält und glänzt. Sonst könnte nicht der Bug
> der Brust nicht blenden, und im leisen Drehen
> der Lenden könnte nicht ein Lächeln gehen
> zu jener Mitte, die die Zeugung trug.
>
> Sonst stünde dieser Stein entstellt und kurz
> unter der Schultern durchsichtigem Sturz
> und flimmerte nicht so wie Raubtierfelle;
>
> und bräche nicht aus allen seinen Rändern
> aus wie ein Stern: denn da ist keine Stelle,
> die dich nicht sieht. Du musst dein Leben ändern.
>
> We did not know his head, a thing unheard of,
> in which the eye-fruits ripened. But
> his torso still glows like candelabra
> in which his gaze, just forced back,

withholds itself and gleams. Otherwise breast's bow
could not have blinded you, and in the hips' gentle
turn, no smile could have gone
to their center which once held generation.

Otherwise this stone would stand defaced
and short beneath the shoulders' transparent plunge,
not gleaming like pelt of beast of prey,

nor bursting out from all its margins
like a star: so that there is no place
that does not see you. You must change your life.

Rainer Maria Rilke, "Torso of an Archaic Apollo"

The poem begins its account by displacing the event into the past, the tense of a report: "We did not know his head." And yet we had not noticed its absence when we first came into that hall and turned our gaze upon the famous body of the god. We had not noticed because we had all seen sculpted torsos before, both those simplifying mutilations worked by time and art's willful imitations of such inevitable simplicity. Long habit had made such absences invisible to us. Realization that the head was missing came only later, in our shock at the gaze impossibly returned. And to see all those broken places and absences was already a gift of sorts, an uncomfortable blessing from the god.

In the poetic report we restore the missing parts by naming them: the head and most of all the eyes that somehow still see, not mere absent shapes of stone but "eye-apples" (Augenäpfel, "eyeballs"). Those eyes were fruits that once grew to ripeness, Eden's apples that made possible both true seeing and "knowing." Such apples had not been eaten by us, who could look on the statue's nakedness and not see; it seemed such eyes were no longer offered to us, having been consumed by simplifying habit and time, *edax rerum,* "devourer of things."

The wonder was, of course, how once the eye-apples had been eaten the whole face underwent a metamorphosis and withdrew into the remaining body, which gazes and blinds with that gaze and smiles. Perhaps the smile is an erotic one, whose center is the god's broken loins—something else which, being missing, withdraws its force into what remains. But in the mutilated contraction of the body's margins, there is also a concentration that bursts upon the unexpecting spectators, dissolving the communal safety of the first person plural and making each of us a "you" before the god.

Let us imagine how it must have been for him, the god, gazing out from his pedestal and trying to address such a blank audience, that first person plural who looked but did not see, who listened but did not hear. Now he looks into the crowd, focuses his attention on one, and says "you." Suddenly the relation is changed, not just for the person singled out but for the others as well, realizing at that moment that their own protective anonymity is lost. No one is ever so entirely a "you" as at such a moment, trapped in a crowd by an act of address that cannot be escaped.

We had all been standing around this lump of stone, secure in our museum habits and aesthetic distances, taking notes on the period style and commenting on the torso's primitive vigor. Suddenly the god looked out and said: "You! I mean *you!*" That's how it must have felt in the Garden, just after eating the fruit and finding oneself torn from the background fauna by the look of the beloved or the god: "You!" Eye-apples eaten, broken loins.

This is not the poem. The goddess never softens stone to life any more, as she once did for Pygmalion; and the god does not look out from poems. Some layer always veils the work of art from Eden's body. The poem can only name what is missing. We can never know whether the poem is flinching from such a gaze or whether it is longing for the gaze's discomforting force, but we do know that the poem does not come into being under such a gaze, nor does it reveal the gaze to us: it is only a road sign that points the way and reports an impossible distance. In detailing every point where the mutilation does not matter, the poet reminds us that the thing is indeed broken; he reminds us of the distance between here and there. It is this mirror of mutilation in the artwork of words, gradually withdrawing from the encounter, which permits him to substitute the present for the past tense in the poem. What had been at first shock and surprise now becomes reassurance, a comfort in the possibility that the god can indeed see you.

Finally the poet gives us a moral, as if to tell us that the encounter had been only a fable for our nurture and education (*trophe*): "You must change your life." This will serve us as an inscription [for] the torso's pedestal in the museum. This too is reassurance—that we have a place to stand from which we can freely receive the god's instruction, and that if we accept the command there is something into which we *can* indeed change. The inscription is the true poetic figure, the consequence of our flinching and withdrawal from the gaze; it is not the god's imperative but our own, words to control the power of such a gaze. We are addressed, perhaps even changed, but not changed in the way the god seemed to command. We are changed in unrecognizable ways quite beyond our control, turning our backs now and driven deeper into the labyrinth of the museum.

Epilogue II (No Exit): Rules to Prevent Our Escape

> On and through the trajectory of rationality, mankind becomes aware through art of what rationality has erased from memory.
>
> Adorno, Aesthetic Theory[1]

> Thus our present age is not propitious in its general conditions for art. Even the practising artist is not simply led astray and contaminated by the loud voice of reflective thought all around him, as well as by general trends in opinion about and judgment of art, led astray to bring more thought into his own work. Rather, the whole of spiritual culture is such that he himself stands within such a reflective world and within its relations, and could not in any way abstract himself from it through will or decision, nor could he devise and bring back for himself a unique isolation, one that would restore what has been lost, either by a unique process of nurture or by a distancing from the relations of life.
>
> Hegel, Lectures on Aesthetics

With these words Hegel forecloses the greatest hope and promise of art and places his seal on history: it is a closed process. Within the sprawling Hegelian system, art is the mode through which Spirit takes on sensuous embodiment; it belongs to a particular phase in the history of Spirit, a phase whose time has passed, inevitably to be replaced by self-conscious, reflective thought. Hegel insists that reflective thought makes its appearance in modern art because the artist is radically a part of this age in which the essence of art is rapidly being supplanted.[2] The blind mechanism of history corrupts the modern artist's work and vitiates it, despite the artist's best intent. There is no escape: there are only broken statues and figures on a crumbling wall that have no third dimension beyond their surfaces.

The particular phases of Hegel's historical order are perhaps less significant than the assumption that becomes unusually explicit in the passage above. It is an assumption, central to Hegel's thought, that has become one of the least-questioned commonplaces of our modern world. We are radically "of" our historical place and moment; we inhabit it and are, in all significant ways, determined by it. Any attempt, such as the artist's, to be elsewhere or otherwise is doomed and futile. Hegel's version of history is the archetype of totalitarian society, in which the individual is constituted by his determinate relations within the total system. It is a powerful assumption, but what force led him to state it so baldly and explicitly here?

There is another question. Is Hegel's point about the modern artist simply one case of the general principle of our radical "historicity," or is there some unique connection between the general principle and this particular case—a connection so uncertain that it compels the philosopher to the strident, redundant, and detailed denial of the possibility of retrograde motion on the part of the arts? Hegel is keenly aware that this is precisely what the artist might attempt to do, to "devise and bring back for himself a unique isolation, one that would restore what has been lost." The possibility is mocked and the attempt proscribed. But the way in which Hegel phrases this impossibility echoes, perhaps unwittingly, a long history in which the artist laid claim to just such a solitude: to be neither of the community nor against it, but somehow separate from it.

The retrograde impulse that Hegel attributes to the artist, the desire to restore what has been lost, seems to follow inevitably from Hegel's description of the situation of art, living on attenuated in a world that has left it behind, a world driven toward reflective self-consciousness. In Hegel's system all the progressive forces of spirit prohibit such retrograde motion. And yet, "playing now before we undertake to be serious," we can raise the possibility that the particular case does not follow from the system, but rather that the whole system is constituted as a response to this particular case—that is, the system which asserts that art must ultimately be supplanted by reflective thought might be a construction made precisely in order to close off the possibility of retrograde motion through art. It is an extravagant hypothesis, but it is only play. We propose that the putative impulse to retrograde motion in art is constituted simultaneously with the system that prohibits it. Art is not an old mode of manifesting spirit that is surpassed by reflective philosophical thought; rather, it has always been mutually constitutive with philosophy and always embodies the particular impulses or desires that philosophy wants to suppress. The concept of historical dialectic becomes an ingenious invention to destroy the dark twin, to displace him into the past and tell him he is obsolete, dead and still dying. But, in fact, art's claim to isolation (from present relations) comes into being with the idea of historical determination; art's retrograde impulses are inextricable from the idea of progress. Art's claim to stand apart (or at the very least, the passionate desire to stand apart that is manifest in art) is a gap in the totalizing impulses of philosophy and a totalitarian culture. It must be jailed in the museum and enclosed within a frame.

Hegel recognizes exactly where the danger lies: he senses that art wants to restore what has been lost. Art attends to losses and, in doing so, makes a silent critique of the present and the present's momentum. Hegel knows that art's retrograde is an insidious rebellion, not the mere palliative force that Nietzsche describes it as:

> Art incidentally performs the task of preserving, even touching up extinct, faded ideas; when it accomplishes this task it weaves a band around various eras, and causes their spirits to return. Only a semblance of life, as over graves, or the return of dead loved ones in dreams, results from this, of course, but for moments at least, the old feeling revives and the heart beats to an otherwise forgotten rhythm. Because art has this general benefit, one must excuse the artist himself if he does not stand in the front ranks of mankind's progressive *maturation*. He has remained his whole life a child, and has stood still at the point where his artistic drive came upon him; but feelings from the first stages of life are admittedly closer to feelings of earlier eras than to those of the present century. His unwitting task becomes the juvenescence of mankind: this is his glory and his limitation.[3]

Like Plato, Nietzsche is torn between awe and contempt for this power of art, yet even less than Plato can he explain why there should be such allure in it.

Then let us play on and suppose that only in the retrograde motion of modern art is dialectical movement really possible. The desire implicit in art's recognition of losses, the desire that Hegel tries to block and thereby bring history to a standstill of perfection, is the mark of an encounter with what is other. The pseudodialectic (that is, the common notion of dialectic) by which we project into the future—our utopias, social plans, and operations of "self-consciousness"—is only a thinly disguised extrapolation from the determinate present. Under the disguise of hope and free will our projections surrender to our determinacy, in a melancholy fatalism that has supplanted tragedy. Truly dialectical movement can be possible only in the encounter with a realized otherness, a substantial and unsubsumed elsewhere; we may discover these in other people, other cultures, and other times, but we cannot produce them out of our own mind and out of our own self-conscious present. If we use the example of the past as our paradigm (since the historically retrograde impulse of art caused Hegel the greatest anxiety), we freely admit that the past we encounter is radically mediated by our determinate present; but in saying that, we admit that there is something equally determinate and other that is mediated, something we may try to interpret away that stubbornly refuses to be completely subsumed.

In warring with that retrograde impulse by system and scorn, Hegel is attempting to quell powerful stirrings of rebellion. Were such retrograde motion possible, it would be possible in some small way to stand "elsewhere," to be engaged with something outside of our historically determined relations. Such a possibility would shatter the determinative and totalizing power of history and all the repressive social forces that justify themselves through a claim to historical necessity. Art's desire for isolation is a threat to collective control because, as Hegel well knew, such solitudes would be available to all. If one person can successfully refuse Hegel's version of history, before you know it whole populations will go drifting through the cracks, discovering "what has been lost," and returning to the historical present with dangerous dissatisfactions and desires.

The most forceful aspect of Hegel's critique of the possibility of art's escape from the determining historical present is what became the modern commonplace: the notion that each of us and all parts of our world are determined by a system of "living relations" (*Lebensverhältnisse*), and that we have no place to stand outside that totality. Society and the received structures of our thought are totalized in an immense ecology. Unlike smaller social ecologies, such as the family or group, in which each individual member shapes the whole as well as being shaped by it, this totalized ecology of the historical present is of such a magnitude that it determines the individual without itself being perceptibly determined by the individual. Nor can a totalized historical present entirely be separated from the totalitarian aspects of the modern state, in which all the small groupings of human life are broken, undermined, and devalued to reinforce the impotence of the individual in any social relation. It is Kafka's world, in which the individual rises through layers upon layers of the ecology, seeking a place where power and influence are exercised, only to find that power lies still a few levels higher or has been diffused into some unreachable space.

This notion that we are a determined part of a system of relations without ourselves determining the system becomes collectively true by our being collectively persuaded that it is true. It is not a demonstrable condition of our being but a hermeneutic, a richly elaborated structure of interpretation by which everything that is disparate can be shown to be merely deviant or irrelevant.

Art remains a threat to that persuasion; it is ostensibly safe because it offers only a shadow, as Nietzsche says, of some alternative empowerment, but it remains a disturbing symptom of unsuppressed resistance and illegitimate desire, something that refuses to be subsumed into its interpretations. Art can catch us up in relations as alive as all the living relations of the historical present, alive and more alluring because art aims for our seduction, not our subjugation.

Any empirical opposition to repressive power is empirically successful to the degree that it assumes repressive and totalizing power in its own right: the cure feeds the disease and perpetuates it. Art renounces power and efficacious control. In doing so it occupies a peculiar position, in complicity with a repressive society while at the same time offering the only true resistance to it. The paradox of that truth is troubling only in a world of repressive totalization.

Hegel saw clearly that the threat lay precisely in modern art's retrograde impulses, which offer a different interpretation of history. By raising the possibility of going back, or refusing to go on, or going elsewhere (and art can raise these only as possibilities), art creates an idea of history that works not by replacement and supersession, or even by cyclicality, but by a blind aggregation without reconciliation; it is the chaos that opens at some point in every structure of order. Art cannot deny temporality—if it did there would be no possibility of otherness and hence no desire—but instead of abolishing and erasing the past, art includes the past in the present as an acknowledged loss, and hence as possibility.

Coda: Going Elsewhere

Tan-fu the great King was dwelling in Pin when the Ti tribes attacked. He offered them tribute of skins and cloth, but they wouldn't accept it; then he offered tribute of dogs and horses, but they wouldn't accept it; he offered them pearls and jade, but they still wouldn't accept: for what they wanted was his land. Then Tan-fu the great king said: I could not bear to dwell among elder brothers whose younger brothers I had sent to death, or to dwell among fathers whose sons I had sent to death. You my people endeavor to continue living here—what's the difference between being my subject and a subject of the Ti? Besides, I have heard it said that one should not destroy that which one nurtures for the sake of the means by which one nurtures it. And then he left, leaning on his staff. His people all followed him in a long line, and a new state was established below Mount Ch'i.

Master Chuang Chou, "Renouncing the Throne"

NOTES

CREDITS

INDEX

Notes

1. Seduction/Invitation

1. From the literal translation of Ruth P. M. Lehmann, trans. and ed., *Early Irish Verse* (Austin: University of Texas Press, 1982), pp. 65–66.
2. Following a venerable Chinese practice of rewriting old poems for new melodies, this poem is translated more or less to the tune of "The Hollywood Waltz": the idioms are remarkably similar. The Chinese *tang-tzu* is quite literally a "traveling man," but also the figurative "traveling man" of country music.
3. In the Chinese way, once this poem grew "old," it could have been easily transferred to some analogical situation, such as a retainer disappointed with his old lord and seeking a new one.
4. John Keats, "Time's Sea Hath Been Five Years at Its Slow Ebb."
5. Translated by Stephen Kessler, from Lewis Hyde, ed., *A Longing for the Light: Selected Poems of Vicente Aleixandre* (New York: Harper and Row, 1979), pp. 66–69.
6. Cedric Whitman, trans., *Fifteen Odes of Horace* (Cambridge, Mass., privately printed, 1980).
7. See by way of comparison and contrast Pablo Neruda, "*Pequeña America,*" in *Los versos del Capitán.*
8. Friedrich Nietzsche, *The Gay Science,* trans. Walter Kaufman (New York: Vintage, 1974), p. 215.
9. Jacques Lacan, "The Function of Language in Psychoanalysis," in *The Language of the Self,* trans. Anthony Wilden (New York: Dell, 1968), p. 9.

2. Interlude: Pastourelle

1. For a fuller comparison of Chinese and Western *pastourelle,* see Jean-Pierre Diény, *Pastourelles et magnarelles: Essai sur un thème littéraire chinoise* (Geneva, 1977).
2. Frederick Goldin, *Lyrics of the Troubadours and Trouvères: An Anthology and a History* (New York: Doubleday, 1973), pp. 150–153.

3. Woman/Stone, Man/Stone

1. Even in impalpable thought we distinguish between what has rigor and is hard, or what is soft and perhaps too tenderhearted. It is a hard world out there; and in the hard sciences, as opposed to the soft disciplines of the humanities, points must be made (a fencing metaphor, *touché*, "touched") rigorously, avoiding soft thinking and mushy arguments. In wartime there are lines which the enemy tries to penetrate, and the guerrilla war, without hard boundaries, becomes a quagmire that sucks a nation in. And to avoid dissolution we must beware of being soft on threatening ideologies.

2. These myths of metamorphosis between human and stone are abetted by a Greek pun, the delight of poets, made by mixing declensions of *laas*, "stone" and *laos*, "the people," who softened from the stones that Pyrrha and Deucalion cast behind them.

3. So Goethe writes in the "Roman Elegies":

   Do I not educate myself, as I reconnoitre shapes
     of my lover's breast, guide my hand down her hips?
   Then I first understand marble well: I think, I compare,
     I see with tactile eyes, touch with seeing hand.

4. As John Marston rewrote the myth, the animated woman was little more than a collection of lusty body parts, the "agents" of a desire that mirrored Pygmalion's own: "Then arms, eyes, hands, tong, lips, & wanton thigh, / Were willing agents in Loves luxurie" ("The Metamorphosis of Pigmalions Image," stanza 37). When George Bernard Shaw reformulated the myth, allowing the discovery of a human being behind the cultural "artwork," the myth instantly became ironic.

5. Even that fierce revisionist of the taboos, Adorno, at moments understood the lure: "Perhaps the most important taboo in art is the one that prohibits an animal-like attitude toward the object, say, a desire to devour it or otherwise subjugate it to one's body. Now the strength of such a taboo is matched by the strength of the repressed urge. Hence, all art contains in itself a negative moment from which it tries to get away . . . Indeed, there is much to be said for the thesis that the dignity of works of art depends on the magnitude of the interest from which they were wrested." T. W. Adorno, *Aesthetic Theory*, trans. C. Lenhardt (London: Routledge and Kegan Paul, 1984), p. 16. The only question, I suppose, is the decision as to which is the "negative moment"? "Dignity" is a dubious virtue, the sole ornament of despair. Its rigidity permits no indulgence, not even in the pain of its self-denial.

   Aesthetic distancing is not the only possible negation of desire in the experience of art. The doubleness of approach and recoil can be inscribed within the poem itself: desire acknowledged, then destroyed on the hard

point of mockery, as in Hsiao Kang's (503–551) "Song to 'Crows Come
to Roost,'" observing the painting of a lovely woman on a screen:

> There was fashioned a folding screen,
>> whose hinges were of silver:
> the red lips, alabaster face
>> emerged in lamplight;
> as I look, the breath comes hard,
>> gazing on my desire—
> but who could be so hesitant, so shy
>> as not to come forward?

It is a desired surface without depth, illusion known as illusion. And yet
the breath comes hard, even as he mocks his own desire and impotence,
unable to animate the painting's cold coyness. In the love game, too, one
must arrive from behind hard surfaces; games that require two players
become ironic when played solitaire.

6. Stephen Mitchell, ed. and trans., *The Selected Poetry of Rainer Maria
   Rilke* (New York: Random House, 1984), pp. 48–53.
7. *Pensées,* Lafuma 529; Brunschwicg 105.

4. Replacement

1. This is essentially the myth of the naive in Schiller's *Naive and Sentimental Poetry.* Here, for example, is the way Schiller describes the operation
   of language in the naive mode: "It is a manner of expression of the sort
   in which the sign disappears entirely into what is signified and in which
   language leaves the thoughts it expresses still bare, so that one cannot
   represent them any other way without simultaneously concealing them;
   it is this mode of writing that is generally called one of genius and replete
   with spirit." As Schiller well knew, the fitness of everything in the naive
   mode humiliates (*beschämt*) our artfulness and makes us feel uncomfortable. Against this feeling of inferiority, some new superiority must be
   discovered in the latecomer, some virtue in the very struggle by which
   place is held. Such free struggle becomes the strength of the sentimental.
   In fact, Schiller's position is the metamorphosis of an old religious trope,
   by which the very absence of divine signs in this late age of the world
   becomes our glory, our ability to have faith as a private achievement
   without external confirmation. Thus Lancelot Andrewes, writing in the
   nativity sermon of Christmas 1622, expounds the Wise Men's vision of
   the star, and concludes:

   > We cannot say, *Vidimus stellam:* The starre is gone long since; Not
   > (now) to be seene. Yet (I hope) for all that, that *Venimus adorare,*
   > we be come hither to worship. It will be the more acceptable, if not
   > seeing it, we worship (though). It is enough, we read of it in the

Text; we see it, there. And indeed (as I said); It skills not for the starre in the firmament, if the same Day-star be risen in our hearts, that was in theirs; and the same beames of it to be seene, all five. For then, we have our part in it, no lesse; nay, full out as much as they.

2. And later, even with the unmarried man addressing the unmarried woman, the love lyric called for a passion, often a sexual relation, specifically outside of socially legitimate matrimony.

3. *Horn of Oberon: Jean Paul Richter's School for Aesthetics*, trans. Margaret R. Hale (Detroit: Wayne State University Press, 1973), p. 29.

4. Friedrich Nietzsche, *Human, All Too Human*, trans. Marion Faber (Lincoln: University of Nebraska Press, 1984), p. 20.

5. Some commentators say that his flower will be the flower of Ronsard's arms, the flowering stalks of blackberry, *ronce*, burning, *ard*. Recall once again that other metamorphosis of a complexion made pallid into a surface of art. Michelangelo: "If it is so, that in hard stone / one likens every other's image to oneself, / ashen and often pale I make it, / just as I am made by her. / And thus I ever take model from me, / intending it be she."

6. Lost arms again: one might add that in the process of Odysseus' traveling the arms of Achilles were lost, and made their own "homecoming" to where they rightfully belonged, as Ronsard told in a translation of a Greek epigram (*Gayetez, Traduction de quelques autres epigrammes grecs*, 10):

> When Ulysses was hanging tossed by the waves,
> to its watery bosom the tempest received
> the Pelean shield, broad, weighty, big,
> and ill-fitting the arm of coward Laertides,
> for which Ajax, self-murderer, by his own hand died.
> But the seas that keep with more justice the laws
> than the Atreides and the rest of the Greeks,
> cast up from its breakers Achilles' shield
> on Ajax's tomb, not on the coast of Ithaca.

7. "Suleika" is the cover name for Marianne von Willemer, Goethe's beloved, who contributed some of the "Suleika" poems.

8. It was early recognized that Goethe's "universality" lay in his capacity to swallow up all historical difference within himself. Friedrich Schlegel, "Dialogue on Poetry":

> Nevertheless there was here preserved at least one tradition, that one must return to antiquity and to nature, and this spark took flame among the Germans after they had gradually worked through their prior models. Winckelmann taught the consideration of antiquity as a whole and provided the first example of how an art should be

founded on the history of its formation. Goethe's universality casts a soft reflection of the poetry of virtually all nations and periods: an inexhaustible and exemplary series of works, studies, sketches, fragments, and experiments in every genre and in different forms . . . The translation of poets and the recreation of their rhythms has become an art, while criticism has become a form of knowledge that has obliterated old errors and opened new points of view in the understanding of antiquity, against the background of which a perfect history of poetry appears.

Nothing is wanting but for the Germans to carry these means further, that they follow the model that Goethe has set before them and to pursue all the forms of art back to their source, in order to be able bring them back to life or combine them anew.

9. Goethe's version of the East ironically and unwittingly assimilates Islamic poetry's version of "orientalism": a poetic Bedouin world of caravans and oases that was to the supremely sophisticated Hafiz, the urbane and urban Persian, what the Islamic world as a whole was to Goethe.

10. Socrates, in the same situation, made precisely the opposite choice. Perhaps for this reason the philosophers could never forgive the poets: the choice reminded them that the soul becomes. Moreover, under pressure the soul is utterly craven, witnessed to by the ingenuity it displays in declaring its courage, cleverness, and good sense. In this way Odysseus won the arms of Achilles.

11. *Mystical Poems of Rumi,* trans. A. J. Arberry (Chicago: University of Chicago Press, 1968), pp. 143–144.

12. This indecision is abetted by the absence of tense in Chinese poetic language: a statement of the past, of the present, or of the continuative and eternal present are all the same.

13. Sylvia Plath, *The Collected Poems,* ed. Ted Hughes (New York: Harper and Row, 1981), pp. 235–236.

14. Thomas H. Johnson, ed., *The Complete Poems of Emily Dickinson* (Boston: Little, Brown, 1960), no. 546, p. 266.

15. This is the archetypical lover in Islamic poetry, Majnun ("the mad one"), whose secular passion blurs into its religious counterpart in erotic mysticism and the divine love poem. Yet in the case of erotic mysticism, the "lover" turns the community's own complacent claims against it. They may have piously professed their belief in subjugation to the absolute One, but now they are placed in the difficult position of resisting its implicit and dangerous abrogation of social relations. Passion for the human beloved is more radical because it can claim no other right than the lover's desire.

16. Theodor Adorno, *Minima Moralia,* trans. E. F. N. Jephcott (London: Verso, 1974), p. 164. The sentences that follow are beautiful in their own

way, despite their Teutonic opacity: "In such distress he who is rebuffed becomes human. Just as love uncompromisingly betrays the general to the particular in which alone justice is done to the former, so now the general, as the autonomy of others, turns fatally against it. The very re-buttal through which the general has exerted its influence appears to the individual as exclusion from the general; he who has lost love knows himself deserted by all, and this is why he scorns consolation. In the senselessness of his deprivation he is made to feel the untruth of all merely individual fulfillment. But he thereby awakens to the paradoxical consciousness of generality: of the inalienable and unindictable human right to be loved by the beloved."

17. *Plotinus,* trans. A. H. Armstrong (Cambridge, Mass.: Harvard University Press, 1967), p. 375.

5. Nakedness/Fabric

1. Robert Burton, *The Anatomy of Melancholy,* ed. Holbrook Jackson (New York: Random House, 1977), p. 71.
2. Li Shang-yin understands that this occasion is deeper than a simple conflict of duty and desire, a replay of a Restoration Anthony and Cleopatra. What he observes is an entire history of causes and consequences concentrated in a moment and a scene—it is the explicit alternative to and collapse of narrative (which survives only as a possibility refused: "Why bother to wait . . . ?"). The structure is significant: the abrogation of public ethics can occur only in an event of "partiality," limitation and the negation of perspective. Like a framed work of art, this engrossing body somehow appears within the larger world, but at the same time manages to close itself off from its external relations; there is a discontinuity, a little world made cunningly, an Eden. The discovery of such a separate space threatens the collapse of the larger world, which requires seamless totality. Like the fable of the little boy and the dike, the world will be washed away in flood if even the smallest breach is permitted.
3. *The Collected Poems of William Butler Yeats* (New York: Macmillan, 1956), p. 324.
4. Geoffrey of Vinsauf, *The New Poetics,* trans. Jane Baltzell Kopp, in James Murphy, ed., *Three Medieval Rhetorical Arts* (Berkeley: University of California Press, 1971), p. 35.
5. There has been deep apprehension about the possibility of nature's complete disappearance from both man and woman, apprehension consequent to the encounter with woman / stone or man / stone. The capacity for passion and an openness to nature's compulsion is presumed to belong to other countries, hotter climates, and earlier times, all more alluringly savage than our own too civilized world. Such civility, a conscious control that Herrick calls "art," may in its perfection threaten to extin-

guish nature altogether; and "lively expression" can be body's replacement instead of mere covering. Michael Drayton's *Idea, 27,* protests:

Is not love here as 'tis in other climes,
And differeth it as do the several nations?
Or hath it lost the virtue with the times,
Or in this island alt'reth with the fashions?
  Or have our passions lesser powers than theirs,
Who had less art them lively to express?
Is nature grown less powerful in their heirs,
Or in our fathers did she more transgress?
  I am sure my sighs come from a heart as true
As any man's that memory can boast,
And my respects and services to you,
Equal with his that loves his mistress most.
  Or nature must be partial in my cause,
  Or only you do violate her laws.

6. Literally, "without using a matchmaker." All legitimate sexual unions must be proposed, arranged, and sanctioned.

7. Immanuel Kant, "Conjectural Beginning of Human History," trans. Emil L. Fackenheim, in Lewis White Beck, ed., *On History* (New York: Bobbs-Merrill, 1963), p. 57.

8. *The Collected Poems of William Butler Yeats* (New York: Macmillan, 1956), p. 125.

9. Martin Heidegger, "The Thing," in *Poetry, Language, Thought,* trans. Albert Hofstadter (New York: Harper and Row, 1971), p. 165.

10. In our reports we often pretend that we were completely alone, that our Eden is decorously solitary, transposed into a quiet garden behind the house, where the tree of knowledge bears "intellectual fruits" in a new and sublimated sense of the adjective. Thus Edward Young in "Conjectures on Original Composition": "It opens a back-door out of the bustle of this busy, and idle world, into a delicious garden of moral and intellectual fruits and flowers; the key of which is denied to the rest of mankind ... How independent of the world is he, who can daily find new acquaintance, that at once entertain, and improve him, in the little world, the minute but fruitful creation, of his own mind?"

11. William Carlos Williams, *Collected Earlier Poems* (New York: New Directions, 1938, 1951), p. 354.

12. "They employ in their productions the most profound thought, which is equivalent to everything hidden in the fruit, and admirable and splendid language, which corresponds to the rind and leaves." Boccaccio, "The Life of Dante," in Allan H. Gilbert, ed., *Literary Criticism: Plato to Dryden* (Detroit: Wayne State University Press, 1962), p. 211.

13. Archibald MacLeish, *The Collected Poems* (Boston: Houghton Mifflin, 1962), p. 50.

Epilogues

1. T. W. Adorno, *Aesthetic Theory,* trans. C. Lenhardt (London: Routledge & Kegan Paul, 1984), p. 99.
2. "Modern" from Hegel's point of view and encompassing all art since Hegel's time.
3. Friedrich Nietzsche, *Human, All Too Human,* trans. Marion Faber (Lincoln: University of Nebraska Press, 1984), p. 104.

Credits

Index

Harvard Studies in Comparative Literature